Tom Feiling spent a year living and working in Colombia before making *Resistencia: Hip-Hop in Colombia*, which won numerous awards at film festivals around the world, and was broadcast in four countries. In 2003 he became Campaigns Director for the TUC's Justice for Colombia campaign, which organizes for human rights in Colombia. His first book was *The Candy Machine: How Cocaine Took Over The World*, which was based on over sixty interviews with people involved in all aspects of the cocaine business and the 'war on drugs,' and was published by Penguin in 2009.

WITHDRAWN

Short Walks from Bogotá

Bogotá

Journeys in the New Colombia

TOM FEILING

PENGUIN BOOKS

PENGUIN BOOKS

Published by the Penguin Group
Penguin Books Ltd, 80 Strand, London WC2R ORL, England
Penguin Group (USA) Inc., 375 Hudson Street, New York, New York 10014, USA
Penguin Group (Canada), 90 Eglinton Avenue East, Suite 700, Toronto, Ontario, Canada M4P 2Y3
(a division of Pearson Penguin Canada Inc.)
Penguin Ireland, 25 St Stephen's Green, Dublin 2, Ireland (a division of Penguin Books Ltd)
Penguin Group (Australia), 707 Collins Street, Melbourne, Victoria 3008, Australia
(a division of Pearson Australia Group Pty Ltd)
Penguin Books India Pvt Ltd, 11 Community Centre, Panchsheel Park, New Delhi – 110 017, India
Penguin Group (NZ), 67 Apollo Drive, Rosedale, Auckland 0632, New Zealand
(a division of Pearson New Zealand Ltd)
Penguin Books (South Africa) (Pty) Ltd, Block D, Rosebank Office Park,
181 Jan Smuts Avenue, Parktown North, Gauteng 2193, South Africa

Penguin Books Ltd, Registered Offices: 80 Strand, London WC2R ORL, England

www.penguin.com

First published by Allen Lane 2012
Published by Penguin Books 2013
001

Copyright © Tom Feiling, 2012

Typeset by Jouve (UK), Milton Keynes
Printed in England by Clays Ltd, St Ives plc

ISBN: 978-0-241-95990-9

www.greenpenguin.co.uk

MIX
Paper from
responsible sources
FSC™ C018179
www.fsc.org

Penguin Books is committed to a sustainable
future for our business, our readers and our planet.
This book is made from Forest Stewardship
Council™ certified paper.

Contents

Acknowledgements   vii

Introduction   ix

Map   xvi

1. The View from Bogotá   1

2. Meeting the McCormicks   30

3. The Last Nomads   49

4. An Imaginary Place between Macondo and Medellín   81

5. The Armed Strugglers   106

6. Downriver to Mompós   133

7. Going Back to San Carlos   161

8. 'NN': No Name   183

9. From Valledupar to the Cape   200

10. The Emerald Cowboy   226

11. Merry Crisis and a Happy New Fear   249

Acknowledgements

For their insights into the history of the conflict, I'd like to thank Luís Eduardo Celis Méndez of the Corporación Nuevo Arco Iris, Omar Gutierrez, Michael Reed of the International Center for Transitional Justice, Timothy Ross and everyone at the Fundación Fenix.

In helping me to understand the plight of the Nukak Maku, I'd like to thank Giovanni Lepri of the United Nations High Commission for Refugees in Villavicencio, Dr Albeiro Riano, and Richard McColl. On the impact of the conflict on the department of Meta, my thanks to Edinson Cuellar Olveros and Carolina Hoyos of the Colectivo Sociojurídico Orlando Fals Borda.

I'd like to express my gratitude to Carlos Gómez for inviting me to hike the Canyon Chicamocha with him and for letting me quote from his book *Desde Aquellos Días*. Roddy Brett at the Universidad del Rosario was great company in my first days back in Bogotá and put me in touch with Gonzalo Patiño at the Universidad Industrial de Santander, whose insights into the rise of the ELN guerrillas were much appreciated, as were those of Joe Broderick.

My trip to San Carlos, Antioquia was instigated by Oystein Schjetne from the Golden Colombia Foundation in Bogotá and wouldn't have been possible without the assistance of Pastora Mira García from CARE San Carlos and Miguel Ángel Giraldo. My trip to Puerto Berrío was organized by the photographer Paul Smith in Medellín, who worked incredibly hard and let me take a back seat throughout the time we spent in the town.

On the coast, I'd like to thank Carlos Sourdis, and in Valledupar Stefani Jiménez Mora and the *vallenato* historian Tomás Dario Gutierrez Hinojosa.

For feeding me leads and stories from the emerald mining business, thanks to Nicolás Lazzarelli, Ralf Leiteritz at the Department of Political Science at the Universidad del Rosario and Jacinto Pineda Jiménez of ESAP Boyacá in Tunja.

My thanks to friends in Bogotá who kept me company and distracted me from writing – Simone Bruno, Tiziana Laudato and Nate Russo, who was also good enough to offer tips on my pitch. For bringing my Spanish back up to scratch, my thanks to Luz Ángela Castelblanco. For sharing the many stories he heard while working at *El Tiempo*, as well as his gin and tonic, thanks to Richard Emblin from the *City Paper* in Bogotá. Thanks too to Maribel Lozano, who was as generous as ever with ideas and contacts. Special thanks to Ricardo Andrés Sánchez Mosquera, my best friend in the city, whose meanderings through time and space it was my pleasure to share.

Back in the UK, I'd like to thank my agent, Broo Doherty, for fighting my corner and my mum, Deirdre Feiling, who patiently listened to a line-by-line reading of the first draft of this book. Thanks too to Michael Ryan, Sam Low, Adam Fausset, Geoff Grint and my editor Helen Conford, who gave me precious feedback on the first draft.

Wherever I have mentioned monetary sums, I have worked from an exchange rate of £1 = 3,000 Colombian pesos, which was correct at the time of going to press.

Some names have been changed to protect the identities of people at risk of stigmatization, intimidation or worse.

Introduction

'Do they have skyscrapers?'

It was my last night in London before leaving for Colombia, and I was having a drink with a friend in the West End. He knew that I'd been coming and going between London and Bogotá for several years and that I'd lived there for a year in 2001. He knew that I'd made a documentary about hip-hop in Colombia and that I'd worked for a human rights NGO called Justice for Colombia. On hearing that I was going back he had given me a wink and tapped the side of his nose — a reaction that I was well used to — but until now, he'd never expressed much interest in the place.

With his question, it dawned on me that my friend knew next to nothing about Colombia. He knew that it was where cocaine came from. He also knew that the Medellín cartel had had Andrés Escobar killed when he scored an own goal for the national team in a World Cup match with the United States in 1994, though his ignorance was no worse than Alan Hansen's. Watching the highlights of the game the next day, the football commentator had said (innocently) that 'the Argentine defender warrants shooting for a mistake like that'.

I daresay most of the millions of casual cocaine users in the UK don't know much about Colombia either. They turn a blind eye to the trade that carries their Friday night entertainment from some remote Andean hillside to the toilet in the pub at the end of the road. The British press, which routinely ignores news from Colombia, bears much of the blame for this benightedness. In the 1980s and '90s our newspapers couldn't get enough of the sensational, bloody war that Colombia's cocaine cartels were waging. That war exercised a grim fascination and set a precedent for news reporting from Latin America, which has veered between the comic and the grotesque ever since. Such is our love of the macabre details of 'real-life crime' that, according to the Norwegian criminologist Nils Christie, depictions of organized crime in films, books and video games are currently worth more than organized crime itself.*

Pablo Escobar has become a modern-day legend, but since he was gunned down on a Medellín rooftop in 1993, the business that he pioneered has become more discreet and less entertaining. Colombia's cocaine traffickers have become yesterday's news.

The same might be said of the Revolutionary Armed Forces of Colombia (FARC), who were long ago relegated to the status of 'insurgents', then 'narco-guerrillas', and are now just plain old 'terrorists'. Despite having rumbled on for the last fifty years, the FARC's struggle with the Colombian government is a low-intensity war. It threatens no strategic western interests and the numbers are never really spectacular – at least, not until you look at the cumulative totals.

So the foreign correspondents were transferred from Bogotá to more newsworthy capitals. News editors turned their gaze towards Mexico, where the never-ending 'war on drugs' has decamped for its latest, gruesomely compelling chapter. Colombia is left with a war that most outsiders show no interest in and a reputation for crime and violence that is second to none. It is both demonized and ignored. Most people can't even spell its name properly.

I quit my job at Justice for Colombia in 2005, and in time I too stopped following the news from Latin America. Notwithstanding the enormous changes taking place in Venezuela and

---

* See Nils Christie, *A Suitable Amount of Crime* (Routledge, 2004).

Brazil, I thought that perhaps the French writer Dominique Moisi had been right when he wrote that 'Latin America is not where the future of the world is being decided, nor will it become so in the immediate future.'* My Spanish got rusty, my memories faded and I moved on to other things. It still irked me when outsiders judged Colombia to be a basket case: that its cocaine traffickers, guerrillas and death squads seemed to capture, in a neat précis, all that they might want to know about the place. But the thrill I had once felt in immersing myself in that most obsessive and introspective of countries seemed gone.

Then, one day in the summer of 2010, while I was queuing for a pint of milk in my local newsagent's, my eye was caught by the latest edition of *Newsweek*. For the first time in what seemed like years, Colombia was front page news. I bought a copy, and idled home with my nose stuck in its lead story. 'In the past eight years, the nation of 45 million has gone from a crime- and drug-addled candidate for failed state to a prospering dynamo,' it said. President Uribe's 'hardline policies on drugs and thugs' had rescued the country from 'almost certain ruin'. Colombia was 'stable, booming and democratic'. It was 'the star of the south', one of the six emerging markets singled out by canny investors as 'ones to watch'.†

Clearly, things had changed in the years since I lived in Bogotá. Back in 2001, all eyes had been on the peace talks that then-president Andrés Pastrana was holding with the FARC. Ultimately, the protracted negotiations and the well wishing of

---

* Dominique Moisi, *The Geopolitics of Emotion: How Cultures of Fear, Humiliation, and Hope are Reshaping the World* (Doubleday, 2009).
† 'Colombia Becomes the New Star of the South', *Newsweek*, 16 July 2010. The article went on to praise Colombia as one of the CIVETS, the emerging economies destined to follow the rise of the BRIC countries: Brazil, Russia, India and China. The CIVETS are Colombia, Indonesia, Vietnam, Egypt, Turkey and South Africa.

the hundreds of diplomats, politicians and journalists who made their way into the remote plains of Caquetá to see the guerrillas in the flesh came to nothing. After months of standing by and watching the government talk, the Army lost patience. The government called off the negotiations, and within hours the Air Force was bombing the FARC's encampment.

President Pastrana had come bearing an olive branch, but Manuel Marulanda, the FARC's commander-in-chief, never intended to lay down his weapons. Instead, he callously exploited the goodwill of millions of Colombians, stalling the government in peace talks while his high command drew up plans for a military takeover of Bogotá. Or at least, that was how the papers explained things.

After the talks collapsed, peace became a dirty word in Colombia. In 2002, not long after I returned to London, an openly belligerent candidate won the presidential election for the first time in twenty years. Álvaro Uribe had no intention of talking to the guerrillas. The way he saw it, the FARC were no more than terrorists. They were also responsible for the bulk of the cocaine production and trafficking that had so destabilized the country. If only they could be defeated, he reasoned, Colombia would soon be on the road to peace and prosperity. Uribe struck a chord with many Colombians, who were by now so desperate to live in peace, free from the threat of kidnap, robbery and extortion, that they happily voted for a man who promised yet more war.

When Álvaro Uribe came into office, most of the Colombian countryside was a no-go zone. Even the biggest roads were liable to be commandeered by FARC guerrillas on the look-out for passing millionaires they could kidnap for ransom, a venture they called *la pesca milagrosa* – fishing for a miracle. By the time Uribe stood down in August 2010, just a few weeks before I flew back to Bogotá, his country had seen ten years of Plan Colombia, a multi-billion-dollar programme of military aid from the

United States. The Colombian Army had doubled in size and the FARC had been pushed back, up the remotest mountain slopes and into the densest jungle expanses. When I had lived in Bogotá in 2001, 400 of the country's thousand or so mayors found themselves forced to share power with either left-wing guerrillas or the right-wing paramilitary armies that had sprung up to counter them. Now all the country's mayors could work unhindered by 'the men of violence'. Wealthy Colombians no longer lived with the constant threat of kidnap and the country's once-notorious murder rate fell to its lowest level for twenty-five years. Even the wealthy now felt safe to drive into the mountains that divided Bogotá from Medellín and Cali. Encouraged by the peace that followed in the wake of Uribe's war, they began spending at home what they had long invested in Miami. Before long, the skylines of all three cities were dominated by cranes, as Colombia enjoyed a boom in construction.

The multinationals weren't far behind. Between 2002 and 2010, foreign direct investment in Colombia jumped fivefold, from $2 billion to $10 billion per year. The value of Bogotá's stock market shot up, as news spread of the abundance of natural resources Colombia had to offer the world. Tourists also cottoned on to the country's natural bounty. In the first half of 2011 alone, the number of Britons holidaying in Colombia rose by 40 per cent.*

By the time I got home, milk and *Newsweek* in hand, I had all but booked a flight back to Bogotá. Not only were the roads safe to travel for the first time in thirty years, I knew that visitors to Colombia would search in vain for a book that explored its fascinating and little-known history. This was my chance to write that book: to venture into Colombia's hamlets and villages, and

---

* 'In Pablo Escobar's Footsteps', *Guardian*, 13 September 2011.

get to grips with the stories their people had to tell. I was already itching to get back.

A few weeks later, I was sitting outside a coffee shop near the Hotel Tequendama in Bogotá with a man who had once been a member of the FARC – my London friend would probably have assumed that he was a drug trafficker. Funnily enough, we were surrounded by skyscrapers. I had been telling him about the general lack of interest most foreigners had in a country that remains a byword for general nastiness.

'We are at war in Colombia,' he told me sternly. 'But the way you Europeans see it, no war fought in the Americas can ever be as dramatic or as testing of a nation's moral fibre as World War Two was to European nations.' He had a point: if Colombia was an unknown to my friend in London, perhaps it is because we judge the issues at stake in its various conflicts to be trifling, at least when compared to the titanic struggle between democrats, fascists and communists that dominated Europe for most of the twentieth century.

But now the tables have been turned. I can imagine few causes that might inspire Londoners to take up arms – thankfully, Europe has had no reason to go to war with itself for more than sixty years. But London has become home for thousands of people fleeing foreign wars, many fought by soldiers convinced that war offers the only solution to the challenges their people face.

As a young man, the former guerrilla had certainly thought so. He had fought to achieve 'true independence' for his country, he told me. Now middle-aged, he was all too aware of the FARC's role in making his country the epitome of festering, futile conflict. But his optimism for what was still for him 'the New World' was undimmed.

'By the European reckoning, the nobility of a war is measured by how much blood is spilt. Colombia was conquered by Spaniards with great bloodletting. But it was liberated by Americans with comparatively little blood spilt.' The wars of independence, at least, were something that Colombians could feel proud of, he told me.

He quoted a favourite author: 'For the last two centuries this country has been known by a name that, if the history of the world weren't a sequence of absurd coincidences, would have been given to all America: Colombia.'* He smiled and let out a sigh. Somewhere between the euphoria of the New World and the tragedy of the real one, Colombia's story was waiting to be told. It was good to be back.

---

* The quote is from *Angosta*, by Héctor Abad Faciolince (Planeta, 2003), p. 12.

COLOMBIA

Caribbean
Sea

Cabo de la Vela

Santa
Marta

Cartagena

Valledupar

Caracas

VENEZUELA

PANAMA

Mompos

Bucaramanga

Medellín

Los Santos

San Gil

Honda

River Magdalena

Bogotá

Pacific
Ocean

Cali

Villavicencio

San José
del Guaviare

Quito

ECUADOR

BRAZIL

PERU

Leticia

River
Amazon

1. The View from Bogotá

I had a few preparations to make before I could hit the country roads, as well as some old friends I was keen to catch up with, so I paid £220 for the month and moved into a little flat in La Candelaria, Bogotá's old colonial quarter. It was on the fourth floor of Casa Los Alpes, a new apartment block, just around the corner from Casa Los Andes, the warren of Andean cottages where I'd lived back in 2001.

The Andean version had offered Eduardo the limping handyman a template, but the flats he had built at Casa Los Alpes had none of its rustic charm. The ceiling and the roof were made of great concrete slabs that he had pebble-dashed and whitewashed. The windows had metal frames, into which he had gummed squares of glass with silicon. Since the frames ran flush with the outside wall, they took the brunt of the winter rains, which seeped between the glass and the metal. I liked Eduardo and didn't have the heart to complain about his craftsmanship. The puddles that accumulated at the foot of the window evaporated soon enough and I soon got used to drawing the green nylon curtains whenever it rained – which, as I soon discovered, was all day every day. The curtains, the rings they hung from and the poles on which the rings were strung were all home-made too. Eduardo had also made the kitchen counter, the shower cubicle and the single sheet of corrugated steel that was my flat's front door.

The building was owned by an old Italian with bristling eyebrows, who would eye me suspiciously whenever I passed him in the street. If there was a ranking among the expat community, the old man was at the top, whereas I was just a rung

above the dreadlocked backpackers who lived in the hostel at
the top of my street. The old man shared a tiny office with his
son Guillermo, who was the more amenable, public face of the
enterprise. Tacked to its walls were various pithy *bons mots*, all of
which hinged on the folly and menace of the global communist
conspiracy.

Over the course of October, I found a tutor who helped
me to get my Spanish back up to scratch and scoured the newspapers to re-accustom myself to the intricacies of the political
scene. After eight years in power, Álvaro Uribe had left office
in August 2010 as far and away the most popular president in the
history of the republic. To his defenders, he was the greatest
Colombian of modern times, the cattle farmer who restored the
good name of a proud country. He was credited with building a
dedicated, professional Army that had taken the war to the
terrorists. His belligerent treatment of the guerrillas seemed to
have secured the peace and prosperity that years of negotiations
had not.

Once out of office, however, his star was quickly losing its
lustre. An American court had called him to testify at the
trial of alleged paramilitaries who had been extradited to the
United States to face cocaine trafficking charges. Protesters had
disrupted the lectures that he had been invited to give at George-
town University in Washington, DC. And in Spain lawyers were
preparing to prosecute him for human rights abuses. Back in
Bogotá, the intelligence agency officials who had served under
him were being called to account for the *chuzadas* or wire-
tapping scandal. In the last year of his second presidential term,
Uribe had tried to change the constitution so that he might run
for a third time. Colombia's intelligence agents (and, by implica-
tion, their boss) stood accused of bugging the journalists, judges
and opposition politicians who had spoken out against the
constitutional amendment.

In terrorizing the terrorists, Uribe had strayed a long way from the constitution he had sworn to uphold. But inadvertently, he had also made it possible for journalists to visit the villages that had been on the front line of the conflict. On my map, whose greens, beiges and deep browns hinted at the dramatic peaks and troughs of the unseen country, I began to plot a route.

My abiding memory of Bogotá had been of a city rendered pin-sharp by blazing Andean sunshine. In my fondness I'd forgotten how cold and damp the capital could get. On most days it rained so heavily and for so long that the narrow streets of La Candelaria became rivers that left those without rubber boots and umbrellas stranded on whichever city block they happened to be standing on. Come evening the rain would finally let up, allowing the storm drains to swallow the last of the floodwater. Mist descended from the surrounding mountains like a cloak, enveloping my neighbourhood in fog.

Yet it seemed that the city had got used to life without central heating. So one morning I walked down to the clothes shops below the Plaza Simón Bolívar, hoping to find a decent jumper. All I could find were hoodies and tracksuit tops – it seemed that *bogotanos* also lived without wool. So I jumped on a bus heading north. After the huge riots that had gripped Bogotá in 1948, anyone with any money had deserted the traditional barrios of the city centre to settle the north of the city. The banks, embassies and corporations had followed them. Their employees moved into pleasant tree-lined streets of brick low-rises, where their wives could spend their afternoons in beautifully appointed boutiques and patisseries styled after those of Paris and Miami. They left the accumulated architectural heritage of the city centre and its rather gloomy history behind, to be blackened by exhaust fumes and soot.

I jumped off the bus outside the Andean Centre, Bogotá's best-known upmarket shopping mall. I padded its marble floors, cautiously eyeing the expensive imported clothing in the shop windows. Eventually I found a sweater in Benetton and paid the equivalent of £50 for a fluffy mixture of every warm thread imaginable, including alpaca, which is what kept most Andeans warm over the centuries before the arrival of cheap Asian polyester.

I'd arranged to meet an ex-girlfriend in the city's nightlife district, a square mile of bars and clubs around the Andean Centre that is known as the Zona Rosa. I had some time to kill before we were due to meet, so I found a seat overlooking the atrium and ate a burger. A pair of replica monkeys were gliding up and down electric-green jungle creepers, watched by twin infant boys in matching school blazers and caps. I cast an eye around at my fellow diners. Notwithstanding the tropical theme, I could have been in Madrid. Everyone was impeccably dressed, and nonchalantly watching one another as they tucked into their barbecued ribs and stuffed-crust pizzas. Of course the illusion was dependent on there being no poor people in the Andean Centre, which meant that there were no Andeans to be seen either. There was no trace of the Muisca, the original inhabitants of Bogotá, nor any of the other ethnicities native to the highland capital, much less the black Colombians who make up a fifth of the country's population.

Apart from a cleaner and a security guard, nobody was watching the television in the corner, so I bought a coffee and pulled up a chair at their table. The newsreader was a statuesque blonde woman with a steely, penetrating gaze. I had the feeling that her beauty was a deliberate ploy to distract viewers like me, who knew that the news was important, but found their coverage of it rather boring.

Over the years, she said, the FARC had been instrumental in

kidnapping dozens of soldiers and police officers. The picture cut to a press conference, where an Army general was addressing a bank of cameras and microphones. 'The FARC should know that we are coming after them. We won't let our guard down. We still have a long way to go.'

The cleaner harrumphed and shuffled off with her bucket and mop. The security guard stayed where he was and together we watched more stories of neighbourhood criminals and disasters brought on by the winter rains, with a familiar cast of pleading locals and resolute policemen. Then the news segued into *Farán-dula,* a daily roundup of celebrity gossip presented by a woman who might have been the newsreader's equally svelte twin sister.

A girl of nineteen or so asked if she could share my table. I nodded and watched as she began eating her soup with a delicacy that I didn't usually associate with Colombians. Perhaps it was her flawless skin, or the braces on her teeth, or the long thin arm that she rested on the table, but she struck me as being almost Japanese. It seemed ridiculous to sit there wordlessly, especially since the table was so small, so I asked her what the soup was. '*Ahuyama,*' she told me. I'd never heard the word before – I later found out that it was squash.

Her name was Katalina and she lived in Los Rosales, an exclusive neighbourhood of modern redbrick apartment complexes on the lower slopes of the northern hills. When I told her that I lived in La Candelaria, she said that she'd be worried to live there, especially after dark. I smiled, groaning inwardly at the fearfulness of the city's gilded youth, whose sanctuary this was. The poor were like ghosts to people like Katalina – rarely seen, but ever-present and often malevolent.

Of course crimes were committed at night in my neighbourhood. One morning I found my landlord clambering over the terracotta tiles on the roof, trying to salvage what was left of the telephone lines. The thieves had been after the copper wires, which they sold for scrap, he told me. Night-time marauders would steal the neighbourhood's manhole covers too, to the same end. At the end of my street, some good citizen had used the branch of a tree to warn oncoming drivers of the hole in the road. Guillermo, my landlord's son, told me that in the late 1980s, when the capital was passing through its darkest times, he used to venture out wondering not if but when he would be mugged.

Even my friend Ricardo, who liked to scoff at upper-class paranoia, was quick to tell me how dangerous the city streets could be. His cousin had been walking in La Candelaria in the middle of the afternoon when someone on the flat roof of the market building had thrown a stone at him, which split his head open. Before the ambulance came to take him away, his attacker had come down onto the street and emptied his pockets.

But those days were gone. Despite the widespread perception of Bogotá as a dangerous city, in the years since I last lived there it had emerged to become one of the safest cities in Latin America. These days, you were more likely to be robbed in Caracas or Quito.* Venturing out at night still had its risks though: many of the street lights in La Candelaria didn't work and the combination of holes and darkness made any night-time wanderer a hostage to fortune. Only in the last twelve months had the city's mayor come up with the idea of fitting plastic manhole covers, though I had yet to see one for myself.

I left Katalina in peace and found a quiet coffee shop, where I spent the afternoon on the phone, trying to find a tour guide or local historian who might help me find out more about Bogotá. I didn't come up with much. The shelves of the bookshops

---

* There are more kidnappings per person in Mexico, Ecuador, Haiti, Trinidad and Tobago, and Venezuela than in Colombia; see http://bigtravelweb.com

groaned under the weight of the memoirs of Pablo Escobar's mistress, the Franco-Colombian politician Ingrid Betancourt's account of her time as a captive of the FARC and hundreds of analyses of the conflict, but there was nothing that might have told me more about the capital.

The light was fading from the sky by the time I got back to the Andean Centre to meet Maribel. We had some dinner and went to see *The Social Network*. The entire country seemed to be on Facebook, so I wasn't surprised to see that the auditorium was packed. After the film, we walked over the road to a bar in the Zona Rosa. The hardwood panelling on the walls and the stark, skinny plants, dramatically uplit by spotlights buried in troughs of big grey pebbles, were reassuringly nondescript. I had the giddy feeling of being in an airport terminal, a secured bubble of globalized good taste, divorced from any indication of where on the planet I was.

We had a few whiskies, or at least I did. Maribel had a lychee martini before switching to vodka. As the night wore on, the salsa got louder and couples took to the dance floor behind us. I was tempted to join them, but something in the atmosphere that night kept me in my seat. Young guys in designer denim and herringbone shirts eyed their fellow dancers steadily from under pristine felt cowboy hats, as they shuffled and kicked their way around the room. They clung to their partners possessively, as if they were human shields in a carefully choreographed battle scene.

On our way out at three in the morning, a smaller, slighter figure than any I'd seen that evening opened his jacket to show me an iPhone. He whispered a price, I shook my head and he darted away into the crowd. I was reminded of something that a friend had once said to me: 'If I go to Norway, I can see that their experience isn't a universal one. No Norwegian lives like poor Colombians do. But go up to the Zona Rosa in Bogotá and you can see that the people there live much as people do in

Norway. That's why what's happening in Colombia is of more universal importance than what's happening in Norway – because we have first, second and third worlds living side by side.'

It was strange to be back in a country that seemed at once universal and isolated. Despite its particular history of fratricidal conflict, spending time in Colombia had often felt like being in a microcosmic version of the world at large. Both are run by a white-skinned elite that makes up about 10 per cent of the population. In both, the privileged one in ten lives in the cooler climes and owns about 80 per cent of the mines, farms, industries and banks. He eats and lives well, studies at the best schools and universities, receives medical treatment in the best hospitals and usually dies of old age.*

Below him on the social ladder are another four out of ten Colombians, generally a little darker-skinned than the privileged one, who spend their lives working as hard as they can, not so much to join the privileged one, as to stave off the possibility of falling into the poverty endured by the remaining five in ten. This bottom half live in the hottest regions, on the worst land, in the most isolated parts of the countryside or on the neglected margins of the big cities. They are black, Indian, white or mixes of the three. The poorest of them live from day to day, never sure of where their next meal will come from. That's the way the world is, and Colombia is a small-scale version of it.

I'd met few Colombians who had the will or the means to move between the three worlds to be found in their country. Maribel was one of them, but she was as careful as anyone to get a taxi that the security guards outside the bar could vouch for.

---

* See Héctor Abad Faciolince, 'Colombia: Boceto para un retrato', *El Espectador*, 9 March 2009.

Everyone seemed to have a story to tell of a friend who had taken a taxi and agreed to a short cut, only for the driver to turn into a darkened street, where he stopped to let in his two accomplices. They called it *el paseo de los millonarios* – the millionaires' stroll: a midnight ride around the cash points of the city, a pistol digging into the victim's ribs, until the account was empty.

With Maribel safely homebound, I spent twenty minutes waiting for a taxi driver who might take me south, but none of them wanted to leave the uptown neighbourhoods. So I started walking; all this watchfulness was making me feel claustrophobic. All I had to do, I told myself, was stick to the Avenida Séptima; if I kept up a good pace, I reckoned on being home in a couple of hours.

Over the first ten blocks I passed groups of well-heeled young men and women who were trying in vain to hail taxis home. A pair of young businessmen were propping up a third who was being sick into a bin. 'Not on your shoes, Raúl!' said one. After half an hour I came to Chapinero, euphemistically known as 'the theatre district', where I passed same-sex couples walking home arm in arm. A face peeped out warily from the doorway of an innocuous-looking house whose windows were shaking to the sound of techno. For the next few blocks, I could have been in Camden Town circa 1978, as the street was crowded with leather-clad punks waiting for southbound buses.

Beyond Chapinero there were roadworks under way, so pedestrians had to cross and re-cross the avenue. I ended up walking down the badly lit streets that run parallel to the Avenida Séptima. I walked fast, dodging the potholes in the road, the shoots of rainwater that gushed from the gaps between the paving stones, and the empty spaces once capped by manhole covers. The horror stories I'd heard from Katalina, Ricardo and Maribel ran through my head. I tried to reason my way past them. The story here was not crime, but *bogotanos*' exaggerated fear of crime, I told myself. But a nagging voice in my head told

me that I was *dando papaya*. It was an expression I had heard time
and again. Its literal meaning was to 'give somebody a papaya',
but Colombians use it to describe anybody who gives a thief an
opportunity: in other words, a mug. It seemed very *bogotano* to
blame not the fox but the rabbit silly enough to venture into
his path.

The gloomy backstreets were empty – anyone venturing out
at this hour would be in the back seat of a car or taxi. In fact,
with Chapinero behind me, the entire city seemed to be empty.
Perhaps this was the solution to night-time crime: with most of
the city having taken to their beds long ago and the revellers
behind closed doors, muggers found that their only would-be
victims were homeless old men.

Maybe the silence of the city and the fear it inspired explained
the great sentimentality with which my Colombian friends
talked about their own patch: their family, friends and the
neighbourhood they lived in. In time, I'd come to recognize the
wariness with which one region eyed another. If I were going to
Cali, *bogotanos* would tell me to be careful; it was '*muy peligroso*' –
very dangerous. Once in Cali, people would warn me of the
same danger being particular to Bogotá, Medellín or Barranquilla. I had thought that people might have grown accustomed
to the violence, but in fact, they seemed more scared than I did.
Whatever lay beyond the end of the street was potentially
dangerous.

I soon came to the barrio of Teusaquillo. In the days before
the first Europeans reached the Andes, when the Muiscas
ruled the city then known as Bacatá, their tribal leaders would
bathe in the springs here. By the 1950s Teusaquillo had become
a pseudo-English garden suburb of bungalows and faux-Tudor
houses with neat front gardens. Though faded, it still had some
charm. Behind a barred window and muted by lace curtains, a
bare bulb shone. A security guard stood outside his kiosk on the

corner of the empty street. Through the half-light cast by a flickering street lamp, I could make out a solitary local, who was walking his dog.

I came to the Avenida Caracas. Running down the middle of the avenue were two new concrete highways that had been built for the *Transmilenio*, the name *bogotanos* give to the gleaming fleet of bendy buses, harbingers of a twenty-first-century version of the city, that shuttle from the wealthy north to the impoverished south and all points in between. A depot-bound bus was waiting at the traffic lights for a man who was pushing a cart laden with offcuts of wood, metal poles and bags of empty plastic bottles. The weight of the cart, and his skeletal frame, which was bent double by the effort, meant that it took him ages to cross the road. The bus hummed patiently.

On the other side, an indigent man was squatting at the kerb, picking through a bag of scraps that had been left outside a shuttered restaurant. With him was a teenage boy who was inhaling glue from a plastic bag. A boy in rags strode past me on a mission, singing at the top of his voice, alone, free and seemingly oblivious to anyone who might have been listening.

These old men and teenagers, dressed in tattered hand-me-downs, their toes poking out from cast-off shoes, and a sack of tin cans for the scrap merchant slung over one shoulder, had been here when I was last in the city. Despite the signs that Colombia was emerging from its twenty-year-long crisis, they were still here. They were short and skinny, with matted hair and furrowed, greasy faces tanned by the Andean sun. Solitary walkers through the night, they slouched with downcast eyes, hoping to avoid other members of their tribe. In the early mornings, as the commuters returned to take the city they half-owned, the homeless they would shrink away to sleep under cardboard boxes at the back of car parks. They re-emerged in the afternoon, but confined themselves to the backstreets, where I'd occasionally be asked for the price of a bread roll or a cup of coffee.

When the Hotel Tequendama came into view, I knew that I'd soon be home. It was five in the morning and the sky was growing light. There was still no sign of the stark Andean sunshine that had illuminated my memories of the city. That morning, the city was hemmed in by cold, grey clouds that swept over the mountains from the east. A lone man eyed me up as he spoke into a lapel mike. Ahead, a security guard with a muzzled Rottweiler slowly paced around in front of the hotel's grand main entrance. I made it back to the Casa Los Alpes just as the first of the day's commuters were coming into the city centre.

Two days later I woke to news that Air Force bombs had killed the man known as 'Mono Jojoy', the commander of the FARC's Eastern Block. After breakfast I logged on to the FARC's website. 'It is with profound remorse, clenched fists and chests heavy with feeling that we inform the people of Colombia and our brothers in Latin America that Commander Jorge Briceño, our brave, proud hero of a thousand battles, commander since the glorious days of the foundation of the FARC, has fallen at his post, at his men's side, while fulfilling his revolutionary duties, following a cowardly bombardment akin to the Nazi blitzkrieg.'

It was a morning of glorious sunshine. It picked out the pine trees on the steep, wooded hills that rise up from the plain of Bogotá to form a north–south wall for the city. The white-washed walls of the church of Monserrate gleamed from the summit. I made my way through the Journalists Park, with its statue of Simón Bolívar under a neglected limestone cupola, and followed the creek upstream, past the students making their way to the Universidad de los Andes, to the Quinta de Bolívar.

This is where Simón Bolívar, the hero of Colombia's wars of independence, lived when he was in Bogotá. I had come to catch up with the thinking of the academics and NGOs that have been faithfully monitoring, measuring and struggling to come up with solutions to Colombia's convulsions since the fifties. Unfortunately, I'd got my timing wrong: the conference had ended, not started, at 10 a.m. I'd forgotten what a nation of early risers this was.

On my way back down into the city, I fell in with Lucho, an old friend from the Arco Iris Foundation, one of the most respected of Colombia's NGOs. He seemed less than surprised by the morning's news. 'The death of any soldier is to be expected,' he said solemnly. 'Every FARC commander has his understudy waiting to replace him should he fall in combat. Mono Jojoy is sure to have agreed his own treaty with Death.' Lucho's easy recourse to metaphysics sounded exotic to my ears, accustomed as they still were to the talk of Londoners, few of whom have agreed to anything as grand as a treaty with Death.

'And anyway,' he went on, 'the guerrillas don't count for much these days. The real problem facing the country is the mafia. They've bought out half of Congress.' In a country that practically defined itself by its 'war on terror', this came as something of a surprise.

We hit the news-stands on Calle 19, where Lucho asked for a copy of *El Tiempo*. Colombia's oldest daily newspaper has long been a cornerstone of its democracy, except for a brief period in 1955 when it was shut down by the military dictator Gustavo Rojas Pinilla. For a while, *El Tiempo* reappeared as *Intermedio*, 'The Times' becoming 'The Intermission', before Rojas Pinilla was booted out of office and normal service was resumed. It was Colombia's first and last experiment with dictatorship.

But at one kiosk after another we were told that that day's

edition had sold out. A young boy with a bundle of newspapers under his arm was winding his way between the cars waiting at the traffic lights. 'Extra, extra!' he shouted. Lucho snapped up the eight-page supplement while I ordered us a couple of *tintos* at a street-side coffee bar. He propped his elbow on the counter and began hungrily scanning the pages.

Perhaps I was expecting cars to be honking their horns in jubilation at the news, but there was nothing so palpable. The politicians and journalists might have been celebrating the death of Mono Jojoy as another blow to the terrorists, but Lucho seemed less than impressed. 'The newspapers are always saying that peace is just around the corner. Today, it's Mono Jojoy. A couple of years ago it was Raúl Reyes.* When I was a kid, my dad used to tell me about *Capitán Desquite* and *Tarzán* and Efraín González. These days, they'd call them terrorists, but back then they were just bandits. Colombians have always had short memories.' I later found out that *Capitán Desquite* – Captain Revenge – had been a Liberal guerrilla in the 1950s and that Efraín González was a Conservative guerrilla from the same period.

Mono Jojoy's death had come just a few weeks after the inauguration of Colombia's new president. To untrained eyes the Air Force's strike might have confirmed that Juan Manuel Santos had adopted the hardline tactics of his predecessor, Álvaro Uribe. But Lucho suggested that it signalled a change in strategy. 'Hugo Chávez and the FARC high command would have been aware of the strike in advance. Maybe they even gave it their blessing.'

The idea that the Venezuelan president might have colluded with senior FARC commanders sounded far-fetched, but Lucho

---

* Raúl Reyes was a high-ranking FARC commander, killed by the Colombian Army in a cross-border raid into Ecuador in 2008.

was adamant. Mono Jojoy had been one of the hardline leaders of the FARC's military wing. With Jojoy out of the way, the FARC's leader, Alfonso Cano, who had always been more open to negotiations with the government, had a free hand to talk to President Santos.* Unlike his predecessor, Santos seemed keen to talk to the enemy, or at least keener than he might admit to his supporters.

'It may well be that Santos hammers out a deal with Cano some time next year, perhaps with Chávez acting as intermediary.' Lucho drained the remains of his coffee and stuck his hand out for a cab. 'Maybe the FARC will demobilize in return for a toughened up Land Law. Who knows? In Colombia, nothing is impossible.'

I was still nodding, struggling to take it all in, when Lucho jumped in the back of a taxi with a wave and sped off into the traffic. I clearly had some catching up to do. I reached for the copy of *El Tiempo* that Lucho had left on the counter. The front-page story celebrated the 'monumental blow' that the Army had dealt to the guerrillas; the man that President Santos described as 'a symbol of terror' was finally dead.

Mono Jojoy was the latest name to be added to the list of FARC commanders killed by the Army or extradited to stand trial on cocaine trafficking charges in the United States. To the optimists in the new government, the guerrillas' surrender was only a matter of time. As and when they turned in their weapons, their country would once again become 'the Athens of South America', a beacon of democratic moderation in a continent that has long been prone to populist excess. *El Tiempo* didn't have to spell out the alternative: that Colombia remain the guerrilla-infested, cocaine-addled basket case depicted by foreigners.

---

*Alfonso Cano was killed by the Army in November 2011. At the time of writing, the FARC was led by Rodrigo Londoño, alias 'Timochenko'.

Although the official line on the war with the FARC was straightforward enough, I had a feeling that I wasn't getting the full picture. The triumphalist pride and unspoken humiliation were worryingly familiar. The media bombast that followed the death of Mono Jojoy only encouraged me to find out more about the man and his struggle. I thought about going to his funeral. No date had been announced, since his body was still in the Army morgue in Bogotá, but in time his remains would have to be handed over to his family. Lucho had said that the FARC commander would probably be buried in Cabrera, the small town southwest of the capital where he had been born.

But every journalist that I spoke to in the days that followed told me that the trip would be too dangerous. Cabrera was in Sumapaz, the high moors that overlook the capital, where local farmers have spent years arguing the relative merits of Marx and Bakunin. Both the FARC and the state intelligence agents likely to be monitoring the mourners would be highly suspicious of a foreign journalist asking questions.

It was clearly going to be difficult to pierce the united front the government was intent on building. I had every intention of avoiding danger, if only because it would leave me open to fear, which seemed to cripple the faculties of all those it touched. The Colombians that I had met since my return were delighted to see a tourist defy their country's awful reputation. But they wanted me to see the sights, not go rummaging through their dirty linen.

I would however get occasional clues to the stories that complicated the official line on the country's 'war on terror'. Buried in the city news pages of *El Tiempo*, I found a small piece about nine people who had been shot and killed across Bogotá the previous night. Most of them had been killed by paramilitary death squads. Masked men in a park in Ciudad Bolívar had shot three teenagers, including a thirteen-year-old boy.

On clear days I could see Ciudad Bolívar from my window.

It was a huge barrio, built high on the treeless southern slopes of the city. Over the past twenty years it had absorbed many of the millions of Colombians driven, whether by political violence or poverty, to seek new lives in the capital. Nobody wanted to live in Ciudad Bolívar, but those who had no choice in the matter had built, plumbed and wired a neighbourhood that the utilities companies and town planners largely ignored. Infamous for crime and violence, most taxi drivers wouldn't even go near it.

I knew that Nidia, the housekeeper who had a little room on the ground floor of Casa Los Alpes, lived in Ciudad Bolívar. When I got back, I found her sweeping the already spotless stairs. I asked her if she knew anything about what had happened in her neighbourhood the previous night. She'd heard the news, she said in a whisper; the death squads often took it upon themselves to root out anyone they believed to be working for the guerrillas.

I balked; it was hard to believe that after eight years of a nationwide Army offensive that had pushed the FARC into the mountains and along the rivers that run out into the jungle, the guerrillas still had operatives in the capital. Whether through fear or ignorance, Nidia couldn't tell me what the guerrillas' urban militias did, bar some mutterings of the type I'd heard from her on previous occasions, about rowdy teenagers swigging beer at the bus stop outside her house. To her mind, revolutionary violence and under-age drinking were of a kind; they were the doings of *subversivos*.

Nidia always called me '*su merced*' – 'your honour', an archaic term of address that was no less surprising for being so widely used. Such deference might have sounded strange outside the highland departments around Bogotá, but it was quite common to hear poor people in the capital address their social superiors as '*su merced*'. Whenever I heard the expression, I couldn't help but ponder the question posed by a Frenchman who visited Bogotá in 1840: 'What is one to expect from a republic where every man calls "master" any individual whiter or better dressed than himself?'

One hundred and seventy years later, La Candelaria was full of very short, very old people living in cramped, unheated houses that had seen little change since the coming of electric light. Their poverty and instinctive deference to anyone with more money or education than themselves went back further still. A visitor to the city in 1900 had found it divided between energetic modernizers and hidebound devotees of the Catholic Church. It was 'a world in which confusion and clarity walked together, as did superstition and faith, arcane ritual and logical deduction'.* That year, the parents of half of all the children born in the city were unmarried, despite the fact that Bogotá had more priests per head of population than anywhere else in Colombia. The city's clergymen railed against the sin of illegitimacy, as they did against the dangers of drink, but were widely ignored on both counts and with good reason. The municipal government had a monopoly on the production of booze, and depended on the revenue for the bulk of its wages bill. Despite the outward signs of piety, it was said that farm workers around Bogotá got half their intake of calories from corn liquor.

The days in which 'pigs, chickens, horses and cows lived intermingled with families of all classes and conditions' were long gone, as was the Church's control of Colombia's education system. But the humility, reserve and durability of the elderly were as apparent as ever. What *was* new, at least to them, was the FARC, the terrible response they had provoked and the all-pervading fear that Colombians of all classes had learned to live

---

* Marco Palacios, *Between Legitimacy and Violence: A History of Colombia 1875–2002* (Duke University Press, 2006), p. 44.

with. Their fear was fully justified. Unlike Al-Qaeda, the IRA and the Basque ETA, Colombia's insurgents had come close to toppling a government. Although they were much less powerful than they had been in 2001, The FARC was still the largest guerrilla army in the world.

Their military power had been doubly frightening for having risen in tandem with their reliance on kidnapping the wealthy for ransom. Many of the students that I had taught at the private Universidad Externado in 2001 had had some personal experience of kidnap, as I found out when I asked them, unkindly I admit, to write an essay about the time they were most frightened. The story that stays with me is that of a girl whose father had received a letter from the FARC, stating that anyone with assets worth in excess of $1 million would be considered a legitimate target for 'detention'. Only by paying a 'war tax' would his name be struck off their list. The girl's father was keen to pay the tax and live in peace, but had no way of locating the tax collectors. So he set off into the countryside, a manila envelope full of cash in his briefcase, to find his would-be abductors. He was lucky, in that he wasn't robbed en route and somehow found a FARC front on the moors of Sumapaz. The girl's father handed his money to the commander of the front, who gave him a receipt, and the millionaire was able to return to the city with some peace of mind.

Others weren't so lucky. I remember too a conversation with David Hutchinson, an English banker and long-term resident of Bogotá, who had been kidnapped by the FARC in May 2002. He spent his first month in captivity camped on the moors of Sumapaz. From his tent he could even see his own house, a graphic illustration of just how close the guerrillas had come to overrunning Bogotá.

The government was locked into peace talks with the FARC at the time. To the guerrillas, it must have looked like a reprise of

Cuba in 1959, or Vietnam in 1975: a moment when the balance of power between old and new creaked towards the latter. And yet, in the years that followed the collapse of the Soviet Union, the idea that communist insurgents might overthrow what upper-class Colombians liked to call 'the oldest democracy in Latin America' wasn't just an affront, but an anachronism that only further isolated their country from the rest of the world.

The peace talks of 2001–2 were a fascinating time for me, even if the near overthrow of the Colombian government went largely unremarked upon elsewhere. For the privileged families that have governed Colombia since independence, however, it was a humiliation that they vowed never to revisit. When the peace talks broke down in acrimony and mutual blame, the Air Force was sent in to drop bombs on the FARC's encampment. The hundreds of envoys from the United Nations and European governments, who had been hopeful of a negotiated solution to the conflict, scuttled for cover. Since then, they have either professed themselves impotent or simply lost interest in Colombia.

The United States, as potent and interested as ever, seemed to greet the return to war with relief. The political life of Colombia has been subsumed by its internal conflict ever since. The barrage of propaganda, designed to exhort the population and marginalize dissenters, has come to seem normal. Somewhere, far from the capital, volleys of gunfire echoed the rhetoric.

The following Sunday morning, I was no sooner out of bed than off to the Avenida Séptima and on a bus heading north. I felt a need to run, to find a vista beyond the claustrophobia and paranoia of life in Bogotá, which the death of Mono Jojoy had only heightened. Half an hour later I got off at the Avenida Chile and walked a few blocks up the hill to Quebrada La Vieja – the Old Woman's Brook – a stream that runs down from the mountains that border the eastern edge of the city.

A beautifully manicured path wound its way along the course of the brook, past the grand apartment buildings of Los Rosales and then up into the forest. It was a steep climb to reach the crest of the hills, but there was a well-trodden trail, crowded with soaring eucalyptus trees and thick groves of bamboo. Within a few minutes all I could hear was the breeze in the treetops. As the air grew cooler and damper, the mosses grew thicker. A family of well-shod *bogotanos* with waxed jackets and Labradors passed me on their way down, but by the time I reached the top, I'd not seen another soul for an hour.

Looking east from the summit I could see only thick woods covering steep-sided valleys. I headed south along a less used path that followed the crest, passing under pine trees that had carpeted the ground in a thick bed of dry brown needles, and came out onto a bluff that finally gave me the view I'd been waiting for. Below me lay Bogotá in the haze; its drone, emitted by big cities everywhere, was reminiscent of the sea. Behind me lay only wilderness.

I had often wondered why the conquistadores chose to build their capital here. Although it sits on a verdant, sheltered plain, 2,625 metres above sea level, many of the mountains that surround Bogotá are dry and windswept. The capital is over 450 miles from the north coast, and the River Magdalena, which until well into the twentieth century was the country's main trade route, was hundreds of metres below me. Cali and Medellín were both prettier cities, with easier climates and better access to the outside world.

Colombia's topography has dictated the course of much of its history. It has been a blessing for its farmers – the mountains and the tropical lowlands that separate them include all varieties of climate, so all kinds of crops can be grown in them, from kale and broccoli to mango and pineapples. But the crumpled landscape has proved a curse for its traders. Since cities like Cali and

Medellín have always been able to feed themselves, they have had little need for commerce with the rest of the country. Internal trade was also prohibitively expensive. As the crow flies, Bogotá is only 190 miles from Medellín, yet until the 1950s it cost less to carry a sack of coffee beans from Medellín to London than it did to take it down to the Magdalena and then up to the capital.

So Colombia developed as a nation of isolated provinces. When it was a colony of Spain, cities like Popayán, Tunja and Mompós were provincial capitals. After independence, power increasingly accrued in Bogotá and they became backwaters. They were notable for their piety, haughty disdain for the modern world, and frequent ambushes of the tax collectors sent from distant Bogotá. Such was their poverty that foreigners visiting Mompós in the nineteenth century remarked that the town elders' sense of superiority was all that separated them from their former slaves.

For most of its history, Bogotá has been one of the smallest capital cities in Latin America. Even in 1900 it was home to no more than 30,000 people. I'd seen postcards of the city as it appeared in the 1950s, when its streets were unbroken and lined with villas with front gardens, and cars were few and far between. Yet even then, the appearance of prosperity was deceptive. Peering beyond the gleaming new buildings that housed the government ministries, I could make out the slums of Egipto and Las Cruces.

Since the fifties, the city has grown like a boil, filled with millions of country folk escaping the poverty and violence of the hinterland. Today Bogotá is a city of 7 million people that sprawls north, south and west from the colonial hub like the dusty spokes of half a bicycle wheel, each spoke a highway that runs out past warehouses, factories and car showrooms. And yet the neighbourhoods of the south still feel like annexes of the city, villages that have been uprooted and dumped in the mountains.

A huge amount of work has been done over the past ten years to try and catch up with decades of unplanned, chaotic growth. A succession of bold and visionary mayors has laid pavements and cycle paths along the highways, and built parks and libraries in the windswept neighbourhoods of the south. But they face huge challenges, not least of which is the indifference to others that seems to pervade this city of strangers.

Generations of *bogotanos* have grown up regarding the city government – indeed, all government – as corrupt and ineffectual. It has become a self-fulfilling prophecy, in which few people pay their taxes and those elected to govern the city routinely pilfer the treasury. The public realm has been starved; hence the wasted people the size of children, lying filthy and emaciated in the doorways of shops, and the security guards who look out at them, their pump-action shotguns protecting anything of value that can't be shuttered for the night.

If only, I thought from my hilltop lookout, the night were reclaimed. If only an army of workers set about fixing all that has gone neglected for so long. If only the pavements were repaired, the houses painted and colour brought back to the grimy walls that line the avenues. If only the streets were lit and *bogotanos* felt safe to walk their city. As it was, many of them still called a taxi just to go to the supermarket.

I clambered down the rocks from the ridge towards a mountain brook. Close by were the huge, straight trunks of eucalyptus trees that had tumbled over waterfalls and been blackened by the water. The winter rains must have washed away whatever hold they had on the hills. If I were to slip and break a leg, I too might lie here unseen. There was no sign of human life to appeal to: no mountain huts or roads; no dogs; not even a telegraph wire to follow.

In the distance, I could see three huge residential high-rises that were being built on the ring road, each twenty or thirty floors high. Being Sunday, they were deserted. They offered great views over the plain of Bogotá, but I could see that anyone who bought an apartment facing the hills would look down on a slum.

Friends had warned me not to walk in the hills alone. Although they looked empty, they bordered a series of invasion settlements. Unplanned, unauthorized and un-policed, the slums act as a buffer between the city and the empty expanse behind the mountains. The kids who live there, I was told, would rob anyone who strayed onto their patch. I could have turned back and retraced my footsteps, but instead I carried on, trying to look purposeful. The ring road was only a few hundred yards away, I told myself.

When I saw the first people, I instinctively stopped, stood still and waited for them to go. But as I got closer, I saw that to get to the main road I had no choice but to walk through the settlement. Once on level ground, I soon got lost in the warren of muddy paths that meandered between the zinc-roofed shacks. The further I walked, the more stupid I felt. Luckily, the first person I came across was an old man, dressed in a grey woollen poncho, brown trilby and rubber boots. He looked surprised to see me, but gladly pointed me in the right direction.

Twenty minutes later, I was back in the fug and racket of the buses racing along the Avenida Séptima. I recognized a couple of teenagers I'd passed in the shanty, who were sitting on a wall. 'What did you make of the neighbourhood?' one of them asked with a wry smile. We chatted for a while. As I turned to go, they asked me, as if it were always worth a shot, if I could spare some change. I was about to reach for my wallet, but then I thought that they might snatch it. I didn't want to *dar papaya*. '*Que pena, no tengo*,' I said, and kept on walking.

*

Since I'd not been able to find a book about Bogotá, I'd started reading a novel by Héctor Abad Faciolince, one of Colombia's best-known newspaper columnists. *Angosta* is a dystopian vision of a not-too-distant future Medellín. The city is governed by *Los Siete Sabios* – the Seven Wise Men – a shadowy clique of businessmen, landowners and senior police officers who monitor and eliminate all possible sources of dissent. The poor of Angosta are confined to the ravines at the bottom of the city by a high wall that is guarded by gun-toting Chinese guards. Transit to the upper slopes is strictly controlled. There, both the temperature and the mood are more congenial: people can walk the leafy streets without fear of being robbed. The gully dwellers are kept out of sight, at once ever-present and easily forgotten.

Angosta, which is the Spanish word for narrow, is a gripping depiction of the constraints of life in a paranoid city, something like a tropical version of George Orwell's *1984*. But the author hadn't had to stray far from the reality of modern Colombia to create what outsiders might regard as a fantasy. The Seven Wise Men were based on the Twelve Apostles, a group of wealthy landowners from Antioquia, the department of which Medellín is capital, who had been prominent cocaine traffickers and paramilitaries in the late 1990s. Santiago Uribe, brother of former president Álvaro Uribe, was alleged to have been among their number, a charge that he has always denied.

While Angosta's Seven Wise Men might have been inspired by the recent history of Medellín, the walls they raised and policed aren't specific to any one nation. Internal barriers, no less real for being invisible, divide American cities from São Paolo to Los Angeles to Kingston. Across North and South America, the public realm is being gradually suffocated; those who find themselves unable to pay for private services are left outside the city walls.

Colombia is the single most unequal country in Latin America, which is, in turn, the most unequal continent in the world. Only in Haiti, Sierra Leone, Namibia and South Africa is the gap between rich and poor wider.* It's not that Colombia is poor: its GDP has doubled over the last twenty years, as has public spending. Plenty of countries are poorer and enjoy less economic growth than Colombia. But in spite of (or because of) the accumulation of wealth and power in so few hands, the Colombian government has done less than any other in Latin America to reduce the poverty in which 20 million of its citizens – almost half the population – live from day to day.

Winston Smith, the anti-hero of *1984*, is rooted out by the state and ends his days contemplating 'a boot stamping on a human face – for ever'. After years of devising his own subtle forms of resistance, he finds that any organized challenge to the tyranny of Big Brother is impossible. Like George Orwell, Héctor Abad Faciolince didn't seem to think that revolution was a realistic prospect. The malcontents of *Angosta* only find something like peace when they are driven into exile.

What then of those Colombians who have decided that the only way to effect meaningful change is by force of arms? Most of their countrymen regard the Revolutionary Armed Forces of Colombia as dinosaurs: antiquated and all the more dangerous for being on their last legs. Yet as seen from the uninhabited hills overlooking Bogotá, the wrangling of rich and poor, and left and right, seemed overshadowed by a more elemental conflict, between the known and the unknown. The geography of this country throws up obstacles to all human endeavour, whatever its inspiration or purpose.

* Inequality is measured by the Gini coefficient, a number between 0 and 1, where 0 corresponds with perfect equality (where everyone has the same income) and 1 corresponds with perfect inequality (where one person has all the income, and everyone else has zero income). Colombia had a rating of .59 in 2008.

I thought again of what David Hutchinson had told me about the ten months he spent as a captive of the FARC. A few weeks after arriving at their camp in Sumapaz, he was taken on a long march towards the southeast, over the easternmost range of the Andes and down onto the *llanos*, the huge plains that run towards the border with Venezuela. They spent months on foot. Although they travelled by day, they didn't come across a single soldier or policeman. 'No satellite saw us. Nobody came and killed us. Nothing at all,' David told me. 'Colombia is a very big country with a very small state. It's a one-way mirror. Behind the one-way mirror is over half the territory of Colombia, where the state can't see anything.'

I'd flown over the eastern plains myself, and had marvelled at the unbroken tropical savannah rolling out towards the horizon. In Britain, people often complain about the omnipresence of the state and its incessant surveillance of daily life. If there is a one-way mirror in Britain, it is obvious who is doing the watching and who is being watched. But in Colombia, people complain about the absence of the state. Away from the big cities, the state is not so much a nanny as an absent father.

Colombians take their one-way mirror for granted, for it has always been there. Those looking into that mirror see only familiar and reassuring reflections; but behind it, never to be seen, lies a sparsely inhabited, frequently lawless country. Few seem willing to admit just how deep the division runs; fewer still, to acknowledge the inevitable violence that division inspires. Despite the surveillance and control the Colombian government aspires to exercise, it is on the wrong side of the mirror.

I asked David how the guerrillas had rated their chances of overthrowing the government. 'I asked one of the commanders when it would all end for him,' he told me. 'He said, "When we are marching on the Avenida Séptima in Bogotá." That's their dream – that one day they'll win.'

Understandably, David didn't like them much. 'They know nothing about anything at all,' he told me. 'They can't read or write. They've never heard of England. They've never been to the sea – they don't even know what the sea is.' His voice betrayed a residual disbelief at what had happened to him, as well as the fear that the guerrillas had instilled in him. 'Well, that's not true,' he said after a moment's reflection. 'They know a lot about some things. They know a lot about birds and fish and the forest. They know natural remedies for when you get ill. So they have a sort of Indian knowledge, which is sometimes quite interesting. It's very like reading the *Odyssey*. They live in a world of five thousand years ago.'

To say that the shoppers wandering the polished marble floors of the Andean Centre and the guerrillas of the FARC are separated by 5,000 years might be an exaggeration, but it gives some indication of the obstacles faced by anyone hoping to build a nation in this corner of the continent. Most of the conflicts of the post-Cold War world have drawn on ethnic or religious divisions for fuel. The Colombian conflict, as well as being older and easier to ignore than most, is also harder to explain. It certainly isn't religious: nearly all Colombians are Catholic. Nor is it ethnic: the Europeans who came here five hundred years ago took wives or mistresses wherever they found them, and at street level at least, no one hue dominates the others. Most black and native Colombians live in the margins, but their struggle for racial equality has been subsumed by other, broader agendas, principally grounded in region and class. Perhaps that explains the near-invisibility of Colombia's war: it is a long-running, unchanging, old-fashioned class war.

I pulled out my map and set to wondering about all the forgotten villages dotted along Colombia's jungle rivers or perched in its distant mountain valleys. For the past twenty-five years, exotic-sounding places like Playboy, Putumayo; Balmoral,

Casanare; and Berlín, Santander have been too dangerous to visit. But even as the guerrillas have been pushed back, the countryside remains largely unknown, even by Colombians. In the remotest departments, the only way to get around is by boat. Other regions have roads, but many of them are unpaved, so even those wanting to get to know the countryside find themselves stymied. The mountains, jungles, swamps and rivers that frustrated the conquistadores when their galleons first made land in the early years of the sixteenth century still resist those who seek to govern them.

One of the few foreign authors to have struggled to make sense of modern Colombia has called it 'a nation in spite of itself'.* From their mountain capital, its rulers might catch echoes of the war rumbling in the tropical lowlands. The city's lawyers, Congressmen and political pundits might digest its causes and effects and pontificate over what should be done, just as they have since declaring their independence from Spain two hundred years ago. But to this day, much of the rest of the country considers the *bogotano* elite to be overweening meddlers, inscrutable and bloodless, somehow a breed apart. I couldn't help thinking that they were spectators in their own country, and that the confluence of indigenous, African and European peoples on which the nation was built lay elsewhere. For those seeking to govern it, Colombia is still, as one journalist called it, 'an act of faith'.

---

* David Bushnell, *The Making of Modern Colombia: A Nation in Spite of Itself* (University of California Press, 1993).

2.   Meeting the McCormicks

I first met Ricardo Sánchez in 2007, when he had been my research assistant for a book I was writing about the cocaine business. He'd come up with lots of stories, none of which had any relevance to my project, but they were always interesting and Ricardo soon became my talking guidebook. We spent hours walking the streets of Bogotá. One day he might point out the house where William Burroughs had once stayed; the next, the spot where Jorge Eliécer Gaitán, Colombia's one and only populist leader, who claimed to be 'not a man but a people', had been gunned down in 1948. Ricardo gave the history lessons and I bought the drinks.

Our impromptu strolls, which invariably ended up in one of the pokey student bars of La Candelaria, were a habit I was keen to pick up again. After immersing myself in the news-papers, TV news and political goings-on of Bogotá, my forays into its old neighbourhoods were a welcome relief. Ricardo walked everywhere, partly because he enjoyed it, but also because he never had any money for the bus. Although he was in his late thirties, he had only enrolled at the National University a couple of years before and still lived with his mum and dad.

One Sunday, a week before I was due to leave Bogotá on my travels, Ricardo and I decided to climb Moguy, the highest of the hills that border the western edge of the city. It was an exhausting two-hour ascent over steep, bracken-covered slopes. Dozing at the summit, and seemingly incapable of moving a muscle, much less returning a greeting, were three young hippies who we guessed to be tripping on the local magic mushrooms. We walked a little further, beyond the TV mast that crowned the hill to the lookout that gave us a panoramic view over the deep green of the plain of Bogotá. Towards the horizon, sunbeams broke through the brownish fug and lit up the distant city. Below us, we could see a silver river running down from the hills, and beyond, the flooded fields where it had broken its banks.

Before the arrival of the Europeans, the highland plain of what was then called Bacatá was occupied by the Muisca. Ricardo told me that the entire plain had once been a huge lake and that those who lived on its shores had called themselves 'the frog men'. Later, the Muisca frog men had managed to dislodge a huge rock, by what combination of leverage and manpower nobody knew, which allowed the lake to drain over what is today the Salto de Tequendama waterfall. The Muisca were frog men no more. Ricardo was hoping to stumble across some of their petroglyphs, which might prove his point. As we combed the bracken for tell-tale signs on the weathered rocks, he went on to say that in modern times, the 157-metre-high falls had become a favourite spot for jilted lovers to jump to their deaths. 'But as the city outgrew its sewage system and the River Bogotá became polluted with shit, the stink of the waterfall became so overpowering that even the suicidal stayed away,' he said with a grin.

Ricardo was steeped in the history of his home city, which offered him some refuge from the dispiriting present. He revelled in the stories of bar-room brawls, crooked police officers and the mayor's shenanigans. He had a keen eye for the grotesque, as well he might, for Bogotá was a city whose patrician elite was as proud as it was sordid. Over the garb of the underdog Ricardo wore the mantel of the radical intellectual. Had he been born fifty years earlier, he might have become a follower of

Che and Fidel, but this being 2011, his convictions were in limbo.
The corruption and brutality of the ruling elite hadn't changed,
but Ricardo had no faith in the guerrillas' high-flown rhetoric
either.

He told me that the first European to enter the land of the
Muisca had been the Spaniard Gonzalo Jiménez de Quesada,
who went on to found Bogotá in 1538. Jiménez de Quesada's party
spent six months trekking up the River Magdalena from the
Caribbean coast. By the time they reached the plain of Bacatá
there were just 170 of them left – by coincidence, Francisco Pizarro had had almost the same number of men when he conquered
the Incas of Peru.

How had such a tiny band gone on to conquer an entire civilization? Disease was to play its part in the years to come, but
the conquest of the Muiscas was only possible because they, like
the Incas, regarded the Europeans with reverent awe. They
called them *usachies*, meaning 'sun-moon', since they regarded
the sun and moon as creators of the world. According to a Spanish chronicler, 'The Indians said to one another – as was later
learned – that our men must be sons of the sun and must have
been sent to punish their shortcomings and sins.'[*]

In each village they came to, the Spaniards accepted the adu-
lation of their Muisca hosts and took on board more gold. On
their way south to Bogotá, the Spanish stormed and looted the
palace of the Zaque of Tunja, throwing his precious objects into
a pile so high that it was said to have hidden a mounted horse-
man. The booty amounted to 621 kilos of fine gold, 14,000 pesos
of base gold and 280 emeralds.

At Guachetá, sixty miles northeast of Bogotá, the invaders
found that the residents had retreated to a fortress on a crag
above the town. Wandering the abandoned buildings, they came

---

[*] John Hemming, *The Search for El Dorado* (Michael Joseph, 1978), p. 77.

across an old man who was sitting in front of a cooking fire. Jiménez de Quesada concluded that he must have been left as an offering. The townspeople had supposed that the invaders, being gods, were sure to enjoy human flesh. Sure enough, when the Spaniards passed the old man by, the locals sent down younger, fresher meat. The Christians made signs to them to indicate that this was not their kind of food and moved on.

Their kind of food proved impossible to find. The land of the Muisca was certainly intensively farmed. Being higher than the tropical forests but lower than the treeless *páramo*, the cool and misty highlands were perfect for growing maize, potatoes and quinoa. The Muisca were great traders and every village would have centred on a busy marketplace. In an area no bigger than Belgium, the Muisca's villages supported a population of at least a million. Since the natives had no pack animals and no wheeled vehicles, they had no need of roads. Instead, a web of stone paths linked the many villages dotted across the plain of Bacatá.

With the single exception of cotton, everything on offer would have been strange to the Europeans: tomatoes, runner beans and squashes; sweet peppers, pineapples and avocados. There were none of the cattle, pigs, sheep or chickens that sustained a Spanish diet in the sixteenth century. The only meat the conquistadores found was guinea pig; according to one observer, they got through 1,000 of them a day.

But the single greatest discovery made by those first explorers was undoubtedly the potato. To this day, the value of the world's annual potato harvest far exceeds that of all the gold, silver and precious stones ever exported from South America. Yet many of the plants that the conquistadores encountered – protein-rich quinoa, arracacha, and camote sweet potatoes – are still little known outside the Andes. These unknown highland crops and the clean mountain air soon restored Jiménez de Quesada's band of emaciated, half-naked men to good health.

As Jiménez de Quesada and his men moved south, word of this party of strangers was sent to the Muisca's supreme ruler, the Zipa of Bacatá. Unlike the villagers they'd encountered up to that point, the Zipa harboured no illusions about the new-comers' intentions. In full battle array, with the mummified bodies of all the previous *zipas* at their head, his soldiers rushed into battle against the Spanish. They were quickly repulsed, overwhelmed by a combination of Toledan steel swords, battle-hardened soldiers and mounted horsemen (which the Muisca initially took to be a single, terrifying creature).

A few days after their defeat of the Zipa of Bacatá, the Span-ish came within sight of his city. 'They began to see beautiful and magnificent buildings, houses and palaces of wood more ornate and better than all they had seen before.'* Many of these buildings had high, conical thatched roofs that were topped by a central mast, dyed red with annatto and adorned with sail-like vanes. As Jiménez de Quesada gazed across the broad plain of Bacatá, he gave it the name *Valle de los Alcazares* – the Valley of Castles. He said that it reminded him of the tiered battlements of Spain's Moorish castles.

On 21 April 1537 his party reached the Zipa's palace at Mue-quetá. They found it empty; before meeting the invaders in battle, the Zipa had hidden his treasure in the mountains. The Spaniards asked the remaining Muisca where they might find more gold, but the locals couldn't help. Although they traded salt and cotton cloth with neighbouring tribes in exchange for raw gold, which their smiths worked with great skill and artis-try, they had no source of gold of their own.

So the Spanish set out to interrogate the Muisca's neighbours, but they remained obstinately tight-lipped about the location of their mines. According to a report from 1560, 'if they see that

* Ibid., p. 86.

one of them is about to reveal where the mines are, the others kill him with poison. For they say that if the mines are revealed they will all perish by being forced to work in them, just as all Indians are finished in any places where mines exist.'*

On our way back down from Moguy, Ricardo suggested that we pay a visit to his Uncle Alejandro, who had invited the Sánchez clan over to celebrate his daughter's first communion. After a half-hour ride on one of the gleaming buses of the *Transmilenio*, we came to a quiet residential neighbourhood. I could have been on a British housing estate. The semi-detached houses looked to have been built in the sixties. In a cul-de-sac, a dad was teaching his baby daughter how to walk. Teenagers on Choppers were pulling wheelies. Even the rich green grass and the silver grey clouds drifting overhead looked familiar.

By British standards, it was striking how little stuff there was in Uncle Alejandro's front room. The walls were bare and the floor was of plain ceramic tiles, which is not to say that he was poor. He was a doctor, and the Sánchez clan's most successful member. Money had been spent on the stucco marbling on the walls, the recessed lighting and the elaborate coving. The furniture was some distant relative of Louis XV and there was a dresser that might from a distance have passed for mahogany, with a tin-dressed-as-silver platter on display inside.

The front room was just a step up from the indoor garage, though I didn't realize it was a garage until Alejandro backed his car into it. He didn't stop backing up until he'd near enough hit the dining table. I thought that perhaps he'd had one too many rum and cokes, but he looked sober enough when he joined us. He explained that to get the car's nose clear of the garage door, he had no choice but to stick its tail into the dining room.

* Ibid.

After I had been introduced to everyone, Ricardo's mum asked me what I thought of Colombia. I sensed a loaded question; what Marta really wanted to know, I told myself, was whether I might make her happy by saying something nice about her country. So I did: '*Pues, me encanta* – I love it,' I said. Everyone smiled. The ice was officially broken.

Over a few rum and cokes, Ricardo, his mum, dad and assorted relatives settled into family gossip. The communion had gone well. Alejandro's daughter had behaved herself. Not that it would have mattered if she hadn't, his dad joked, since God didn't exist anyway. The Sánchez family, I later discovered, came from a long line of anti-clerical Liberals.

'And do you like the food?' Marta asked me. Who could argue that the food was anything but delicious? Lunch certainly always got off to a good start, I told her. The plantain soup, maize soup, barley soup and fish soup I was served at the cheap restaurants I frequented were hearty and warming and the main course was always filling. But Colombian food was let down by its chefs' aversion to herbs and spices. The Spanish seem to have a similar lack of interest in seasoning, I added, so as she wouldn't feel too put out, though the truth of the matter is that at least the Spanish use garlic.

In fact, given the huge variety of foods that can be grown in Colombia, the gamut of flavours on a typical plate was depressingly small. Potatoes, rice, cassava and plantain were the staples. Meat was grilled, fried or sometimes boiled, generally without adornment. I might be lucky enough to get a thick slice of avocado or a token salad, but oil and vinegar didn't often make it onto the table and there seemed to be a nationwide ban on green vegetables. They weren't much good at bread or cheese either.

'Yes, we like our food natural,' Marta said with some pride. Perhaps it's something about the enduring myth of Latin passion, but the British always imagine that Latin food is hot and spicy. It isn't, at least not in this corner of the continent, perhaps because the traders who brought eastern spices like cardamom, cloves and cumin to Europe never made it to the Andes.

Or perhaps a legend I once heard better explains the Colombians' suspicion of spice. In colonial times, the witches of the Caribbean towns would pray to a god called Fot to give them the power of flight. At night, they could be seen on their broomsticks, flying to Jamaica to bring back the green chillies they used in their potions. One day, some local men decided to cut down the tree where the witches used to rest mid-flight. After felling the tree, the men took a break. Sitting on the stump of the tree to sip some rum, they felt something land on their heads. It was human excrement. Looking up, they saw the witches cackling as they flew away on their broomsticks.

To finish my meal, I was often given a slick of figs with a dollop of sweet *arequipe* toffee, but more often a cube of jelly. I'd seen no custard, but all the same a Colombian lunch often felt like a school dinner. Both spurned sensual delight for stodge, as if culinary pleasure were affected, or even intoxicating. Whatever the origin of the naturist streak in Colombian cuisine, there was no Colombian Jamie Oliver.

The good news was that there were plenty of juices to choose from. Some, like strawberry, raspberry, passion fruit and mango, were familiar. Others were novel. *Lulo* was a delicious combination of apple and pear flavours, while *feijoa*, a personal favourite, looked like cut grass, and *borojo* was a muddy aphrodisiac with a game-like aftertaste. Away from Bogotá, there would be yet more juices to try: *zapote* (sapodilla plum), *curuba* (a variant of the passion fruit) and *nispero* (medlar, or Japanese plum). Everything, it seemed, except apple, orange and grapefruit juice.

'And what do British people think of Colombia?' Marta wanted to know.

'Well, being so far away, most people don't even have a conception of the place,' I said, not wanting to confirm her worst imaginings by telling her that most of my British friends still thought of Colombia as a gangster- and terrorist-infested war-zone.

'And what do Colombians think of the UK?' I asked, and Marta started talking about Margaret Thatcher and Lady Di – 'who the whole world loved, of course' – and King Juan Carlos, who she wasn't so fond of. Her picture of Britain, like ours of Colombia, was stuck in the eighties (and Juan Carlos is the king of Spain). Perhaps she, like me, was just trying to be polite. When I'd asked Ricardo the same question, he'd said that he was a little frightened of the British. His picture of us was still col-oured by the Falklands War and football hooligans.

Ricardo told his mum that I was planning to write a book about Colombia, and the smile on her face faded somewhat. 'Many foreign journalists come here and tell lies about how bad the place is,' Marta said. I sympathized, even though the badness of the place was inescapable – it was no lie that Colombia was the world's biggest producer of cocaine. Nor was it untrue that in the 1980s Pablo Escobar had gone to war with the Colombian government on a scale that dwarfed the worst excesses of the Mexican drugs cartels today. That Colombia once had the high-est homicide rate in the world, and still exported more prostitutes, printed more fake euros and planted more land-mines than any other country in the world was all true too.

But Marta wouldn't have denied any of that. What she wanted to say was that the international cocaine business was none of her doing. It had no impact on her, nor she on it. What she wanted to say was that she and millions of other Colombians felt demonized by the outside world. No passport raises more suspicion at international airports than a Colombian one.

'It is important to tell the truth about this country,' Marta told me. 'Most people here are good. They are hard workers' (which isn't quite the same thing, but still, much of the developed world depends on Colombia for cheap labour as well as cocaine). 'And Colombia has made big contributions to literature, medicine, art and music,' she added. Well, enough talk of truth and lies, I thought. The point is that this is still the New World. Ricardo's ancestors, willingly or not, had come here to build a nation. Colombia, like the United States, is a project, not an inheritance. The current generation wanted the outside world to acknowledge their achievements, as well as the beauty that surrounded them.

When I had first met Ricardo, he told me that his dad's side of the family had come to Colombia from Scotland. But Mr Sánchez Snr. said that the McCormick brothers had in fact been Irish. Julio's could well have been an Irish face: it was lean, with a long bony nose and a prominent forehead that hung over keen, deep-set eyes. The McCormicks had arrived in 1812, he told me, to fight with the British Legion. 'Without British soldiers, armaments and finance, Simón Bolívar's campaign to free South America from Spanish rule would have been doomed to failure,' he said.

This was news to me. In fact, as I found out from later forays at the National Library, Simón Bolívar had been such an Anglophile that after declaring independence in 1819, he considered making Colombia an English-speaking country and was only dissuaded from doing so by his second-in-command, General Francisco de Paula Santander.

After the defeat of the Spanish forces, Julio told me, the McCormicks set out to make their fortunes in the newly independent republic. They built Colombia's first iron bridge, which still spans the river at Sube, a village in the department of Santander. Later, they built and ran the country's first radio station, which they called Radio McCormick. But after an auspicious start, the family's fortunes took a turn for the worse. At the turn of the twentieth century, they lost several members in the War of a Thousand Days, the last and bloodiest of the civil wars that convulsed the country for most of the nineteenth century. In the early 1960s, all of their male descendants joined the guerrillas of the Ejército de Liberación Nacional (ELN) – the National Liberation Army, inspired by the Cuban revolution that swept Fidel Castro to power in 1959. Shortly after, they were killed in fighting with the Army, their bodies only iden-tified by the red roses that they wore in their berets. The family name died with them.

While some of the McCormick brothers had sought their fortunes in Colombia, others had gone to the United States. Julio told me that the North American branch of the family had met with better luck. They gave their name to McCormick Spices of Chicago, as well as the McCormick truck company, which produces the famous Mac trucks.

I knew from past conversations that Ricardo wanted to visit Scotland and/or Ireland, to see whichever land it was that his forefathers had sailed from. But he struggled with mixed feel-ings. He had long borne the McCormicks a grudge for the way they'd treated his mum's side of the family, who were black and from Cali. The only protest Ricardo could make was by his refusal to learn his European ancestors' language. English, he told me, was the language of Empire. That was true, I admitted, but it was also the language of globalization. Facebook and the worldwide web had brought the world to Bogotá; together they had rescued Ricardo from the straitjacket imposed by the Andes, his lack of money, the end of socialism and his country's never-ending war on terror.

Hearing that I was curious to find out more about the British contribution to Colombia's story, Marta – who was an avid and refreshingly non-partisan football supporter – had mentioned a *Señor Greenfell*, an Englishman who had been one of the first managers of Santa Fe, the more likeable of the two big *bogotano* football teams. Even their most ardent fans admitted that Santa Fe had had a terrible season, some of which I'd witnessed for myself, but I was intrigued when Marta said that Mr Greenfell was buried in the British cemetery.

The following day, Ricardo and I walked to the cemetery. If Marta hadn't mentioned it, it would have been easy to overlook. Although it occupied an annex of the city's Cementerio Central, it was surrounded by high walls, there was no sign, and the front gate didn't even offer peeping room. The groundsman opened the gate warily, as if accustomed to turning people away.

'Is this the British cemetery?' I asked him.

'Yes,' he replied.

'Is it open to the public?'

'No, it's private. You have to get authorization from the British embassy,' he said, and made to close the gate.

'Even if you're English?' I asked.

He ushered us in. Ricardo got in too: clearly, Colombians were allowed in if accompanied by a Briton. I was chuffed that my nationality was opening doors for me, if only to a graveyard, and chuffed too that the groundsman had, at least at first, taken me for a Colombian. He made a quick call to the British embassy, explaining that a fellow countryman wanted to have a look around. He gave my name as 'Thomas UK Passport Office'. The '*coronel*' must have given him the go-ahead, because the groundsman, who introduced himself as Edgar, gestured for us to follow him, before turning on the heel of his rubber boot and trudging up the brick path that led through a short avenue of yews to the cemetery.

'This is officially British soil,' Edgar said, pointing to the British and Colombian flags, wet from the rain, that were hanging limply from their poles. 'Though it's strange that the British put their flag on the left.' I asked why that was strange, but neither of us understood his reply. What I did understand was that the plot of land occupied by the cemetery had been a gift to Britain, by way of thanks for the contribution made by British volunteers to the wars of independence fought between 1810 and 1820.

When the first revolts against Spanish rule were heralded on the Caribbean coast in 1810, Madrid rushed reinforcements across the Atlantic and they were quickly put down. In 1815 the colony was up in arms once more, the rebels in Cartagena only capitulating to the Spanish after a 108-day siege of the city in which a third of its 18,000 people died of starvation and many of those who survived were reduced to eating rats. In desperation, the city even proclaimed itself to be part of the British Empire, a suggestion that the British government politely rebuffed.

Britain was a beacon of freedom to many of the natives of Gran Colombia, the huge colony that covered modern-day Colombia, Venezuela, Panama and Ecuador. The British government wanted to help the rebels who were seeking to wrest themselves free of the Spanish yoke. London had not forgotten the support that Spain lent to the rebels of the Thirteen Colonies in North America. But as long as the British government was at war with Napoleon Bonaparte in Europe, it could not afford to offend the Spanish crown, which was a key partner in the anti-French alliance.

Even after the defeat of Napoleon at Waterloo in 1815, the British were unwilling to openly defy the Spanish. So they reverted to the policy first devised by Elizabeth I, when English traders and pirates had harried the north coast of Colombia, and Colombians had bought contraband English goods in defiance of the Spanish monopoly. They formally banned trade with Spain's colonies, while informally allowing it to go ahead. By a proclamation of 1817 the British decreed that 'no subject of His

Majesty may take part in the disputes between the King of Spain and those who govern or attempt to govern his American colonies.' Meanwhile, they turned a blind eye to the Latin Americans who came to London to foment support for Simón Bolívar's liberation army.

Their cause was trumpeted by the British press. 'Come quick to avenge the dead, to give life to the dying, confidence to the oppressed and liberty to all!' Simón Bolívar declared in *The Times*. Bolívar is remembered as a brilliant general, who led his troops up and over the Andes not once but several times. Had he not also been an idealist, his name might not inspire the devotion that it still does. 'The freedom of the New World,' he said, 'is the hope of the universe.' It was a phrase I would find myself repeating under my breath in the weeks to come.

Bolívar's right-hand man in London was Don Luis López Méndez. To him Bolívar entrusted responsibility for finding the volunteers and equipment they would need to defeat their colonial masters. Such was López Méndez' importance that in later years, Bolívar would call him 'the true liberator of Colombia'. In the early stages of the liberation campaign, López Méndez could only offer his British recruits the uniforms cast off by soldiers returning from the Napoleonic wars. But as the South Americans secured funding for their recruitment drive, the volunteers saw conditions improve. Recruits were soon provided with sabres, rifles, gunpowder and strikingly luxurious uniforms, styled on those of the Royal Artillery.

They were paid for with short-term loans, which the London banks made to the revolutionaries with some wariness. The bankers had little confidence in the nascent government or its ability to repay the loans, so they charged extortionate rates of interest. British support came at a price and the infant republic would be saddled with huge debts for years to come.

Initially, López Méndez recruited 1,200 soldiers to what

became known as the British Legion. He enticed them into making the two-month-long journey across the Atlantic with offers of land in Colombia and 500 American dollars for any man who stayed in the Americas for more than five years. In time, more than 6,500 English, Irish, Scots and Welsh soldiers signed up, among them many unemployed soldiers, recently back from the fighting at Waterloo, as well as hundreds of former convicts keen to start over in the New World. Some enlisted for the nobility of the Colombian cause, others for the adventure, glory or gold. With the exception of a 300-strong detachment of German soldiers, the soldiers of the British Legion were the only foreigners to come to the aid of Simón Bolívar's rebel army.*

The first contingent to reach Colombia was led by General Edward MacGregor, who arrived in Cartagena at the end of 1817 with 600 men. This time, the British were instrumental in defending the main square against the Spanish. Once on American soil, many members of the British Legion succumbed to the tropical illnesses prevalent on the coast, but as they trekked inland, the mountain air restored the survivors to good health.

At the Battle of Pantano de Vargas, which was fought in highland Boyacá in 1819, the British Legion under the Irishman Colonel James Rook earned a reputation for valiance. Colonel Daniel Florencio O'Leary, the young Irishman who served as Simón Bolívar's aide-de-camp, wrote that 'in the most difficult circumstances and in the presence of the greatest danger, the English officers showed noble perseverance and loyalty to the cause that they had embraced: the liberty of Gran Colombia.' The rebels inflicted a significant defeat on the Spanish at Pantano de Vargas, but the battle took a terrible toll on the British

---

* 'Legión Británica en la independencia de Colombia', unpublished article by Coronel Guillermo Plazas Olarte; also General Álvaro Valencia Tovar, 'La Legión Británica', *El Tiempo*, 18 April 2005.

contingent. Colonel Rook survived, only to die a few days later, just hours before the Spanish were decisively beaten at the Battle of Boyacá. Though the British contribution to Colombia's wars of independence has been largely forgotten in both countries, it supplied the winning blow to colonial rule. Indeed, more Britons died fighting the Spanish than did Colombians.

One Englishman who served for a time in Bolívar's army was 'the Cornish Giant' Richard Trevithick, who sailed from Penzance on the whaling ship *Asp* in October 1816, bound for Peru. The man who had given the world the high-pressure steam engine and the railway locomotive sailed for the New World in the hope of finding work in the silver mines at Potosí. But he was swept up by the wars of independence and eventually found himself in Cartagena, where he designed and built a gun for the rebels.

By chance, while in the city he ran into Robert Stephenson. The last time they had met, Trevithick had bounced the baby Stephenson on his knee at his house in Camborne. Thirty years later, the two men's prospects couldn't have been more different. Stephenson was a world-renowned engineer who had come to Colombia to build a railway, while Trevithick was ailing and broke. When the younger man offered to lend him £50 for his passage home, Trevithick gladly accepted.

Richard Trevithick died penniless in a rented room above a pub in Dartford in 1833, but not before he had alerted his fellow Cornishmen to the opportunities awaiting them in the mines of South America. Cornish tin miners were the first wave of what was to become a tide of informal British imperialists who crossed the Atlantic to build the roads, railways, tunnels, bridges and ports of the new republic. They were also the first to dig for gold in the mines of Antioquia. In 1857, Cornishmen founded Frontino Mines, to this day one of Colombia's biggest gold mining companies.

The relationship between Colombia and Britain was formalized by the Treaty of Friendship, Commerce and Navigation of 1825. Until the opening years of the twentieth century, Britain was Colombia's principal trading partner. Of course, the formal equality espoused by opening each country's ports to the other's goods benefited the British rather more than it did the Colombians, since Colombian merchants had little worth exporting until they began growing coffee in bulk in the early years of the twentieth century. Nor did they have the means to carry what little they produced, either within or beyond their own borders. The previous year, the Colombian Navy had bought two magnificent US frigates at a cost of $1 million, but the Colombians had no money to maintain them or sailors to sail in them, so they were left to rot in the harbour at Cartagena. Still, Colombia needed official recognition, bank loans and foreign technology, and the treaty ensured it got all three.

Beyond the yews, the British Cemetery was bound by a row of spiked railings, fashioned, Edgar told me, from the bayonets of those early British volunteers. At the far end was a low adobe wall, most of which had crumbled away over the years. Beyond, a wall of breeze blocks separated the cemetery from a car park. It was a tranquil spot, and the sight of moss-covered gravestones soon had me feeling wistful. In all, more than 500 Britons were buried there. There was a Scot from Aberdeen, an Englishman from Sutton Coldfield and a Welshman whose gravestone had been carved, presumably by the stonemason next door, in English and Welsh.

The earliest grave I found went back to 1836. In the second half of the nineteenth century, as a steady trickle of foreigners ventured to Colombia to start over in the New World, the British Embassy allowed foreign Protestants to be buried in the cemetery too. There were the graves of Americans, Germans, French and Poles, as well as their offspring, signs of the intermingling they'd done on the Caribbean coast and in departments like Santander and Boyacá. There was the family plot of the Wells Castillo family, the head of which was credited with being 'the father of the Colombian flower business'. Next to it was the grave of one Julian Velásquez Jones, who had been born in Barranquilla and died in Bogotá. A little further along was Dora Golding de Vélez, who had been born in Manchester and died at Sogamoso, Boyacá.

There was a grave shared by two English brothers, who had died just weeks apart in 1900, at Girardot, a town on the River Magdalena. I wondered whether they'd fought in the War of a Thousand Days. Perhaps they had worn *niños en cruz*, the cross of tiny stones that soldiers on both sides of the war used to stitch under the skin of their wrists? I'd read of several fighters who had sworn that bullets bounced off them thanks to their *niño en cruz*. It was a telling sign of the melange of shamanism and Catholicism that once held sway in the Colombian countryside.

Today's soldiers, guerrillas and paramilitaries would be more likely to carry a *fajada* – a laminated picture of a favourite saint – but many would still have it blessed by a local witch before putting it down their pants and heading off into battle. Foreign soldiers still come to Colombia to fight, though these days most of them are American and work for private defence contractors. But the British Army contributes advisors and SAS men to the Colombian front of the so-called 'war on drugs'. I have a photo of the then-Defence Minister Kim Howells, posing with troops from the High Mountain Battalion, one of several Colombian Army units to have received training from their British counterparts. It is hard to know just what they were doing, as the MoD is reluctant to divulge any details.

The High Mountain Battalion, however, is an easier book to read: in May 2006, troops from the battalion were ordered by

their commanding officer to ambush and kill ten counter-
narcotics police officers near the town of Jamundí. The police
had been preparing to seize 200 kilos of cocaine that reportedly
belonged to Diego Montoya, one of Colombia's leading drug
barons. Subsequent investigations showed the commander of
the High Mountain Battalion to be in the pay of Montoya.*

I couldn't find the grave of Señor Greenfell, the Englishman
who had valiantly tried to save Santa Fe from ignominy. On my
way out, Edgar asked me to write the name down for him, just
in case he spotted it while he was cutting the grass. Back in the
traffic on Avenida El Dorado, Ricardo and I negotiated our way
around the roadworks and watched the diggers for a while. A
skinny young engineer in a fluorescent jacket was supervising
what might have been another, shorter and stockier race of men
who were shovelling mud from a huge hole in the ground. Just
short of the bridge that carried the *Transmilenio* buses over Calle
26, they'd excavated a small round mud-brick hut, which they'd
been careful not to demolish. I hadn't expected to see layers of
Bogotá's history unearthed, as I might the remains of London or
Rome. Had it been built by the Muiscas? Nobody could tell.
As Lucho had said on the day Mono Jojoy was killed, Colombians have short memories. The present, it seems, demands their
undivided attention.

---

* 'Colombian Army Accused in Massacre of Drug Police', *Washington Post*,
18 June 2006.

3. The Last Nomads

Back in the 1980s, when Pablo Escobar first started making his – and his country's – name for all-round nastiness, nobody gave much thought to bio-diversity. Now that they do, and with Escobar long gone, environmentalists are paying more attention to Colombia. Per square foot, it is the most bio-diverse country in the world. It has more species of birds and frogs than any other country, and were it not for the conflict botanists would doubtless have found many more. Colombia's mountains, and its location just north of the equator, make it supremely wet and verdant. Its rivers and lakes contain more freshwater than those of the United States and Canada combined.

I was keen to see some of this natural wealth, after so many years in which the best bits were reserved for the country's guerrillas and cocaine traffickers. I particularly wanted to visit the Caño Cristales. I'd seen the photos, of a river flowing over red jasper and blooms of blue and yellow algae, and heard more than a few people call it 'the river that ran away from paradise' and 'the most beautiful river in the world'. The Caño Cristales runs through the national park of La Macarena, a 60-mile-long loaf-shaped range of hills. It is one of the world's oldest geological features, a stranded relative of the Guyanese plate, which sprouts as *tepuis*, or table-top mountains, on the border between Brazil and Venezuela, hundreds of miles further east. The park is home to hundreds of species of animals and plants to be found nowhere else on the planet.

Until recently, many of the farmers around La Macarena made their living from growing coca. Now they had set up an eco-tourist venture to lure visitors to the river. Such a thing would have been unimaginable when I last lived in Colombia, but it illustrated just how far the country had come, as well as the natural bounty the country had to offer. A trip to La Macarena wasn't without its problems: the northern half of the park was still host to FARC guerrillas, as well as plenty of coca growers who had yet to 'get' eco-tourism. All the same, I booked a flight in a biplane that would give me a bird's-eye view of the park and had my bag packed, when I was told that since the death of Mono Jojoy, the whole region was once again off-limits. The FARC commander had been killed in the national park only a week before, and the guerrillas were even warier than usual of potential spies and informers. I thought it best to leave the Caño Cristales for another time.

Beyond La Macarena, however, lies San José del Guaviare, a small town on the open plains about 170 miles southeast of Bogotá. It is the last outpost before the roadless Amazon basin. In the past three years both the guerrillas and the coca farmers have been forced out of San José del Guaviare and into the dense rainforests to the south and east. Many jungle dwellers have had to make way for them, among them the Nukak Maku, the last nomadic tribe in South America. I had heard about a refugee camp on the outskirts of San José, where several Nukak clans were living. A visit offered a good introduction to the tangle of cause and effect that had made Colombia's conflict so long and intractable. I headed for the bus station.

Leaving Bogotá for San José, the road follows one of the many rivers that flow down from the eastern Andes on to the plains, or *llanos*. In the latter stages of the descent from the highlands, the valley sides become steeper and the road is forced through a series of tunnels and bridges. By the time we left the last tunnel and emerged onto the open expanse of the *llanos*, the light was fading from the sky, leaving clouds of amber, pink and violet. The heat of the plains and the smell of dry grass seeped into the bus as the street lights of Villavicencio came into view. From there to the Atlantic, thousands of miles to the east, was a flat expanse of savannah, jungle and isolated *colono* settlements.

Known as the 'Gateway to the Plains', until the 1950s Villavicencio was no more than a village. Only in the years that followed did migrants from other parts of Colombia begin to colonize the virgin land in large numbers. Sixty years of unstinting toil later, those *colonos* had made the city's cattle ranchers rich.

I'd decided to break my journey here. I found a cheap hotel, took a room and channel surfed for the hour before dinner. Most of the channels offered familiar transnational fare: CNN, Discovery and BBC World. On the Latin version of MTV, a Mexican *ranchera* singer with a silver moustache and a velvet jacket covered in gold sequins was crooning from the saddle. He was singing about the women of his life, '. . . *unas buenas, otras peligrosas* . . . some good, others dangerous'. It was a sad song, which he wrapped up with the line '*mi caballito es mi mejor compañero* – my little horse is my best friend.'

On channel 35, I found one of the ubiquitous *telenovelas*. A woman was crying her eyes out; her husband had been having an affair with her best friend. The camera lingered on the tears streaming down her face for a mawkishly long time. There was another *telenovela*, with yet another tear-soaked protagonist on channel 36. On 38, I found a discussion programme, in which one of the guests was criticizing the president for riding roughshod over the wishes of Congress. This was a novelty: I'd never heard such open dissent on Colombian television before; sure enough, it turned out that I'd picked up a Venezuelan channel.

I settled for the evening news, which began with a report from the southern department of Nariño, where the Army was fighting running battles with the guerrillas. Next, the cameras

turned to the presidential palace, where the recently inaugurated president Juan Manuel Santos was introducing his cabinet
to the press. Judging by their complexions, I could have been in
Spain. Plenty of Colombians had told me that the mix of black,
white and indigenous people was the essence of their country,
but you'd never have guessed that this was a *mestizo* nation from
watching television.

The news was interrupted by an ad break. The men and
women in white coats were extolling their latest marvel. As
they explained the benefits of using their new and improved
painkiller, a microscopic graphic of a neural transmitter throb-
bing in the background, I couldn't help but notice a parallel
with the news. Sometimes the threat was internal, at others
external, but whatever form it took, Colombians could rely on
white people to warn and protect them.

The Argentinian writer Jorge Luis Borges was once asked on
a trip abroad if he was Spanish. 'I'm sorry,' he replied, 'but I
made the decision fifty years ago to stop being Spanish.' It
seemed that the more Colombia struggled with New World
problems, the more tightly its leaders clung to Old World solutions. They might have fought a war to free themselves from
rule from Madrid, but they were far from reconciled to the
mixed-race nation they governed. For loyal defenders of this
outpost of European civilization, there had only ever been one
language, religion and culture worthy of the names. Even their
war of independence had been whitewashed. All the accounts
I'd read had Spanish tyrants pitted against their American-born
descendants. The struggles of black Colombians, let alone the
country's indigenous people, barely got a look in.

The conflict between the native peoples of South America
and the descendants of those who conquered them is less notice-
able in Colombia than in countries like Bolivia or Peru because
indigenous people make up just 2 per cent of the population.

Most of their forefathers were either massacred, worked to an early death or fell victim to the various illnesses that the Europeans brought with them. But many indigenous women survived, to be kept as wives by the conquistadores. As a result, five hundred years later most Colombians are *mestizo*. In Antioquia – after Bogotá, the most powerful and influential of Colombia's thirty-two departments – nine out of every ten people can trace their descent to a Spanish father and an indigenous mother.[*] Perhaps this explains the frequency with which I heard Colombians say, 'One's mother is a saint, but one's father is any old son of a bitch.'

I ventured out to have a look around Villavicencio. The city centre was orderly and neat, with an abundance of shops selling trainers – in fact, the whole town seemed to be wearing new trainers. I found a table on the terrace of a pizza restaurant and settled down with a cold beer to watch the world go by.

At a neighbouring table, a gaggle of teenagers were flirting with one another. The girls wore skin-tight jeans studded with sequins or plastic gold letters. The boys wore T-shirts emblazoned with gothic lettering. 'Punk Rock Club', said one; 'Revolution: Real Attitude', said another. I could have been anywhere, watching kids brandish their pseudo-affiliation to the political traditions of the twentieth century in clothes manufactured by the tailors of communist China.

But the slogans seemed especially ironic here. In the poor neighbourhoods that ring Villavicencio, a paramilitary army known as ERPAC – Ejército Revolucionario Popular Antisubversivo de Colombia – is waging a real, albeit simmering, war on the FARC. The name – at once popular, revolutionary and

[*] Héctor Abad Faciolince, 'El puñal y la herida', *El Espectador*, 18 December 2010.

anti-subversive – is a telling bundle of contradictions. Only occasionally do ERPAC's fighters take on the guerrillas in open combat. The FARC are seasoned combatants, as well as elusive targets, so the paramilitaries spend most of their time rooting out 'subversives', a term which sometimes refers to community activists, but more often means young glue sniffers, thieves and prostitutes. Over the last twenty years, paramilitary groups like ERPAC have killed almost 3,000 Colombian children.

At its most savage, the paramilitaries' campaign of violence has been sociopathic, but at times it has also seemed strangely juvenile. All too often, the perpetrators are children in uniform, killing other children for the price of a new pair of trainers. It is playground bullying, with the parents supplying the weapons. For as the rules of engagement in Colombia's long-running conflict have been tossed aside, the recruitment of child soldiers by both guerrillas and paramilitaries has shot up. The boys are used as spies; the girls are recruited as girlfriends, sometimes raped and forced into abortions. When they leave school, many of the boys go on to learn how to handle weapons. By 2010, 14,000 Colombian children had been recruited by illegal armed groups.* The conflict that is spluttering to its gruesome, as yet undecided conclusion is being fought by armies in which one in four fighters is technically still a child.

ERPAC was led by Pedro Oliveiro Guerrero, a powerful landowner and cocaine trafficker in the *llanos*, whose *nom de guerre* was 'Cuchillo' (Knife). In the last days of 2010, three months after I passed through Villavicencio, the Army tracked him to a ranch downriver from San José del Guaviare, where he and his men were enjoying Christmas drinks. Cuchillo drank 21-year-old Chivas Regal; his men drank only *aguardiente* – the

---

* 'Unos 3.000 niños, asesinados por paramilitares en Colombia', *El Mundo*, 19 February 2010, citing a report published by the NGO Tribunal Internacional.

local firewater. As the Army moved in, Cuchillo fled. His body was found face down in a nearby river early the following morning. Drunk, and weighed down by the M-60 machine gun and walkie-talkie around his neck, it seemed that he had got caught in the roots of a tree and drowned.*

The only reason I'd decided to stop in Villavicencio was because the United Nations' High Commission for Refugees (UNHCR) had an office there. I was hoping its director could tell me more about the Nukak Maku, so the next morning I walked out to meet him. Giovanni Lepri told me that the first mention of the Nukak made by outsiders came in 1963, when *El Espectador* reported that *colono* farmers in the department of Guaviare had killed several Nukak, after being attacked with arrows by 500 of them. Three years later, the same newspaper carried a priest's account of a trip he had made to the confluence of the rivers Inirida and Guaviare, where he walked the Nukak's intricate pathways and saw some evidence of plant cultivation.

In 1976, evangelical Christians from a mission called Nuevas Tribus built a settlement in the northern reaches of Nukak territory. One of the missionaries was an American, Kenneth Conduff, who became the first outsider to master the Nukak language. He found it to be far more complex than he'd first thought. It even had a subjunctive tense, like Spanish.† Conduff reported that the Nukak were very sarcastic in their use of words and that although they laughed a lot, their laughter often veiled criticism or scorn.

And yet they received the newcomers hospitably and were

---

* 'La noche negra de alias "Cuchillo"', *El Espectador*, 29 December 2010.
† Strictly speaking, the subjunctive is not a tense, but a mood, used to denote doubt rather than assertion. It is widely used in Spanish, but there are only vestiges of it to be found in English grammar, 'If I were a rich man . . .' being the example that most readily springs to mind.

curious to know more about the outside world. Until the missionaries arrived, the Nukak had assumed that they were the only people on the planet. They didn't know where or what Colombia was. When they saw planes flying overhead, they supposed that they were travelling along an invisible road in the sky and wondered who could have built such a thing. They had no concept of money or property. They didn't even have numbers, so they had no way of measuring age or distance either.

The Nukak told Conduff that for most of their history, they had lived beneath the surface of the earth. One day, a Nukak woman made a hole in the sky and the tribe emerged to live above ground. They believed that those first Nukak had created many of the animals they saw around them. Parrots, for example, were born of an early Nukak woman who liked to sing, as all Nukak did. They believed that they were inhabited by multiple spirits, and that when they died, their spirits returned to various parts of the jungle. The spirit world was ruled over by a god called Mauro. If a Nukak man had been angry during his lifetime, Mauro was sure to eat his spirit when he died, so the Nukak taught their children never to show anger (which might explain their frequent sarcasm).

The missionaries told them that by hiding their anger, they were lying to themselves, others and ultimately to Mauro. They shouldn't lie to God, or to one another, the missionaries told them. God was all-powerful and all-seeing, but he loved mankind. The idea that God loved them impressed the Nukak greatly and when the missionaries told them about the life of Jesus Christ, they were dumbfounded. Christianity had a huge impact on a community accustomed to regarding God as brutal and mean-spirited. They converted willingly and unquestioningly.

Only in 1984 did the Nukak venture to the edge of the forest and make contact with the outside world. As word got out of the discovery of an unknown tribe of 'pristine' people untouched by Western civilization, anthropologists began to visit them, first from Bogotá and then from universities around the world. The police in the town of Mapiripán would give them presents when they came across them. Local *colono* farmers came to eat with them and struggled to learn their language.

When the missionaries had first met the Nukak, the women had gone naked, except for bands that they wore just below their knees and around their ankles, and the men had worn short grass skirts. But as the Nukak spent more time with the *colonos*, they came to copy their dress. Western clothes and metal objects became their most treasured possessions. Sometimes the Nukak would take things from the *colonos*. At first, this didn't provoke any ill will – these jungle people clearly had no concept of private property, the *colonos* said to one another, so their light-fingeredness could hardly be called theft. Besides, they dropped most of what they took on their way back into the jungle and the *colonos* soon got used to picking up after them.

But one day, one of the Nukak walked off with a settler's newborn child. The *colonos* looked for but never found the missing baby. Soon after, many Nukak fell ill. They'd caught the common cold from the settlers, but as they had no immunity to this alien malady, some of them died. The Nukak saw this as divine punishment for their abduction of a white woman's baby. Living in proximity to *colonos* soon brought the Nukak into contact with other illnesses, such as dengue fever and measles. Between 1992 and 1996, many of the older Nukak died, still convinced that God was punishing them for abducting the settler's baby. In 1992, there were thought to be around 3,000 Nukak, but by 1996 the population had fallen by half.

In this sense, at least, the plight of the Nukak has been little different to that suffered by millions of indigenous South Americans over the last 500 years. Most of the rest of the world's population has increased explosively since the sixteenth century. But thanks in large part to the diseases that the Europeans brought to the New World, over the same period the native lowland population of the Americas has declined by about 95 per cent.[*]

Although less than a million Colombians are indigenous, they belong to 104 distinct tribes, each with its own language, history and traditions. Thirty-two of these groups are currently at risk of extinction, nine of which are from the *llanos*. The Jiw, Sikuani, Cuiva, Jitnu, Makaguane and Iguanitos each have less than 1,000 members remaining and less than half of them practise any aspect of their traditional culture. This may not be a bad thing: hunting and gathering is desperately hard work. But rather than being assimilated into Colombian society, these tribes are being forced into a material and spiritual wasteland. Less than a third of them graduate from secondary school and most are jobless.[†]

And yet the single biggest threat to the indigenous groups of the *llanos*, and particularly the Nukak Maku, is not western diseases. It is the cocaine business. Coca cultivation took off in the *llanos* not only because the Army and police were nowhere to be seen, but also because the *colonos* were on the brink of ruin. It could take days to get their produce over the plains to the marketplaces further west. The roads were bad and the prices paid for their crops were derisory. Bereft of any help from the government, many *colonos* hit the road, wandering the plains towns in search of work and sustenance. So when representatives of the big cocaine producers came downriver offering them bags of coca seeds, they didn't need to be asked twice. Coca was a native crop that needed no fertilizers or pesticides and brought a

---

[*] John Hemming, *The Search for El Dorado* (Michael Joseph, 1978), p. 23.
[†] ACNUR, *Comunidades Indigenas en el Municipio de Villavicencio* (2010).

steady stream of buyers to their door. Harvests were frequent and plentiful and the rising demand for cocaine in Europe ensured that prices were only going up.

In the early 1990s, *colonos* began clearing the forests in the western part of Nukak territory to plant coca bushes. They also encroached from the north, so some Nukak families moved eastwards, into territory occupied by neighbouring tribes. Others decided to stay and started working for the coca growers at harvest time. They settled on the outskirts of *colono* villages, where they learnt how to cultivate plantain and cassava.

At first, the FARC tried to stop the *colonos* growing coca. They suspected that the cocaine business was part of some kind of covert imperialist invasion, and that peasants who became prosperous from coca growing would lose interest in the revolutionary struggle. The guerrillas had ruled swathes of the sparsely populated countryside since the mid sixties, and many *colonos* had been persuaded by their programme of rural self-government, land reform and economic development. But the FARC leadership soon realized that if they were to ban coca growing, they risked losing the *colonos'* support entirely. So rather than prohibit coca, the guerrillas taxed it. The *gramaje* is a levy on all aspects of the cocaine trade that has earned the FARC millions of dollars a year, mainly from the traffickers and the more prosperous coca farmers.

The guerrillas' rapprochement with coca fed straight into the hands of their enemies. With the Americans upping the pressure for results in their war on drugs, it was clear that whoever was branded responsible for the cocaine trade would become public enemy number one, not just in Colombia but in Washington, DC. The US ambassador was the first to coin the term 'narco-guerrilla'. But the idea that the FARC were involved in cocaine production or smuggling, or that they were forcing *campesinos* to grow coca, was – at least in the early days – false. The FARC dominated large tracts of the jungle plains long before the first coca bushes were planted in the *llanos*. The *colonos* didn't need the FARC to tell them that the government had no intention of investing in the development of the region; that the politicians they voted into office were corrupt; or that any attempt to organize or protest would be fiercely put down. The life of a community leader has been brutal since the first *colonos* settled the plains, and the FARC seemed to be the only ones willing to address the chronic lack of development in the region.

Still, the 'narco-guerrilla' moniker stuck. Drug-trafficking Marxists became the justification for a multi-million-dollar coca fumigation campaign that sent *campesinos* the length and breadth of Colombia scrambling for cover. By 1996 nearly 200,000 of them had seen the effects of the pesticides that fell from the crop-dusting planes onto their coca plants and whatever legal crops they happened to be growing. In June of that year the FARC mobilized thousands of coca farmers in the departments of Guaviare, Putumayo, Caquetá, Norte de Santander and Bolívar. The Army broke up their protest marches, in full view of the television cameras. For the first time, distant city dwellers were sensitized to the reality of coca producers' lives and the government's indifference to their precarious conditions. The guerrillas, who had taken the coca farmers' side against the crop dusters and the *yanquis* who paid for them, seemed heroic by comparison.

The fumigation planes kept up their sorties over the coca fields. As the poison settled into the jungle foliage, the Army pursued the FARC's battalions ever deeper into the wilderness. In 1997 local paramilitaries began moving into the FARC's coca-growing areas, in an attempt to separate the guerrillas from what had quickly become one of their biggest sources of funding. They mounted roadblocks to stop supplies going into jungle villages controlled by the FARC. In Mapiripán, the Colombian

Army colluded with paramilitaries in the chainsaw massacre of at least forty villagers, a brutal warning that 'subversives' and those who supplied them would not be tolerated. People living along the roads and rivers of the *llanos* fled deeper into the jungle.

The missionaries from Nuevas Tribus had already been threatened by the FARC, and in 1996 they left for good. As the fighting between the Army, the guerrillas and the paramilitaries intensified, local indigenous people were forced to leave their ancestral territories to live in makeshift shacks on the outskirts of Villavicencio.

Nukak territory is vital to the guerrillas, not just because so much coca is grown there, but also because nearly all of their kidnap victims are held there. Fear of informers is pervasive and well founded among the guerrillas. In some jungle villages, all calls made from public phone booths are routed through loud-speakers, so that the local FARC militia can hear exactly what is being said. The FARC have no inherent problem with the Nukak, but they are wanderers and have earned themselves a reputation for talking too much. The guerrillas have tried to explain the importance of not talking to anyone about their whereabouts, but the armed conflict is a mystery to the Nukak. The FARC have tried to stop their wandering, telling them that they can no longer go on hunting and fishing trips and confining them to specific parts of the jungle. But this too is incomprehensible to the Nukak. By way of warning, the FARC killed a Nukak leader in 2005. The Nukak still didn't understand what they had done wrong.

So the FARC forced them out. In 2008, the entire tribe arrived in San José del Guaviare, claiming to have been ordered out by 'the green brothers', presumably a reference to the guerrillas' fatigues. A Nukak man called Mow-be emerged as their spokesman and asked the government to help them to return to their lands. The government offered them humanitarian assistance, but said that it could do little more. The situation seemed hopeless; despairing of ever finding a solution to the crisis his people faced, Mow-be committed suicide.

After my meeting with the director of the UN's refugee programme, I sat at a café and had a cold drink in the shade. Some soldiers were studying a map at the table next to mine. A *campesino* farmer came and shared my table. Héctor must have been my age; he had a thin, rat-like face and light-brown eyes. He was from a village in La Macarena, the national park I had hoped to visit to see the Caño Cristales. Things were bad there, he told me; there was a lot of fighting between the Army and the FARC. People were too frightened to work their fields and their families were getting hungry. Héctor had come north to denounce the theft of his horse by his neighbour to the police, but he didn't hold out much hope of anything being done about it. I bought him a cold drink, wished him luck and walked back to my hotel.

When I'd told the woman at reception that I was on my way to San José, where I hoped to find out more about the Nukak Maku, she told me that she knew an American missionary in the town who had lived in the *llanos* for years and spoke the Nukak language fluently. I wondered if she was talking about Kenneth Conduff, the first outsider to learn their language; no, she said, his name was Jack. She called his number and handed me the phone. He sounded as surprised as I was to be speaking English in the *llanos*. I told him that I was planning to take the bus to San José that afternoon; he told me to give him a ring when I got there.

The journey, which can't have covered more than 120 miles, took six long hours. For much of the way south, the jungle had been cleared to make way for near-empty cattle pastures. Every hour or so, the road would come to a sudden end and the bus inched along what had become a rutted dirt track, past the road-building crews that were laying concrete under the blazing sun.

For a while, we followed the languid River Ariari and then we passed through a town with a clue in its name: Fuente de Oro – source of gold. Between 1530 and 1535 three expeditions of European adventurers left the coast of Venezuela in the hope of finding gold on these plains. They spoke of a land so rich that tufts of grass pulled from the ground had gold dust on their roots.

The first expedition was led by Diego de Ordás, a Spaniard who was convinced that there was a causal connection between the brilliance of the sun and the glow of gold. It followed that gold would 'grow' best at the Equator. By Ordás' reckoning, the source of South America's fabled gold had to lie at the head-waters of one of its two great rivers, the Orinoco and the Amazon, somewhere behind the Andes. Ordás and his men travelled up the Orinoco for hundreds of miles in search of the chimerical gold mines, enduring terrible hardship along the way. One of them was to write, 'If someone was bitten by a vampire or got a small cut, he immediately became cancerous. There were men who, from one day to the next, had their entire feet consumed by cancer, from the ankle to the sole.' They suffered in vain: by the time Ordás left South America, 'his only gain was that most of his followers had lost their lives; and those who escaped alive were left poor and sick, without property in that wilderness.' Ailing and broke, Ordás died at sea on his way back to Spain.[*]

The early explorers' greed and recklessness was only matched by their complete ignorance of the lands they ventured into. They had no maps to guide them and the local Indians had limited knowledge of what lay ahead, so they were constantly

---

[*] Hemming, *Search for El Dorado*, p. 16.

losing their way. In 1530, a German adventurer called Nicolaus Federmann left the Venezuelan coastal town of Coro to look for a route to the Pacific Ocean. When he climbed a small hill and gazed out over the vast expanse of water that lay ahead, he felt sure that he had reached it. Had he waited for the morning mists to clear, he might have realized that he was not on the shore of an ocean, but the edge of the *llanos*, which had been flooded by the annual rains.*

Five years later, another German reached the *llanos*. Georg Hohermuth declared himself 'overcome by the great fame of [the region of] Meta, which was the general objective that explorers pursued in those days'.† After crossing the River Arauca, Hohermuth came to a village called Sarobai, where 'all the Indians said unanimously that the riches were on the other side of the mountains'. His party began to climb into the foothills of the Andes, but the mighty Sierra Nevada Del Cocuy prevented them from going any further west, so they headed south. In April 1536 they came to an outpost on the River Upía, where they found Muisca tribesmen from the highlands trading with the lowlanders. The Europeans had no idea that they were immediately below Bogotá and the sacred lake of Guatavita, origin of the myth of El Dorado. 'The Golden One' was reputed to be a tribal chief so rich in gold that every day he covered his body in gold dust before jumping into the lake.

Of the 400 Europeans who left the Caribbean coast with Hohermuth in 1535, only 160 made it back. The young Philip von Hutten, who accompanied Hohermuth on this disastrous three-year escapade, wrote, 'It is horrible to consider what the poor Christians ate on that expedition: snakes, frogs, lizards, vipers, worms, herbs, roots and other food always of the same

* Ibid., p. 29.
† Ibid., p. 56.

sort and without any value. Some, contrary to nature, ate human meat: one Christian was found cooking a quarter of a child with some greens . . . God dispensed his grace to those of us who managed to save our lives.'*

With the benefit of hindsight, it is easy to pour scorn on the greed and ignorance that sealed the fate of those early explorers. But that would be to overlook the terrible fascination that South America exercised over the minds of many sixteenth-century Europeans. Von Hutten wrote, 'God knows it was not avarice that impelled me to undertake that journey, but a strange desire I have harboured for a long time. I believe that I could not have died in peace without having seen those Indies.'

The myth of El Dorado (and the hope of robbing him of his gold) was to lure Europeans into the plains and mountains of Colombia for centuries to come. The eighteenth-century writer Basilio Vicente de Oviedo wrote that every year the local tribes-men would draw lots to decide who would be sacrificed to their idol. 'They open him up and salt him with gold dust, and offer him as a sacrifice in their church. Because of this they call him *El Dorado*.'[†] As late as 1965, foreigners were still trying to figure out how to drain the sacred lake at Guatavita and get their hands on the gold thought to lie on its silt-laden bed.

For most of the colonial period, however, the gold prospec-tors stuck to the highlands and left the plains untouched, a source only of hostile tribes and legendary beasts. Not until the 1950s did Colombians return to the *llanos*, when they became the sponge that absorbed the labour of thousands of peasants forced to flee the violence then raging in the west of the country. Migra-tion to the *llanos* was always more a matter of expulsion than attraction, as malaria, yellow fever and tropical anaemia were

* Ibid., p. 63.
† Ibid., p. 102.

rife in the lowlands. An American physician by the name of Hamilton Rice travelled across them in 1912 and was amazed at the poverty and sickness he found in the *colono* settlements. In San Martín, every one of the 300 people Rice examined was stricken with malaria.

The bus passed through San Martín a couple of hours after leaving Villavicencio. It looked to be a prosperous little farming town, but I knew that appearances – and particularly the appearance of peace and prosperity – could be deceptive in Colombia. The poverty of the *colonos* has long been the hidden face of the country's progress. Since the fifties they have cleared huge swathes of jungle to make way for cattle pastures; their herculean efforts made many of the local landowners rich. In return for felling trees and draining swamps, the *colonos* were given small plots of land to grow the food they needed to survive. But they have never been granted legal title to anything, and becoming a legal smallholder is still a distant prospect for most of them. As one commentator put it, 'their tribulations and generalized insecurity are the price of free competition for land in a profoundly unjust and viscerally independent society. On the agrarian frontier, the state has always been waiting in the wings, and there it still waits. The weak have no laws to free them from the freedom of the strong.'*

It was dark by the time we arrived in San José del Guaviare. The Hotel Colombia was one of those deeply pretentious places, which every provincial town seemed to have, that catered to the town's honchos and their visitors. Since San José had only sprung up in the past twenty years and was known to be crawling with cocaine traffickers, I assumed that the hotel was an

---

* Marco Palacios, *Between Legitimacy and Violence: A History of Colombia 1875–2002* (Duke University Press, 2006), p. 167.

example of what Colombians called *narquitectura*, the ostentatious style favoured by the country's drug traffickers. The reproduction Greek statues, convoluted water feature, and glamorous older woman owner might have appealed to the suddenly rich, but the place gave me the creeps – though I had to admit that they kept it spotlessly clean.

The next morning, I woke to the chugging sound of the little engines in the park that kept the ice-cream sellers' products cold. I made my way downstairs to the bakery on the ground floor, for breakfast. A dog was lounging on the pavement, enjoying the morning sun. The farmers liked to pat him as they sipped their coffee. He was familiar yet strange, the size of a Labrador but with blacker skin, shorter hair and a heavier brow than I'd ever seen on a dog before. One of the farmers told me that he was an indigenous dog, one of the few traces of the breed that dominated canine Colombia before the arrival of European dogs. Spanish soldiers and priests had devastated South America's dogs as well as its people. The soldiers brought their own sturdy hunting dogs, which either killed the native breeds or contaminated them with diseases to which they had no resistance. The priests, recognizing the sacred status the indigenous tribes afforded to their dogs, were happy to see the last of them go – bound, it seemed, for the relative peace of San José.

After breakfast, I met Edgar Alzate, a short and kindly man with no shoulders who ran education programmes for the indigenous people of the *llanos*, funded by the oil companies that were prospecting across the region. We walked a few blocks to the banks of the River Guaviare and sat at the top of a steep slip to contemplate the great curve in front of us. A dugout canoe was buzzing its way downstream, distant and calming. Thousands of miles to the east, the river would flow into the Atlantic, as one of the hundreds that make up the mighty Orinoco.

'Plenty of *colonos* regard the Nukak as no more than dirty

beggars,' Edgar told me. 'They say that they come into town to steal food or to beg from restaurants. But the Nukak don't even realize that it's a crime to steal. Personally, I blame the anthropologists. They encouraged the Nukak to preserve their system of common property, without realizing the trouble it would get them into.'

Other *colonos* were more self-interested. Many of them had arrived in San José single and on the lookout for potential partners. There had been cases of sexual abuse of Nukak women, some of whom had been forced to live with *colonos*. Some Nukak children had also been abused; others had been abducted, to be brought up in *colono* households, where they quickly lost contact with their families.

Fortunately, most of the *colonos* were more paternalistic. Although the Nukak tended to be quite indifferent to anyone who wasn't a member of their clan, everyone knew that Nukak women were very sensitive and tender-hearted with their own. To illustrate his point, Edgar told me about the disappearance of a 24-year-old Nukak man called Luis. When the women of his clan heard the news, they went to the mayor's office and cried for hours on end. They thought that Luis was dead and were getting ready to kill themselves. The Nukak regard suicide as a way of showing their love for a person, said Edgar. Even a false accusation could lead a Nukak to commit suicide. Indeed, the elderly practically expected their children to kill themselves when they died. Confronted by this group of near-suicidal women, the mayor made some frantic phone calls and soon discovered that Luis had been forcibly recruited by the town's paramilitaries. Luckily, they released him a few days later. He'd been no use to them; he had no idea what a gun was for, let alone how to use one.

Only in the late afternoon did Jack, the American missionary who I had spoken to before leaving Villavicencio, pick up the phone. He seemed reluctant to meet; the time he'd spent with the Nukak was all a very long time ago, he told me. Yes, he'd known Kenneth Conduff, the first outsider to learn Nukak, but he'd long since passed away. No, he'd not got very far with his own efforts to learn the language, despite what the woman at my hotel in Villavicencio had told me. Jack said I'd be better off talking to Albeiro Riano, the doctor who had been sent to look after the Nukak by the national organization for indigenous people in Bogotá.

By good fortune, Albeiro lived in the Hotel Colombia, so I hung up the phone and walked down the long, shiny corridor from my room to his. I found him sitting on his bed, shirtless and cross-legged, reading Patrick Suskind's *The Pigeon*. Albeiro was a calm and serious man in his late thirties who had lived in the same small room for the past eight years. The shelves around him were piled high with medical textbooks, academic reports and manuscripts that flapped in the wind created by the overhead fan.

Albeiro told me that he had given inoculations against illnesses like tetanus and polio to the displaced Nukak. Mortality rates had fallen; but there were no vaccinations to be had for influenza, diarrhoea or malaria. Even with western medical treatment, the Nukak were still five times more likely to fall ill than the *colono* population. Albeiro had watched a lot of Nukak die. 'The only ones left are those that have managed to develop some immunity to the illnesses that killed off the older generation.'

I was curious to know how the Nukak explained their plight to themselves. Did they still put it down to their abduction of a settler's baby? 'Well, they still believe that illnesses are caused by malevolent spirits,' he told me. 'But since western, not traditional, medicine is what has saved them from the spirits, most of them have stopped using the old cures and potions.' The

Nukaks' appreciation of western medicine would make their return to the jungle, which already looked unlikely, harder still. But maybe this was a good thing: the Nukak who lived in the jungle were far more likely to fall ill than those living in the displaced community on the outskirts of San José.

Albeiro was planning on visiting their camp the following morning. Perhaps I'd like to come along and see things for myself? I accepted his invitation, and bade him goodnight.

Back in my room, my attention was caught by the notice on the back of the door: 'Please read this in silence: it's very short and very effective,' it read. 'Lord Jesus: Forgive me my sins. I love you very much. I'll always need you. You are in the depths of my heart. Cover with your precious blood my family, my home, my job, my finances, my dreams, my plans and my friends.' My inherent wariness of the Catholic religion came back with a vengeance. Did the Nukak really have to cover themselves with the 'precious blood' of Jesus? Hadn't this country seen enough bloodletting? 'Pass this prayer on to at least seven other people,' it went on. 'Tomorrow you will receive a miracle. Don't ignore it.'

I ignored it and took a shower. There was no hot water, not that I needed it. The concrete shell of the building had heated up over the course of the day and the shampoo came out of its bottle lukewarm. The single stream of water that gushed down the pipe from the tank on the roof was strangely reminiscent of home for a few moments, before the colder depths came onstream.

Promises and threats; enticement and fear-mongering: perhaps Colombia's conflict had started in its churches? The priests had always tried to mediate between the powerful and the powerless, sometimes siding with one, sometimes with the other. Arguments over the moral and theological right of Spaniards to conquer foreign lands were virulent in the first years after the conquistadores arrived on these shores. Ecclesiastics told King Charles I of Spain that his very soul was endangered by the conquests being made in his name. Driving infidel Moors out of his Catholic kingdom might have been a valid crusade, but occupying the lands of innocent tribes that had never even heard of Christianity certainly was not.

Juan Ginés de Sepúlveda had no such compunction. An erudite humanist and scholar, he argued that the superiority of Spanish civilization and religion justified the conquests. In August 1550, Sepúlveda and Bartolomé de las Casas, the leader of Spain's anti-colonial movement, engaged in a debate to resolve their differences. Bemused judges in Valladolid listened for days on end as the protagonists read hundreds of pages of argument in Latin, with both men turning to the Bible and Aristotle for support. Their to-ing and fro-ing went on for so long that the king issued a decree suspending all expeditions, exploration and conquests from Imperial Spain until such time as the judges could decide on the legitimacy of the competing arguments.

So for the next ten years, the native peoples of the Americas enjoyed some respite from the raids and press-gangs of the marauding conquistadores. Eventually the Christian soldiers hit on a solution to their quandary. The Requirement was a proclamation, to be read aloud, through interpreters if possible, before the Spaniards launched any attack on the native tribes. It began with a brief history of the world, moved on to descriptions of the Papacy and the Spanish monarchy and concluded with the 'requirement' that the native chiefs accept King Charles as their ruler and allow the preaching of Christianity to their people. Failure to comply made the listeners liable to Spanish attack, and – in the words of the Requirement – 'we protest that any deaths or losses that result from this are your fault.' Bartolomé de las Casas confessed that he didn't know whether to laugh at its ludicrous impracticality or weep at its injustice.*

Early the next morning, Albeiro gave me a lift on the back of his scooter to the Nukak's makeshift camp. It was a twenty-minute ride from San José, past one of the military bases where the Colombian Army was co-ordinating their southern offensive against the FARC. A conscript was mowing the grass outside the perimeter fence; another was slapping white paint on the boulders that lined the road leading up to the heavily fortified main gate, where a soldier in shades slouched on the sandbags surrounding an idle machine-gun. Albeiro turned down a sandy dirt track, past grazing brahma cattle and over great slabs of volcanic rock to Aguabonita, the piece of land that the mayor of San José had ceded to the Nukak while everyone made up their minds what to do with them.

There was great excitement at our arrival, perhaps because Albeiro had stopped on the way to pick up a big bag of bread rolls. 'Wash your hands first,' the doctor told them. As well as treating the many illnesses they were prone to, Albeiro had taught them elementary hygiene and rubbish disposal, but this had been hard to do. Still, they did as he asked. Once back with clean hands, everyone was quick to scoff the rolls. There were lots of little children, who played with the wing mirrors of Albeiro's scooter. In fact, apart from a solitary old man, who Albeiro guessed to be seventy-five, everyone was young. Their play quickly turned into a game of not giving one of the older boys his cap back. They threw it from one to another to great hoots of laughter. Everyone seemed so, well, childlike. The old survivor, who walked with two canes, had the happy, smiling

---

* Hemming, *Search for El Dorado*, pp. 38, 139.

face of a child. Even Albeiro had a grin on his face. It was the first time I'd seen him smile.

Their camp was of six open-sided thatched huts. Albeiro told me that they'd copied them from the *colonos*. The Nukak were nomads: in the jungle, they would only spend five or so days in any one place before moving on, so living in a permanent settlement was new to them. In the main hut, T-shirts and shorts hung unwashed from the beams. Western clothes were a novelty that most of the Nukak had taken to with interest, though many of them suffered skin infections because they still didn't understand the importance of washing them.

A girl was peeling *chontaduros*, a starchy orange vegetable, for the pot. Unopened bags of flour and ground coffee lay in the dust next to a bag of meat that a local butcher had given to them. Feeding the Nukak had also created unforeseen problems: they weren't used to eating the rice, beans and powdered milk that they received from Acción Social, the government's welfare agency, so cooking classes had been arranged for the women. At first, the Nukak would cook and eat all they had in one sitting, just as they would have in the jungle. Only in time had they learnt to make their supplies last for a week.

Though rendered childlike by their ignorance of *colono* life, the Nukak have a deep understanding of life in the jungle: in their natural habitat, they regularly eat eighty-three types of vegetable, more than half of which have yet to be identified by the outside world.[*] They consider monkeys a great delicacy, which they hunt with blow-darts tipped with poison prepared from the milky sap of the *bejuco* creeper. On their hunting trips, they also gather the various seeds that they eat as antidotes to

[*] Richard McColl, 'The Plight of the Nukak Maku', *City Paper* (Bogotá), July 2009.

jungle illnesses. But the camp at Aguabonita was surrounded by cattle ranches, so monkeys were few and far between. The people from Acción Social did their best to accommodate them, even organizing hunting trips, for which they would chauffeur the Nukak four hours south into the jungle, where they could hunt monkeys, peccaries and ducks, before driving them back to Aguabonita. It was a pragmatic response to the crisis the Nukak face, but hardly a sustainable one.

A tiny hairless dog was sitting in the dust, frantically scratching itself. Albeiro washed it with some antiseptic that he found in the little shack that served as the settlement's dispensary. Once the door was open, the ailing crowded around with their complaints. A girl with a squeaky, high-pitched, voice had the first signs of the same complaint on her shoulders. Pedro, who must have been in his early twenties, had an abscess on his leg. Some of the infants had distended bellies; Albeiro told me that their light-brown hair was a sign of malnutrition.

Once he had tended to the sick, we walked to the dry bed of a nearby stream. The once stagnant water had been a source of malaria, so workers from the UN's refugee programme had diverted the stream and installed a water pump. It was driven by a windmill and brought water up from the water table thirty metres below our feet. On the side of the storage tank was the dark blue and gold flag of the European Union.

Despite the risks, four of the six remaining Nukak clans had chosen to return to the jungle since their mass exodus in 2008. The other two clans were still living in the camp at Aguabonita, where their culture was on the brink of disappearing. Few of them worked and most were reliant on handouts from Acción Social. They were stuck, unable to go hunting or gather traditional remedies, without enough to eat, and beset by health problems. Albeiro estimated that in total there were only 500 Nukak left.

Even before their displacement from the jungle, the Nukak tended to die young, so anyone who reached the age of forty was considered an elder. But these days, the young were the clan's spokespeople, partly because the elders spoke no Spanish, but more because the young seemed more willing to admit the enormity of the challenge their tribe faced. I spoke to Pedro, who was one of the few Nukak adults that spoke Spanish. 'We can't go back into the jungle because the FARC won't let us,' he said. 'We'd like to grow sugar cane, cassava and plantain, like the *colonos*, but we don't have any land of our own. Some of us have found work clearing land for the cattle ranchers, but it doesn't pay much.'

On our way out, Albeiro and I passed four young Nukak who were on their way back to the camp from a fishing expedition. They were carrying palm leaves and long metal poles, and one of the girls had a baby monkey on her head. It looked to be a simple life and I allowed myself a moment of unthinking envy. Then a Black Hawk helicopter roared over the treetops. It was heading south, towards the FARC, Nukak territory and the still uncharted depths of the jungle. I remembered the director of the UN's refugee programme in Villavicencio and his parting shot as I had got up to leave. When he'd told his boss about the work they were doing to help the Nukak, she'd asked him a simple, inescapable question: 'But they're going to disappear anyway, aren't they?'

Jhon Henry Moreno was the grandly titled People's Defender[*] and a pugilistic graduate of the National University in Bogotá.

His name, not to mention its spelling, might once have surprised me, but I'd heard it said that there are more Henrys than

---

[*] La Defensoria del Pueblo is the ombudsman's office, created by the Constitution of 1991; it is the last resort for any Colombian with a legal grievance against the state.

Enriques in Colombia, as well as thousands of Kevins, Yonathans and Yasons.

We were sitting sat on the veranda of his office in San José, drinking guava juice and watching the burnished gold of the setting sun. Despite his instinctive support for the underdog, the dilemma facing the Nukak had Jhon Henry stumped for solutions too. 'The problem is not a lack of political will,' he told me. 'A lot of organizations have tried to help the Nukak. The real problem is knowing what to do.'

Like many indigenous peoples, the Nukak were given land of their own by the new Constitution of 1991, widely regarded as a model document of enlightened good sense. Colombia's indigenous peoples were also granted their own judicial systems, in which outsiders were not allowed to intervene. Unfortunately, when the guerrillas moved into their reservation in 2002, the Nukak had no way of prosecuting the interlopers or preventing their own eventual displacement.

That year, the Army began their southern push into FARC-dominated territory, but the guerrillas still controlled much of the jungle. The problem wasn't so much that the Nukak's rights were being violated by the FARC. It was that the Nukak had no conception of rights, much less the organizations they would need to defend them.

'The Nukak are nomadic, which means that they're spread out over a very wide area,' Jhon Henry explained. 'Being nomadic, they have never developed a settled, agricultural society or a religious or political hierarchy. Traditionally, they have only organized along family lines and that makes them very fragile.'

The Nukaks' fragility is compounded by the fact that they have done nothing to resist what has happened to them. In the face of systematic violence and injustice, Colombia's other indigenous groups have organized and educated themselves, but the Nukak seem content to live off the paternalistic concern of outsiders. Community leaders from bigger indigenous groups in Cauca and the Sierra Nevada have come to San José to explain how to put coherent proposals to the bureaucrats in Bogotá, but it is a steep learning curve for all concerned. The Nukaks' lack of organization also means that the £600,000 that the government has assigned to them is still being held on their behalf by the mayor in San José.

'Ultimately, there needs to be a regional dialogue between the Army, the FARC and the paramilitaries to facilitate the Nukaks' return,' Jhon Henry said with a sigh. 'But the Army isn't interested in regional peace processes. Even if the Nukak do go back, who can assure them that they won't run into the FARC's landmines? And who can assure the FARC that the Nukak won't tell the Army where they are? At the end of the day, the problem is the cocaine business and the economic under-development of the *llanos*. There's always a steady stream of peasant farmers who come down here from all over the country to grow coca. Wherever they go, the FARC follow.'

I thought of my London friend, the cheeky wink and the tap of the nose he had given me when I told him I was going back to Colombia. Somewhere, in a land far from this one, members of an advanced civilization were stuffing their noses with cocaine, inadvertently hastening the demise of some of their most distant relatives. Rarely can the clash between old and new have seemed so stark or so intractable.

It was dark by the time I left Jhon Henry. I planned to catch a bus back to Bogotá the next morning, but I had one more appointment to keep before turning in for the day. Albeiro had told me about Lina and Johan Aguillón, two evangelical missionaries who have spent the past sixteen years living with the Nukak. This was my last chance to speak to them.

I found them in a large, apparently empty house opposite the town's football pitch. The solitary lantern and the cooking stove on the kitchen counter suggested that they were camping indoors, as if still unaccustomed to life out of the jungle. They both seemed to harbour some mistrust of my intentions, and spoke in a dry, matter-of-fact way that suggested they had endured more than enough barbs from secular urbanites like me.

They told me that they'd lived with the missionaries from Nuevas Tribus until they abandoned their settlement in 1996. Then they'd moved to a Nukak settlement at Chekamo, two days away from San José by boat and dirt track (the Nukak chose to walk, which took them eight days). Once there, they converted the Nukak to Christianity. They would have stayed in Chekamo, but in 2008, the Army ordered them out, shortly before they went into Nukak territory to spring the Franco-Colombian politician Ingrid Betancourt from the clutches of the FARC. The Nukak chose to stay in the jungle, but Lina and Johan were worried for the safety of their two teenage daughters, so they came back to San José. Like their parents, the girls both spoke fluent Nukak.

I was surprised to hear Lina say that the threat posed to the Nukak by the FARC had been exaggerated. 'The guerrillas are much less of a threat to the future of the Nukak than the *colonos* of San José,' she insisted. 'The Nukak should return to the jungle. It is their only chance of a sustainable future.' Lina and Johan were glad that the converts they left behind in Chekamo still lived as jungle nomads.

'Some people complain about the work that we do, but in fact, Christianity has saved the Nukak from the degradation they face living alongside the *colonos*,' Johan told me. The Nukak of Chekamo still paint their faces when they feel happy. They still cut their hair square, using the jawbone of a river fish, and burn off their eyebrows with the gum they tap from a jungle tree.

The displaced community at Aguabonita, however, was another story. They seemed to have no interest in the Christian message. 'They've been reduced to beggary and slavish imitation by their interaction with *colono* society. They're losing all sense of their cultural identity. They enjoy being "poor little Indians" and surviving on handouts. There are plenty of NGOs that would have no reason to be there if it weren't for the parasitical relationship that the Nukak have fallen into. Most doctors just don't want to go into the jungle to help them. And most of the young Nukak don't want to go back. They just want scooters and mobile phones.'

Before meeting Lina and Johan, I had had misgivings about their work, but I had to admit that they had challenged not just me, but the whole state-sponsored response to the Nukak's plight. I walked back to the Hotel Colombia slowly, enjoying the night air, along sandy streets lit only by the occasional passing car. Despite its reputation as a frontier town founded by cocaine traffickers and run – until recently, at least – by the FARC, I felt a calm in San José del Guaviare that I hadn't experienced since getting back to Colombia. In the few days I'd been there, I'd got used to the faces around town: the kid with the woven straw *boltiao* cap; the driver of the tiny Hyundai taxi with lights in the door handles and a strip of LEDs running along both flanks who paraded, customerless, up and down the main street every night; the smiling apple road signs, telling people to slow down and not to drink and drive. I'd even grown fond of the only Chinese restaurant in town, despite the awful spaghetti with sweet-and-sour pork I had eaten there.

Maybe the young Nukak felt the same way. Pedro had told me that while some of his friends wanted to go back to the jungle, most of them just wanted to live like the *colonos*. If that meant growing cassava and plantain, driving a taxi or selling ice cream in the park, all well and good. But Albeiro had told me that he'd seen Nukak boys playing games of 'guerrillas versus paramilitaries'. How long would it be before they ran into the real thing, and learned how to use real guns?

By the following evening, I'd be back in Bogotá. There, the Nukak have become the public face of the 'pristine' indigenous people of Colombia. Nukak models have been photographed donning bows and arrows in fashion pieces for the Sunday papers. They made for better photos than the country's other tribes, many of whom have been assimilated into creole culture to some degree. 'Nukak' has even become a brand of camping gear, used by urbanites wanting a taste of the 'real' Colombia.

The young Nukak refugees of Aguabonita have effectively been born in a cage. But they have been quick to wise up to their own value in a country that still prizes racial distinctions between black, white and indigenous people, over the *mestizaje* to which most Colombians owe their heritage. Some of them have started charging press photographers £10 a time to pose for pictures. As and when the tourists make it this far south, I am sure that they will make a killing.

4.   An Imaginary Place between Macondo and Medellín

After polishing off *Angosta* on my way back from San José del Guaviare, I had spent the days since getting back to Bogotá drifting in and out of *One Hundred Years of Solitude*. Before Pablo Escobar came along, Colombia was synonymous with Macondo, the isolated Caribbean village that Gabriel García Márquez conjured into life in his novel. Since publication in 1967 it has been translated into thirty-seven languages, sold more than 20 million copies and won its author the Nobel Prize for Literature.

One Hundred Years of Solitude is the story not of one man, but an entire community, and covers hundreds of years, from the foundation of Macondo to its maturity and eventual decay. Even in 1920, its inhabitants recall the days when 'the English pirate' Sir Francis Drake harried the Caribbean coast as if it were yesterday. In the village's earliest days, Colombia was little more than a series of remote settlements, a name pretending to be a nation. The people of Macondo receive all kinds of exotic visitors, who bring them oddities, inventions and theories from the distant lands of Europe and the United States, which they refashion according to their fancy.

The western world loved the 'magic realism' that García Márquez pioneered in his novel. It is his – and Colombia's – gift to the world. It seems to express something essential not just about Colombia, but about all the villages built by the travelling bands that ventured into the New World. But *One Hundred Years of Solitude* wasn't doing it for me. It didn't chime with anything I knew of modern Colombia. It was certainly a world removed from the dystopian vision that Héctor Abad Faciolince conjured up in *Angosta*. Although both books were fantasies that purported to convey something inimitably Colombian, Faciolince's novel also served as a warning. Angosta was a divided city, not a village of extended families. Its cocaine traffickers had corrupted the traditional elite not just financially, but morally. The Seven Wise Men that ruled the city made no claim to represent the people of Angosta. Their city was modern, but closed. Unlike Macondo, no visitors came to Angosta and those who left went feet first, and for good.

I liked the idea that these imaginary places might teach me something about the real Colombia I was travelling, and was wondering where I might track down other depictions of the elusive country, when I had a call from my friend Carlos Gómez. When I had first met him, ten years before, Carlos had been working for ONIC,* the same organization for indigenous peoples that had sent Dr Albeiro Riano out to San José to treat the Nukak Maku. Carlos was not indigenous himself; he was one of many Colombians, especially those radicalized by their time at one of the national universities, who had taken to indigenous culture as a respite from, and antidote to, the colonial inheritance. I knew that Carlos always had a book on the go, so I asked him if he knew of any other novels set in imaginary Colombian towns. He told me that he had just the book I was looking for. He suggested that we meet for lunch; there was a Pacific restaurant in La Candelaria that he liked and hadn't been to for a while.

The restaurant was at the top of a steep, narrow staircase that led off the street to a low-ceilinged room with walls that had been blackened by greasy smoke from the grill. I left the ordering to Carlos; the list of fish that the waiter reeled off meant

---

* Organización Nacional Indígena de Colombia.

nothing to me and besides, he dropped his consonants, which left me mentally stumbling to put them back again. The waiter was from Chocó, the isolated department on the Pacific coast where African customs have been preserved, as if in aspic, since colonial days. I'm tempted to compare its villages to Macondo, but I know that would be a mistake; although it has long been home to similarly hot and sleepy settlements, in recent years, Chocó's mangrove swamps have become battlegrounds for guerrillas and paramilitaries struggling for control of the cocaine business.

Carlos had many of the characteristics I liked in Colombians. He exuded physical and mental health. He was thoughtful, told a good story and his idealism was tempered by a hard-won measure of pragmatism. He also had a healthy appetite. As we tucked into a big slab of smoked fish, he told me that since leaving ONIC, he'd been wandering Colombia, first to an isolated country school on the north coast, where he had spent a year teaching indigenous Sinu children to read and write, and later to the eastern plains, where he had helped ten indigenous tribes to establish the institutions they'd need to appeal to the government for help, now that the coca farmers had reached their lands. All the while he'd been wondering, like García Márquez and Faciolince, about the essence of his country.

The waiter cleared our plates and we eased back into our seats to digest over a cup of hot *panela* sugar water with lemon. Carlos reached into his bag and handed me a novel called *Desde Aquellos Días* (From Those Days). He had written it a couple of years ago, he said. It was the first from his own publishing venture, which he had called Editoriales Pirata. It cost nothing, but all takers were obliged to pass it on when they'd finished reading it.

'Look, I'm going back to Bucaramanga tomorrow. Why don't you meet me there? There's a wonderful canyon nearby that we can go hiking in.' Bucaramanga is the departmental capital of Santander. It lies in the easternmost range of the Andes, the Cordillera Oriental, about 180 miles north of Bogotá. The mountains and valleys of Santander were the setting for many of the key moments that had determined Colombia's peculiar fate. The villages around Bucaramanga were the birthplace of the ELN guerrillas. Further east was the Magdalena Medio, where paramilitary armies had first mobilized to fight the guerrillas. And the weather had to be better than it was in Bogotá. It hadn't stopped raining in the week I'd been there since getting back from San José.

I'd have liked to take a train to Bucaramanga, but as in most Latin American countries, Colombia's rail network had been abandoned to the elements long ago. So too had the bridges and tunnels, many built by pioneering Britons in the nineteenth century, that once carried the railways over and under the crumpled Andean landscape. Luckily, the country is well served by its airlines. Avianca is the second oldest airline in the world and even the smaller cities have airports.

The flight from Bogotá's El Dorado airport headed north over the rugged green mountains of the department of Boyacá. I settled down to make a start on Carlos' book, but was soon distracted by the girl sitting next to me, who also had her nose in a book. Out of the corner of my eye, I caught the line 'I was obsessed by . . .' before she closed the book to look out of the window. I tilted my head to read the back cover. 'At the age of ninety, I decided that I wanted to make love to an adolescent virgin,' it read. 'I went to see Clementina, the owner of the local brothel, who had always laughed at my oh-so-pure principles. "Morality," she said to me, "like everything else, is just a question of time."'

I turned back to *Desde Aquellos Días*. The story started with a terrible, inexplicable event: a woman walks into the town, her clothes in tatters, her breasts exposed, and blood running from her nose. Yet she remains a woman accustomed to being admired and aware of her own allure. Her father sees his neighbours lean out of their windows to watch her, but only recognizes her when she swaggers past his office. He grabs the nearest material to hand, which happens to be the national flag, and rushes into the street to cover her. 'It was the first time they had ever had any physical contact,' Carlos wrote. And that was just chapter one.

Carlos had set his book in Empalá, a typically hot and claustrophobic village where not much happened. There were none of the fond descriptions of García Márquez's novel. Instead, the author's voice was cool and remote. It struck a chord, in a way that *One Hundred Years of Solitude* never could – partly because there were far fewer unknown words to look up, but also because Empalá seemed to be full of corrupt politicians and soldiers.

As I pushed into the second chapter, the story unfolded of a tyrannical mayor, Don Roque Monteeiro, who is obsessed with the terrorists that are supposedly menacing his town. Although the reader never gets to see or hear anything from the 'terrr-orrr-ists' – a word that rolls off Don Roque's tongue like machine-gun fire – they supply the pretext for a murderous campaign against the landowners and businessmen who are Don Roque's opponents on the town council.

Only when the pilot announced our descent into Bucaramanga did I look up from my book. The plane came down out of the clouds into a landscape quite like the one we'd left in Bogotá an hour earlier. Green hills rolled into deep valleys, patches of which were lit by the morning sun. I was expecting to land in a few minutes' time, but the runway came up out of nowhere and suddenly the wheels were skidding on tarmac. We had landed on top of a mountain.

I'd arranged to meet Carlos at a bus-stop-cum-store called Papi Quiero Piña – Daddy I Want Pineapple. 'All the taxi drivers are sure to know it,' Carlos had told me, and sure enough, mine did. It was a half-hour drive across town from the airport, past hillsides that had given way under the winter rains and the various bulldozers and diggers that were putting them back again.

I wondered if Carlos' imaginary town of Empalá was based on a real town in Santander. At one point in the novel the tyrannical Don Roque hires a band from a town called Aratoca to play at a party to celebrate the birth of his daughter. Spreading my map out in the back of the taxi, I found Aratoca on the road between Bucaramanga and Socorro. I had another clue to go on: midway through the story, two of the main characters are driving back to Empalá in their truck, delivering beer and soft drinks to the local shopkeepers. They try to find some music to listen to on the radio, but the mountains turn the signal to fuzz. Finally they're able to tune in to Radio Chicamocha, and listen to the news, which warns them of roadblocks that the terrorists have mounted up ahead. Carlos had arranged for us to go hiking in the canyon at Chicamocha, just north of Aratoca.

I'd made an early start that morning and yawned my way through the short wait for Carlos. He showed up in a white poncho, a woven straw *boltiao* hat and army-issue boots. We boarded a bus bound for the village of Los Santos, which soon left the city behind us and began climbing into the dry chalk hills. It threw up white dust from the unpaved road as it trundled between fields of pineapple, maize, tomatoes and beans.

At the first stop, a man got onto the bus and walked down the aisle, putting a laminated card on the lap of each passenger. It was a *fajada* of the Virgin of Carmen. Swaying with the movement of the bus and shouting over the roar of the engine, he announced that he was a demobilized paramilitary. 'I really don't want to commit any more crimes,' he said; 'I want to make a legal living, so if you could help out a bit, I'd be ever so grateful'. A few people gave him a few coins for a lucky card and he jumped off at the next stop.

Despite former President Uribe's success in bringing down the once-horrific number of murders committed in Colombia, since my return the newspapers had been talking of crime rates creeping back up. Carlos explained that as more paramilitaries demobilized, handed in their weapons and passed through the process of 're-insertion' into civilian life, many of them found themselves jobless. So they pitched up in the bigger cities, far from their villages, qualified only in dispensing violence. Most were absorbed by the government's programme for demobilized paramilitaries, and went on to find legal work selling *fajadas* and similar trinkets; but more than a few started making their living from the many criminal opportunities on offer.

Los Santos was a pretty village, hotter than Bucaramanga and perched on the edge of the Chicamocha Canyon, which, as we were soon to discover, was hotter still. On the lower side of the village square was an old colonial house that had been built around a courtyard of undulating terracotta tiles. It was offering lunch, so we went inside and sat in the shade cast by the veranda that ran around three sides. It was wonderfully quiet and as we waited for some service, I found myself watching the spiders poised in the dusty rafters overhead. Our hostess emerged in her own good time and shuffled over to our table. She looked to be about seventy and might have passed for Italian or Greek. The women of Santander are famously steely; she wasn't one for an easy smile, but she did what she was there to do with stoicism, as if expecting some idiot to upend the cart at any minute.

When I'd arrived in Bucaramanga, I noticed that many of its people had green or blue eyes. Our bus driver had been a brawny, ginger-haired man who could have been from Newcastle.

I heard about the Germans who had settled in Santander in the nineteenth century, but Carlos told me that the local look was down to the Guane. They were an indigenous people unlike the rest for not having migrated from Asia. The Guane were white-skinned, a racial quirk that nobody seemed able to explain, and were known to have been excellent weavers and stonemasons. Their carvings could still be seen around Los Santos.

Lunch arrived: first a fish soup served with deliciously sweet *arepas con choclo* – maize pancakes with cheese. Then goat, which came with a side dish of diced goat's innards in saffron rice. Tender and succulent with a slightly gamey after-taste, it was the perfect way to start a day of walking.

The dusty path that led down into the canyon started behind the restaurant. At the first switchback we came to, Carlos scrambled over the rocks to a lookout point tucked under an outcrop. I followed and together we gazed out over the vast, silent canyon beneath us. Downriver, the slopes were of white and grey scree, but on the lip of the bowl-shaped upper valley where we were sitting, cacti and all kinds of low trees and shrubs had taken root between the rocks.

'*Punto rojo*,' said Carlos, as he stuffed his pipe. 'All the way from Corinto. Colombia's finest.' It was a name I had heard before. Corinto was a village in the southern Andes, lauded by locals as the only place in the world where chickens had learnt how to swim, supposedly in order to have sex with the ducks that lived on an island in the river that flowed through the village.

Carlos stopped two or three times that day to pack his pipe with Colombia's finest, so my experience of the canyon was a dazed one. Once stoned, Carlos didn't initiate much conversation and replied to my openers with an anodyne 'uh-huh' that didn't encourage a follow up. This was fine by me; my conversation starters were only made to break the silence of the canyon and the sudden strangeness of being stoned in the middle of nowhere. Besides, my Spanish stumbles after a smoke.

Carlos walked ahead, partly because I stopped from time to time to take photos but more because he was accustomed to walking alone. We made our way down the stone path in silence as the sun beat down mercilessly on our heads. It seemed like the kind of bucolic existence that I could let myself be taken in by for weeks.

We passed an abandoned farmhouse with cracked adobe walls and a pitched-in roof of palm fronds. On leveller ground, the stones had been cleared to plant fields of tobacco. A fork in the path was marked by a pile of rocks that somebody had topped with a simple black wooden cross. In fresh white paint were daubed the words 'We are children of God.' I walked on, wondering if it was meant as a consolation or a warning.

After two hours of hiking we came to the bottom of the canyon, where the River Chicamocha flowed through the tiny village of Sube. It wasn't on the map: the first road to connect Sube to the outside world had been completed in 1994. Until then, the only access the villagers had had to the outside world had been over the rough stone paths that led north and south up the steep slopes of the canyon.

The paths had been built in the mid-nineteenth century, at the orders of an entrepreneur called Geo von Lengerke, one of a handful of Germans who fled to Santander in the aftermath of the Revolutions of 1848, when Europe's monarchs rolled back the progressive tide of Liberalism. Lengerke was a giant of a man, hungry to make a name for himself in the New World. The land he found in Santander was good, so he began to cultivate tobacco and the cinchona trees whose bark was the basis for quinine, which in those days was the sole antidote to malaria. The governor of Santander, keen to foster ambitious newcomers, granted him a concession of 12,000 hectares. But Lengerke had no way of getting his crops from the highlands to the River Magdalena, which at that time was the only route to the Caribbean coast and the distant markets of Europe. So Lengerke had his men lay over 370 miles of stone paths, braving the sinister growl of the jaguars in the trees overhead, yellow fever and countless attacks from resentful local tribes.

Geo von Lengerke was overawed by Colombia. He called it 'a country in which everything remains to be done, dedicated to the rush of revolution'. He was determined not to be drawn into the bloody feuds then raging between the country's Liberals and Conservatives, who he disparagingly called 'romantics'. Lengerke was a pragmatist, while the Colombians were 'excessive' and had 'no sense of proportion'. But as a European – and a hard-drinking, womanizing, not very God-fearing one at that – he was an easy target for those jealous of his commercial acumen. When civil war next broke out, the mock-German castle he had built at Montebello was razed to the ground.

Lengerke died broke and broken by the land he had come to call home. His vision and dedication had come to nothing, 'but it is beautiful and it seems it cannot be otherwise'. Though rarely used, the pathways he had built survive to this day. Lengerke said that they incorporated 'the suffering, hope and uncertainty of all those who walk them'.*

Only when I saw the bridge over the river at Sube did I remember the story of Colombia's first iron bridge. When Ricardo's dad told me about the bridge that the McCormicks had built, I imagined that it would look something like the original at Ironbridge: entirely of iron, with countless rivets covered in countless layers of black paint. But the bridge at Sube

---

* Pedro Gómez Valderrama's *La otra raya del tigre,* first published in 1977, is a wonderful, fictionalized account of the life of Geo von Lengerke. Sadly, it is only available in Spanish.

was like nothing I'd ever seen before, at once rudimentary and apparently indestructible. Wooden planks were suspended from thick iron cables that ran sixty feet between the enormous brick ramparts on either side of the milky brown river that coursed below.

Crossing the bridge, we came to the deserted village square. A woman was sweeping the flagstones with a broom of bound twigs. Seeing us, she came over to open up the recently restored *posada*. They were hoping that the inn would bring in the tourists, Angela told us, though few had come to stay yet. She was waiting for an inaugural visit by the governor of Santander, who was due to be helicoptered in that very day. We looked up at the darkening blue of the cloudless sky. 'He'll probably come tomorrow,' she said with a faint smile.

The *posada* was basic but beautiful. A cobbled yard sloped down to a stone basin, where a solitary chicken was washing herself. But the bare rooms and freshly limed walls were hardly cosy, so Carlos and I wandered over to the farmhouse on the other side of the bridge. In a near-empty barn three teenagers were shelling corn and watching MTV. Carlos negotiated some dinner for us and had just put his feet up on the bench running around the veranda when he was interrupted by a phone call.

It was his friend Carolina, calling him from Bucaramanga. He sounded less than pleased to hear her voice. 'It's not a good time to talk,' he told her. Why not? 'I really don't want to talk about that.' Why didn't he want to talk? What was wrong? The more he remonstrated, the more she held on. Nodding and sighing, he drifted into the dark courtyard, where one of the farmhands was washing her hair in a tub.

By the time he re-emerged, I had spent twenty minutes watching the mosquitoes swarm around the single bare bulb that lit the yard and enjoying the evaporation of the sweat that matted my hair. Over a cold beer, I asked Carlos about his novel. I'd taken *Desde Aquellos Días* and the town of Empalá to be products of his imagination, but he told me that in fact, his imaginary town was based on Sube. 'I grew up not far from here. Over the years, I'd hear about Sube from time to time, though I'd never actually visited the place.'

In the late 1990s, Carlos told me, he had taken to walking in the safer parts of the mountains of Santander. When he reached Sube, he heard a quite amazing story. 'The mayor of the village was a tough old bird called Roque Ferrer. Not long after the first road was opened in 1994, Don Roque went on a crusade against his opponents in the village council. One by one, he started killing them off. The local people fled for their lives. By the time I came here, about eighty per cent of the inhabitants had left. Don Roque had died by then. I think the villagers ganged up on him one night and killed him.'

Not long after becoming president in 2002, Álvaro Uribe ordered the police back into the hundreds of villages, scattered over thousands of square miles, that had become virtually lawless in the course of the last twenty years. In Sube, the police moved into one of the grand warehouses that Geo von Lengerke had built to store his cinchona crop. Thirty-three police officers found themselves in command of a village of just five residents. Since then the villagers had started coming back to reclaim and restore their homes, though many of the houses in the side streets were still eerily quiet. When Angela came by later that evening with more beer, she told us that Sube was still ruled by relatives of Don Roque, albeit less murderously.

'The story of Don Roque made a big impression on me,' Carlos said. 'But it was only when President Uribe was running for a third term, uprooting our democratic traditions and allowing one man to speak for all Colombians, that I started to think about Sube again.' By Carlos' reckoning, Álvaro Uribe was entirely driven by his blind hatred of the guerrillas. Once in power, he used that hatred to justify his own brand of increasingly violent authoritarianism. His 'democratic security' policies had brought security to some, but Uribe took anyone who opposed his government to be a friend of the guerrillas. For them, the eight years that Uribe spent as president had brought neither democracy nor security.

Appalled by what was happening in the name of the 'war on terror' in Colombia, Carlos took the story of Don Roque in Sube, turned him into Don Roque Monteeiro of Empalá and wrote a tragedy about a small-town mayor who orchestrates a bogus war on terror as cover for the murder, rape and robbery of the people. 'Roque Monteeiro is corrupted by power. Once he finds that he has no opponents left, he has to mask his true intentions by inventing an imaginary opponent.'

Carlos was warming to his subject. He spoke with great conviction, his voice soaring and diving for dramatic affect. His take on the conflict chimed with what I'd heard from other war-weary Colombians. The guerrilla threat existed, but it was routinely exaggerated because the fear it provoked was such an effective way of turning the public good to private ends. 'More than ever, I believe that the government and the guerrillas need each other. The government needs the guerrillas because they justify the status quo. The guerrillas need the government because they give them their *raison d'être*. The oligarchy wants to maintain the power it has, and the guerrillas want to maintain their army.'

By Carlos' account although both the former president and the fictional mayor wrapped themselves in the national flag, paid warm tribute to the armed forces and swore to uphold the constitution, it was all a sham. 'There are no principles at work in Colombian politics. Everything is open to negotiation,' he said scornfully. 'But there are interests – money, power, even religion – that have to be defended. And there are interests that

transcend immediate interests,' he said ominously. 'Causes that
are bigger than the causes.'

Carlos was from the generation that had come of age in the
eighties. There was still something of the romantic idealist
about him, a thirst for justice that might once have inspired him
to throw in his lot with those committed to the armed struggle.
But as he'd watched the medicine prescribed by the guerrillas do
more harm than the illness it was supposed to cure, he had
become jaded. It wasn't just that the war had lost whatever purpose it might once have had – it was being perpetuated by people
with a vested interest in ensuring that peace was never realized.

'This so-called "war on terror" has been going on for years,
and it has always been used as a way of ducking responsibility
for the big, underlying problems. I've worked with lots of indigenous groups and the government has always told us that things
can't be improved because the guerrillas are too strong and the
state can't function in those outlying regions.'

Now that the FARC have been pushed out of many of those
regions, I wondered who the government would blame for their
lack of development. If President Santos had been having a beer
with us that evening, he might have said that he was making the
countryside safe so that the big foreign mining companies could
invest in the bountiful natural resources that Colombia had to
offer. 'Indeed, Mr President,' I imagined Carlos saying, 'but
judging by the experience of other Latin American countries,
foreign investment and national development are quite distinct
propositions. The wealth generated by the gas-fields of Bolivia
hasn't lifted its people out of poverty. And multinational agricultural corporations are making Argentina's farmers poorer,
not richer.'

Development: it is hard to see how such an anodyne word
could be responsible for so much conflict. Early in his novel,
Carlos warns his readers: 'Generally, understanding how things

end is not as complicated as understanding how they begin.'
Everybody knows the bloody mess that Colombia ended up in,
with guerrillas, paramilitaries and cocaine traffickers thrashing it
out between themselves usually at the expense of ordinary
Colombians. But few seem able to explain how it all started.

In 1978, when the FARC were at the height of their popularity, their struggle had seemed a honourable one, to a sizeable
minority at least. Nobody wanted war, said the guerrillas; but it
had been thrust upon them. The *campesinos* had to protect themselves from the landowners, who had long used violence to
break up any threat to their power and prestige. The guerrillas
claimed to be the protectors of the *campesinos* and had resorted
to arms only when every legal avenue had been closed to them.
Thirty long years later, the FARC have come to embody the
very cruelty and indifference that they deride the oligarchs for.
Any claim they make to be an 'army of the people' is laughable.
Among those they claim to speak for, they have never been so
unpopular.

How has this happened? The short answer is that when the
guerrillas were popular, they weren't powerful, at least not in
military terms; and in the process of acquiring power, they lost
popularity. So was their revolution doomed from the start?
Carlos seemed to think so. When Toño, the young student rebel
of *Desde Aquellos Días*, is asked about the revolution he has in
mind, he says that if it is left to the poor, they'll all be worse off
than before. 'The *campesinos* don't have the worldliness or the
experience needed to exercise power responsibly,' he says. Once
they are in charge, 'they'll just take their revenge and plunge the
country into a civil war.' Toño goes on to say that, 'in the end,
the rich are, in their way, as much victims of the system they
invented as the poor. What we have to do is make them see that,
and get them involved in our cause. Which should be yours.'

By now, Carlos and I were the only ones still awake at the

farmhouse. We left our empty beer bottles on a pile of maize husks and slowly made our way back over the bridge to our *posada*. The planks lurched on their cables; the river churned white water under our feet; the crickets chirruped from the darkness. That night, I had a dream about the old woman who had brought us our lunch at Los Santos. I asked her if I should sit on a cushion when I was writing. She said that I shouldn't – it would make me complacent.

We were perching perched atop a huge boulder in a stream. We were a short way out of Sube, and Carlos was preparing the first of the day's pipes. It was still early and the air was cool and fresh. In the distance, a huge plume of white water was soundlessly cascading over the brim of the canyon. I smiled to myself at the sheer excitement of the place. I felt as if I'd stumbled into Arthur Conan Doyle's *Lost World*. '*Que maravilla!*' I said, not for the first time. It really was a marvellous place, though I only said so because I thought it might lift Carlos' mood, which had been bad since he had woken up.

We set off to climb the other side of the canyon, with Carlos taking an early lead on the rugged stone path, which he kept up for most of the day. Perhaps it was just as well that I was alone, trudging between the switchbacks that carried the path up the ever-steepening incline, when a huge butterfly with electric-blue wings fluttered past me. It seemed a gift, one I tried to preserve with a photo, hoping to share the magic of the moment, but the end-result was just a bright blue blur.

Around noon, we finally reached the top of the canyon and walked to a farmhouse to wait for a ride to take us into the nearby town of San Gil. Exhausted, we sat in the shade of the back porch with a *refarto*, a refreshing mix of beer and Colombiana, a soft drink that tastes of bubble gum. The farmhouse had high-ceilinged rooms and tiled floors that sagged between old joists. I could smell myself. Under that high note rode others, first of dry mud and then of warming wood.

In the yard in front, the farmhands were playing *bola*, a local version of skittles. I watched as they took turns to try and knock down three heavy pins that had been lined up in front of a thick wooden pallet.

In a lull in play, I decided to have a go. It must have been ten metres from pitch to base, which is a long way to throw a heavy iron ball underarm. I did pretty well with my first couple of throws, but my third attempt was a good fifteen feet wide of the mark. I watched as the ball sailed off to the left and knocked a dent in the wattle-and-daub wall of the main house. My next throw was worse: I chipped one of the tiles on the roof. Everyone laughed, but I thought it best not to try again. I didn't want to see their faces if I pitched the ball through the roof.

The men sauntered back to their fields. One of them pulled at the rope that tethered his goat, which threw itself into the air, bleating hopelessly, as if it knew its end was coming that afternoon. Two young boys dragged the marker halfway down the pitch and set to practising with the iron *bola*. Carlos and I chatted with the ref, a kindly farmer who regarded me with infinite curiosity. I don't think he'd met a foreigner before. When the pick-up truck pulled into the yard to take us to San Gil, he touched my arm absent-mindedly, his eyes still searching mine, as if he were struggling to put his thoughts into words.

Until Álvaro Uribe came to power in 2002, many of the villages around San Gil had been too dangerous for Colombians, let alone foreigners, to visit. Now they, like hundreds of others, had seen the benefits of Uribe's much vaunted 'democratic security' policies, which had put a police station in every village and sent the Army out to patrol the surrounding hills. The guerrillas had been pushed out, the paramilitaries had been demobilized and the roads were safe to travel for the first time in a generation.

Gradually, Colombians began to venture onto the country roads, to marvel at the beauty of a country many of them only knew from photographs.

But Carlos wasn't happy with the way his home department was changing. On the way to San Gil, the pick-up passed through Barichara, which every Colombian knows and loves as the country's archetypal colonial-era town. The boutique hotels and up-market restaurants might have employed a few locals, but as more rich Colombians bought second homes in the town, rising house prices had driven plenty of local people out. The neighbouring town of Villanueva, as the name suggested, had no colonial charm to trade in and its people made their living from farming, as the people of Barichara once had. Carlos told me that despite appearances, Villanueva was more prosperous than Barichara.

As word got out of the novel peace that had settled on Colombia, its colonial towns were soon back on the gringo trail. San Gil was one of the Colombian towns highlighted in the Lonely Planet guidebook, billed as the country's adventure sports capital, offering world-class white water rafting, kayaking, caving and paragliding.

Carlos and I checked in at the Hostel Macondo, a single-storey colonial house set on the side of a steep hill overlooking the River Suárez. Despite (or perhaps because of) its decrepitude, its dormitories were full of British, Irish, Australian, German and French backpackers – it seemed the Americans, who until 9/11 regarded this country as the most dangerous on the planet, had yet to hear the good news. Carlos sat at the hostel's dining table, quietly regarding the foreigners, a wry smile playing around his mouth. They were all very young and very well travelled. They swapped tips on catching boats to Panama, extending their tourist visas, and the best cure for the hangover brought on by a night spent drinking *aguardiente*. Twice, I met twenty-something Irishmen who compared the rafting on the Suárez with the rafting to be had on the Zambezi.

Yet no one was reading *One Hundred Years of Solitude* in the Hostel Macondo – or anything else for that matter. Most of my fellow travellers seemed markedly uninterested in what Colombia had been through. Those who weren't swapping travellers' stories were silently peering into their laptops. Thanks to Facebook, their friends were always close at hand, shielding them from the isolation that used to give such journeys much of their meaning. I couldn't help but wonder if they would have gone travelling for so many months in such strange places in the days when the only news from home came in letters written on onionskin paper picked up from *postes restantes*.

The young travellers at the Hostel Macondo seemed to be a hybrid of three distinct traditions. Victorian travellers saw their journeys into distant lands as a way of toughening up their minds and bodies. Such men – and the occasional woman – threw themselves into foreign cultures, partly to better understand them, but mainly to deprive themselves of the comforts of home and thereby strengthen their inner resolve. For them, travel was akin to a military exercise. In the 1960s, a new generation of more peaceable westerners returned to those remote places. They too sought spiritual renewal, but they wanted softening up, not toughening up.

Holidaymakers, on the other hand, were only looking for a chance to rest mind and body, to enjoy the sensory pleasures offered by the sea, the sun and the sand between their toes. Holidays were for workers and holidaymakers had limited ambitions. They didn't want to discover or conquer anything, least of all themselves. They wanted to rest for the couple of weeks they had off work.

It was nice to spend an evening speaking English again, but something irked me about these young backpackers, flitting over South America like butterflies darting between exotic flowers. After so many years of intensive education and self-discipline, they were doubtless looking for a rest and an escape from routine. I'm sure that they were also looking for meaning-ful experiences, as they rappelled down waterfalls and threw themselves into canyons from bungee ropes. But I couldn't help thinking that they treated travelling as another homework task. All those maps and guidebooks and itineraries looked more like a tribute to organization than imagination, as they granted themselves a week or two to 'do' Colombia. Perhaps it was because the country they found themselves wandering was so labyrinthine that they ended up engaging not with the strange but the familiar. They spent their time with others from the same hostel, as if they were on a school trip without their teachers.

Carlos and I had dinner at a sandwich shop down the hill from the Hostel Macondo that an English girl and her American boyfriend had just opened. It was one of a clutch of foreign-owned start-ups in the tourist towns, and an encouraging sign of how far the country had come since 2002. When I told the proprietor that I was planning to catch a boat downriver to the coast, she asked if I meant the Amazon. When I asked about the guerrillas who only a few short years ago had patrolled the hills around us, she had no idea that they had ever been present in Santander. Perhaps it was to the good that the tourists knew nothing about the combatants still fighting it out in the remoter parts of the country. But some of them barely knew which country they were in. Presumably that was what the Colombian tourist board was hoping.

Carlos and I spent our last day at a riverside spot called Pescade-rito, which was a short bus ride from San Gil. It was crowded with day-trippers who had come into the mountains from

Bucaramanga to enjoy the bank holiday. They swam and sun-
bathed in front of the tents that they had pitched along the
banks of the river. Kids splashed their feet in the rock pools
from inflated sun beds, while their mothers barbecued great
slabs of beef and their dads blasted out the sounds of *reggaeton*
and *vallenato*, the accordion-led country music I had heard in
every town and village I passed through. We rock-hopped our
way up the river, hoping to find Carlos' favourite perch, which
he felt sure would be quieter, but that too was crowded with
what he called '*esa mierda de colombianos*'. In the end, he gave up,
found some shade under a tree that leaned out over the river and
prepared his pipe.

Carlos was still thinking about the tourists at the Hostel
Macondo. He told me that he'd spent eight months in Reading
back in 1992, while his then-girlfriend was studying for a master's degree at the city's university. I didn't know that he had
been to the UK. I thought of the platforms at Reading station;
the masses of people on the trains, with their newspapers, iPods
and attempts at privacy in public. No, he'd not liked Reading
much, he said. His attempts to learn English, which he'd never
had much interest in by the sounds, had stopped there. 'But no
matter – your Spanish is perfect,' he said with a beaming smile.

In the days when his country was renowned and feared, Carlos said, the only travellers who came to Colombia were
journalists, botanists and anthropologists. They came to learn
about, and from, what he liked to call 'Locombia' – the crazy
country. But it seemed that those days were gone: the colonial
district of Bogotá now had twelve backpacker hostels, he said
incredulously, all full of tourists whose interest extended no
further than cheap cocaine and the local girls. 'Flashpackers,'
Carlos said indignantly. 'They show up and the first thing they
do is open their laptops. They don't talk to anyone else in the
hostel, let alone visit the Gold Museum!'

To my mind, Colombia needed more tourists. For years, foreigners have been too scared to come here; now that they are braving its fearsome reputation, Colombians should do their part in opening up to the rest of the world. I felt sure that their insularity, though rarely acknowledged, was responsible for much of the political intolerance that fuelled the conflict.

Carlos nodded along when I said this, but like many Colombians, he had grown up with a pervasive—if rarely expressed—mistrust of the outside world, which to him invariably meant *los yanquis*. Despite its wealth of natural marvels, Colombia was a demonized country. Its people struggled to reconcile their national pride with the fear and loathing they inspired in the colossus to the north. So outsiders, whether gringos or not, were periodically made the butt of resentful griping.

Not only were foreigners driving property prices up and locals out, Carlos said, they had also created a market for child prostitutes in Cartagena. And yet the government still kowtowed to them, which was why the Ministry of Tourism sold the country under the slogan that '*Colombia es Pasión*'. To me it seemed an effective, albeit predictable, way to appeal to those commuters at Reading station. The word 'passion' was the perfect bait for those who chose to swim in that sea of greys, dark blues and blacks. To Carlos, however, it was a clear-cut case of inciting lustful Anglo-Saxons to treat his country as a whorehouse.

It was time to change the subject. We started to talk books. Carlos mentioned some of his favourites: Robert Louis Stephenson's *Treasure Island*; Herman Melville's *Moby Dick*; the ghost stories of Edgar Allan Poe: all Gothic, moody and distinctly Anglo-Saxon. His literary tastes seemed to jar with the easy recourse he made to gringo-baiting, but I didn't say a word. Beneath the educated small talk, I could feel an undercurrent of suspicion building. Perhaps some of it was personal: as an outsider, I could afford to be more placatory and less critical than Carlos could. Perhaps he attributed my mildness to my being just another cosseted foreigner, wilfully blind to the true savagery of a world created by and for the likes of me.

Unthinkingly, I asked him how he made his money. He didn't need money, he told me. When he wasn't hiking, he lived with his eighty-year-old mother in the family home in Bucaramanga, where he spent his days watching black-and-white films. Long before I had first met him, he'd tried to build a conventional career for himself. He had worked as a journalist – and then spent ten years trying to forget everything he'd been taught about Colombia in the newsroom.

From what I'd seen of the Colombian press, this was understandable. There is no shortage of sophisticated analysis and commentary in *El Tiempo* and the weekly news magazine *Semana*. But their writers struggle with the same one-way mirror that divides rich from poor and city from countryside. This is partly down to the comparatively privileged, city-dwelling lives that they and many of their readers lead. While the editorial line remains conservative in the extreme, it is left to columnists, not reporters, to uncover the scandalous levels of corruption, collusion and impunity in the country.[*] The columnists at *El Tiempo* and *Semana* are the escape valves for self-censoring journalists who know just how much truth-seeking their editors will tolerate. The columnists are invariably from the same class as the country's rulers – indeed, many are from the same families – and have the good fortune to be able to speak out without incurring the risks run by less well-connected scribes.

This evasiveness stems from fear too. Colombia is still one of the most dangerous countries in the world to work as a

[*] 'El unanimismo de hoy lo hubiera envidiado Álvaro Uribe', interview with Cecilia Orozco in *La Silla Vacía*, 4 January 2011.

journalist. Sometimes the threat comes from cocaine traffickers, but any journalist probing the nefarious ties between the Army and the paramilitary death squads, or local politicians and traffickers, is at risk of being killed.

For less privileged journalists, exposé journalism can lead to reprimands from editors, or worse: death threats from hired goons.

So Carlos turned his back on the newsroom and started working as a photographer. But he soon tired of photography too. 'It teaches you to see the world in a certain way, but it blinds you to other ways of seeing,' he told me. So he'd become 'a photographer who doesn't take photographs'. He had no need of a camera – and little time for mine. In a lull in the conversation, I started scrolling through the photos I'd taken so far. 'Going to post them on Facebook, are you?' he asked me dismissively. I was, as it happened.

He repeated what was once an almost funny line about 'the famous Tom Feeling', which had grated on its third telling, particularly because I'd already told him that people have been mispronouncing my surname for as long as I can remember (it's pronounced 'Feiling', as in 'filing cabinet', by the way). Then he cracked a joke about tom-terias, *tontería* being the word for stupidity. Maybe he was jealous of the book I had had published – though not speaking a word of English, he'd have known nothing about it or what anyone else thought of it.

It was time to go home. When we had arrived in Los Santos on the first day of our hiking trip, Carlos had a hearty greeting for anyone we passed. But on the way back from Pescaderito, he had nothing to say to the holidaymakers, despite a beautiful walk up from the river and then down a dusty track that overlooked the rolling hillside opposite. We found a table at a crowded rustic eating spot, where we wolfed down bowls of *mute*, a local stew. On the way out we grabbed a couple of *patas* –

fresh marshmallows made from the gelatine found in horses feet, which were delicious — and headed for the pool hall on the other side of the road to kill some time while Carlos waited for the bus that would take him back to Bucaramanga.

The young owner kept the tables scrupulously clean, brushing them down and polishing the balls incessantly. We wore three-fingered gloves to play a game with only three balls. The object of the Colombian version of pool is to score points by making your designated ball hit first one colour, and then the other. It was completely novel to have to calculate not just the initial impact of the ball, but also the second and third repercussions. A game that asked you to consider the consequences of your actions seemed a fitting way to end my time with Carlos. *Desde Aquellos Días* was a great book, the first I had come across that suggested that Colombia's conflict was being perpetuated not just by 'narco-guerrillas', but by warlords from all sides with a vested interest in keeping peace and democracy off the negotiating table. I felt for him; he seemed to have cut himself adrift from the prevailing narrative, yet had no viable alternative to hand. So he'd fallen back on his defiant intelligence, which veered from charming and insightful to ambivalent and scornful.

He was quite a shark on the pool table too, and we walked out to the bus stop with victory very much his. In the village square, a boy of eight or so and his little sister came by hawking *empanadas* – small, deep-fried meat pasties. 'How many of them does your mum say you have to sell a day?' Carlos asked the boy. 'Thirty,' he said. Carlos cooed in admiration. He cupped his hands and blew them like a horn. He made farting noises with his armpit. By the time the bus arrived, he had a real rapport with the boy and his little sister. The kids, at least, loved him.

5. The Armed Strugglers

Carlos might have missed the watchful respect that Colombia inspired in its foreign visitors when this was a war zone. But I needed a break and was happy to join the backpackers in San Gil for a few days. I went horse riding in the hills. I went white-water rafting down the River Suárez with the young Irishmen from the Hostel Macondo. I hung from a glider over the Canyon Chicamocha and abseiled down waterfalls. And all the while, I thought about the story of Colombia, the ending that everybody knew, and the beginning that nobody could agree on.

One day, on my way back to San Gil from a day trip, I saw signs for Mogotes. I recognized the name: my friend Ricardo had told me that he had been there in 2001, as part of a convoy of volunteers from an NGO called Red de Paz. By his reckoning, Mogotes was the most democratic village in all Colombia. It was a peace community, one of a handful scattered across the country. The name sounds cosy, but their very existence is an indictment of all the warring parties. The guerrillas and para-militaries were not welcome in Mogotes, and neither were the police or the Army. The villagers had even thrown out their mayor and the town councillors. They were sick of the lot of them and had decided to rule themselves.

Ricardo told me that the first he had seen of the people of Mogotes was the human chain they had formed to encircle the village. They hadn't recognized the minibus that was trundling towards them and were braced for a confrontation. Only when the leader of the volunteers stepped forward to explain the purpose of their visit did the villagers relax for a moment. They listened, nodded and pulled their visitors into the chain.

Ricardo turned to face the surrounding hills. He saw that they weren't alone – he could make out a row of figures in the distance. It was a detachment of guerrillas from the ELN. 'Those villagers held my hands so tight that it hurt,' Ricardo told me. 'Their defiance brought tears to my eyes.' Eventually, the guerrillas retreated from view, the villagers relaxed their grip, and the people of Mogotes accompanied their visitors to the village square. In the mayor's office, which they had renamed the *Palacio de la Democracia*, the people of Mogotes gathered weekly to debate how best to spend the municipal budget. Everyone in the village had a right to join the working groups, including all children over the age of thirteen. Participatory, inclusive and supremely democratic, the people of Mogotes seemed to have come up with a real alternative to the left–right schism dividing their country.

When I got back to San Gil, I had a look at the mayor of Mogotes' official website, but it made no mention of the ELN guerrillas that had once ruled the village or the peace community that had taken their place. The 'history' link took me from 1706, when the town had been founded, until the early nineteenth century, when it had risen up against Spanish rule. It seemed that the struggle to live free of the current armed conflict wasn't worth mentioning. Perhaps the airbrushing was understandable: Santander was pitching itself as a tourist destination and was keen to forget its past.

So was President Uribe: shortly after coming to power in 2002, he declared that he would have no truck with the peace communities. To him, they were an affront: Colombia was a democracy under siege from terrorists, and unity in the face of the common enemy was imperative. He ordered the Army and police back into Mogotes.

Ricardo hadn't been back since, so I had no way of knowing how the people of Mogotes had responded to their return. But I was left with a more pressing question. How had the guerrillas of the ELN – which in 1963 had set up their first unit only a few miles from Mogotes – become so unpopular with the very people they claimed to represent? The same might be asked of the FARC, the Army and the police. What had they all done to become so unpopular?

The towns and villages of Santander have a long history of insurrection. Socorro and Vélez were among the first towns to rise up against Spanish rule. In 1781, 15,000 *santandereanos* took up arms in protest at colonial taxes and the Spanish nobles who depended on them. 'We ought to live in a brotherly fashion and he who attempts to dominate and advance himself more than is suitable to equality will be separated from our community,' they warned. In Socorro they formed a popular assembly, which elected five local creoles as leaders. Their rallying cry was 'Long live the King, and death to bad government.'

But no sooner had their leaders won concessions from the Crown than they renounced them. Unbeknownst to their followers, all five leaders of what became known as the Comunero Rebellion had betrayed the patriot cause. They had put their names to a secret oath, in which they denounced the commune, protesting that they had only accepted their posts under pressure.

The price of that betrayal was paid by their followers. Rebels were executed, and their heads, hands and feet paraded on poles through public squares. The house of José Antonio Galán, a second-rank leader who resisted arrest and ended up with his head on a pole, was razed to the ground and the site strewn with salt, as the Romans had done at the final defeat of Carthage. Other rebels were exiled to Africa. Those lucky enough to escape fled to the upper reaches of the Cordillera Oriental. The betrayal of the Comunero Rebellion is widely acknowledged as the first act of treachery on the part of the creole oligarchy.

It was a less than auspicious start to Colombia's struggle to free itself from Spanish rule. Even after declaring independence in 1819, Simón Bolívar sensed greater troubles ahead. 'The day that we don't fear an external enemy will be the day that all misgivings will begin for Colombia. On that day, the trumpets of civil war will sound.' Bolívar was right: civil wars bedevilled the young republic from its inception.

Ultimately, the origins of today's FARC and ELN guerrillas lie in the earliest days of the republic. Their forerunners had been Liberals. The idea that followers of John Stuart Mill, John Locke and Jeremy Bentham might take up arms in defence of their beliefs is a strange one, but it goes to the heart of Colombia's peculiar history, which until the 1960s was emphatically revolutionary and spectacularly violent without ever being particularly left-wing.

At the heart of that history was the issue of land: who owned it, what they did with it and how they treated the vast majority of peasants who didn't own a thing. Land ownership was tightly concentrated, and so was political power, which ebbed and flowed between the Liberal Party and the Conservative Party, the oldest political parties in South America.* Although both

---

* Much of what follows is from Frank Safford and Marco Palacios, *Colombia: Fragmented Land, Divided Society* (Oxford University Press, Inc., 2001); David Bushnell, *The Making of Modern Colombia: A Nation in Spite of Itself* (University of California Press, 1993); Marco Palacios, *Between Legitimacy and Violence: A History of Colombia 1875–2002* (Duke University Press, 2006); Forrest Hylton, *Evil Hour in Colombia* (Verso, 2006); and Alfredo Molano, 'The Evolution of the FARC: A Guerrilla Group's Long History' in NACLA *Report on the Americas*, Sept/Oct 2000.

parties were dominated by the elite, Colombians of all classes, races and regions were affiliated to one or the other. When wars broke out, everybody seemed to have a stake in the result. Since neither side had the resources to raise large armies, wars tended to be fought with small arms, machetes and swords. And because Liberals and Conservatives were generally equally matched in numbers, neither party was able to keep the upper hand for long. Wars would rumble on spasmodically for years at a time.

The War of a Thousand Days that straddled the opening years of the twentieth century seemed the last lesson in the futility of armed politicking. After seventy-five years of near-constant fighting, the government was bankrupt, as were its opponents. They couldn't even afford to keep the country's three leper colonies going, so the patients were left to wander the countryside. Worse, Colombia's leaders had been so busy fighting one another that they hardly noticed when in 1903, just as Liberal and Conservative leaders were putting their names to a definitive peace treaty, the province of Panama renounced all ties to Colombia and declared its independence. It was a national humiliation, made worse by the opportunity it gave the United States to establish a puppet government on Colombia's doorstep. US president Theodore Roosevelt rubbed salt into the wounds, calling Colombians 'contemptible little creatures' and the 'inefficient bandits' of a 'corrupt and pithecoid community'.

Fortunately, winds from the north were about to fill Colombia's sails and lift the country out of the whirlpool it had floundered in for so long. Global demand for coffee was rising and Colombia was well positioned to become the world's biggest supplier. For the time being at least, the party patriarchs stopped politicking and turned their attention to making money.

But as regional elites turned their attention to the world beyond their borders, the notables of smaller towns retreated into cultural isolationism. Their near-feudal outlook only made the poverty that defined the lives of most Colombians more glaring. Like Spain, Colombia was 'a land without men, of men without land', with the best bits being given over to cattle ranching. Unemployment and under-employment were high, the diet was poor in protein, and disease was rife. It was a land perfectly compatible with an illiterate population.

Those fortunate enough to be able to read and write were easily seduced by their standing. As David Bushnell has written, 'Men of letters produced learned essays and clever conversations on almost any subject except the deprivations suffered by the Colombian masses.'* The elite seemed content to stand the principle of 'no taxation without representation' on its head, as their factions fought over the right to tax a perennially impoverished population.

Between 1930 and 1946, a series of Liberal administrations inaugurated a tentative land reform programme, in an attempt to alleviate the poverty of their *campesino* followers. A handful of neglected or under-used estates were confiscated, broken up and divided among the landless. But the Conservative Party, which had long been dominated by powerful landowners, regarded these reforms as a threat to privileges that they considered nigh on ancestral. When the Liberals were voted out of office in 1946, the new Conservative government took back the land that the Liberals had distributed, by a combination of bribery, intimidation and outright violence.

The Liberals were divided over what to do next. Land reform was key to keeping their *campesino* followers onside, but the party leaders were themselves from an oligarchy that took the country's great estates for granted. These estates were a legacy of the Spanish, but had long sustained the wealthy creole families

* Bushnell, *Making of Modern Colombia*, p. 163.

that had usurped them. Besides, the mass mobilization of increasingly confident and ambitious *campesinos* could only threaten stability and the elite's narrow definition of 'national progress'.

Amidst the confusion, a charismatic leader from the land reform movement challenged the old guard for leadership of the Liberal Party. Unlike most politicians, Jorge Eliécer Gaitán was from the artisans' barrio of Las Cruces in Bogotá. He used the word 'oligarch' as a term of abuse and railed against a Colombia divided between 'the political country' of the creole elite and the 'national country' that the vast majority of Colombians lived in. Gaitán looked likely to be the Liberal Party's presidential candidate. For the first time in history, Colombians would have a credible, populist leader to vote for.

For the old guard, the world looked set to be turned on its head by a godless alliance of the ignorant and the amoral. On 9 April 1948, Gaitán was gunned down outside the offices of *El Tiempo* in Bogotá. His assassination unleashed the *Bogotazo* – several days of great violence and looting in the capital. Popular mobilization was intense, widespread and chaotic. One of those who witnessed the stillborn revolution was a young Fidel Castro, who happened to be in Bogotá for a meeting of the Pan-American Council. Castro remarked that, 'what was absent on 9 April was organization . . . there was absolutely no organization.'

The *Bogotazo* proved to be only the opening salvo in a nationwide orgy of grief-stricken vengefulness, known simply as *La Violencia*. As news of the assassination of Gaitán spread across the country, popular insurrections broke out in virtually every city where his followers were dominant. In the town of Puerto Tejada, south of Cali, *Gaitanistas* decapitated local Conservatives and played football with their heads.

In the period 1930–46, when the Liberals had been in power, they had turned the national police force into an appendage of their party, expelling long-serving police officers and replacing them with loyal Liberals. It was a move that was to have dire consequences during *La Violencia*, when the police were once more 'Conservatized'. Police officers loyal to the Conservatives took their revenge on *Gaitanista* Liberals, setting to with bloodthirsty relish.

Conservative volunteers were known as *chulavitas*, since many of them originally came from the town of Chulavita, where Liberal violence had been widespread in the thirties. Others were simply known as *los pájaros* – the birds – for the way they would 'fly' into villages to exact retribution before 'flying' back to resume their day-to-day lives in the city. In the valley of the River Cauca, their gangs cut out the eyes and tongues of Liberals. *Los pájaros* pioneered 'the necktie cut', whereby the tongue was pulled through the victim's slit throat, and 'the florist's cut', by which the victim's severed limbs were stuffed into his decapitated neck.

Their opponents responded with equal cruelty. In Santander, the Liberal Rafael Rangel returned to San Vicente de Chucurí, where he had been police commander in the 1940s, and massacred 200 Conservative civilians. Bands of Liberal peasants rallied around commanders who sported names such as *Capitán Desquite* ('Captain Vengeance') and *Sangrenegra* ('Blackblood').

Gradually, the Conservatives won the upper hand. With the Army barracks, police stations and mayors' offices all in Conservative hands, Liberals found themselves increasingly ostracized from public life. In 1949 Conservatives led a furious chorus of toy whistles whenever Liberal members rose to speak in Congress. At a later session, bullets took the place of whistles: one hundred shots were fired and two members of Congress were killed. The Liberal Party instructed its members to withdraw from all official bodies except Congress. As one party leader put it, 'For Conservatives, not even a greeting.'

Alberto Lleras Camargo, who was to become president in

1958, described the processes at work with customary eloquence. 'The most typical violence of our political struggles is that which atrociously makes victims of the humble people in villages and in the neighbourhoods of the cities, as a product of the conflicts that alcohol illumines with the livid flames of insanity. But the explosives have been sent from urban desks, worked with cold unconcern, elaborated with guile, in order to produce their fruits of blood.'

It was a pattern that was to re-emerge time and again in the years that followed. While the vigilantes and their victims were overwhelmingly poor peasants, the intellectual authors of the violence were often *bogotano* party apparatchiks, most of whom hailed from the country's ruling families. Thanks to their long domination of political life, it would be another twenty years before any organized alternative to their duopoly made it onto the ballot. The sense of being pawns, to be pushed into battle by the more powerful pieces on the Colombian chessboard, was what inspired many of those peasants to join the FARC in the years that lay ahead.

One of the oddities of Colombian history is that the savagery of *La Violencia* bore little relation to the ideological differences between Liberals and Conservatives. Ostensibly, those differences were real. For 150 years, the party leaders had argued over the role the Catholic Church should play in their children's education. They bickered over how much power should be granted to the regions and how much protection the government should give to the country's native industries. The Liberals' defence of the sovereign individual, religious freedom and free trade irked Conservatives, who trusted in the traditions of oligarchy and deference to the Church. But ultimately both parties were born of that oligarchy, and though they hated to admit it, they had a common enemy in Gaitán.

With Gaitán dead, the need to appease the rank and file of the

Liberal Party receded. The ferocity of the Conservative mobs that were roaming the countryside prompted little concern from the leadership of the Liberal Party. The vulnerability of the *Gaitanistas* was made worse by the fact that the police did nothing to protect them or to prosecute those who attacked them. With little prospect of seeing formal justice done, the violence ebbed and flowed as each side sought to avenge the losses inflicted by the other.

Colombians have long struggled to account for the wanton cruelty of *La Violencia*. At the time, wealthier Liberals tried to distance themselves from their followers and blamed 'criminals who distorted the authentic grief of the people'. But this interpretation was itself a distortion, and allowed the elites of both parties to speak in the most extravagant terms about the impossibility of ever civilizing the Colombian masses.[*]

Ironically, very often it was civilization – or the Colombian version of it – that fanned the violence. The *chulavitas* were among the most upstanding members of their communities. They considered theirs to be a holy war, that pitted the forces of order and authority against the atheists, freemasons and communists travelling under the Liberal Party banner. Their struggle against Liberalism was akin to a crusade, and as such, it tapped into the ancestral passions of a people raised in the company of saints and demons. Far from discouraging the violence, many local Catholic priests gave the killers their blessing from the pulpit.

By 1952, Colombia's cities had returned to something like normality. But the countryside was another story. Once unleashed, Conservative Party leaders found it hard to control their *contrachusma* (counter-scum) forces. That year more than 200 Conservative-affiliated gangs roamed the villages of Colombia

[*] Palacios, *Between Legitimacy and Violence*, p. 142.

in search of scalps. On the eastern plains, thousands of Liberal peasants took up arms to defend themselves. With the assistance of Communist Party activists, they formed a 10,000-man army. These Liberal peasants were an audacious force. They issued the 'Second Law of the Plains', a legal code that combined quick justice with an egalitarian vision of how best to govern land and labour. When an Army patrol was sent to hunt them down, Liberals under the command of the guerrilla Guadaloupe Salcedo ambushed it, killing ninety-six soldiers.

Their belligerence inspired the formation of small guerrilla groups across the country. The government branded them 'bandits without political labels', but this was a hard sell: the small cattle-raising communities of the eastern plains had been among the principal bearers of liberty in 1819, when Colombia was struggling against colonial rule from Spain. Their cowboys embodied the heroic, near-mythic origins of independent Colombia. This only made their turn to guerrilla warfare all the more troubling – and the need for speedy repression all the more pressing. For the time being at least, Washington didn't see it that way and declined the Colombian government's request for 1,000 napalm bombs.

Clearly it was time to put dampeners on the inter-party conflict. It seemed that a brief period of military dictatorship was the only way to calm both sides. In 1953 an anti-communist strongman, General Gustavo Rojas Pinilla, came to power. The General decreed an amnesty for all combatants, bar the communists. The by-now-infamous Guadalupe Salcedo accepted the terms of the amnesty, but shortly after putting his name to the agreement he was shot and killed by a Conservative hit man. The remaining guerrillas saw that laying down their arms would be suicidal and decided to fortify their positions.

In 1955, Rojas Pinilla committed himself to a military defeat of the rebels. This time the gringos were more forthcoming, keen to snuff out a guerrilla organization with clear ties to the Colombian Communist Party. Backed by a $170 million loan from Washington, the Colombian Army began bombing the guerrillas' positions. The Liberal rebels were forced to retreat into the jungles of the Andean foothills. A second column made a long march onto the eastern plains, where they founded *colono* towns like El Guayabero in Meta.

One peasant guerrilla who emerged as a leader of this Liberal uprising was Pedro Antonio Marín. Later known as Manuel Marulanda or *Tirofijo* – 'Sure Shot' – he was joined by Jacobo Arenas, a charismatic ideologue who described himself as a 'professional revolutionary'. Together they built a community based on economic self-sufficiency and military self-defence. Marulanda went on to become commander-in-chief of the Fuerzas Armadas Revolucionarias de Colombia – the FARC – a position he was to hold from the group's formation in 1964 until his death in 2008.

Once the party leaders had agreed to draw a line under their sectarian strife, they no longer needed Rojas Pinilla, and the general was forced from office in 1957. From now on, the two parties would share public office and their leaders would take turns as president. This National Front ensured that once again, the two big political parties dominated the country's politics, while the big landowners dominated the rural economy.

Officially at least, *La Violencia* was over. In the nine years since the assassination of Jorge Eliécer Gaitán it had taken the lives of 200,000 Colombians. But the gentlemen's agreement did nothing to resolve the simmering land disputes and general lawlessness that had fuelled the fighting. In the absence of reconciliation or reparation, much less any attempt to address the underlying causes of the conflict, the two parties simply chose to forget what had happened. Theirs was, as one historian put it, 'a merciless, enforced forgetting, based on historical myth and fantasies of total dominance'.*

In Colombia's cities, the rising prosperity of the post-war world was bringing real signs of progress to a people that had grown accustomed to living much as their grandparents had. But most city dwellers still had close connections to their home villages and couldn't help but brood over the savagery they had been witness to. In 1962 Alejandro Obregón won that year's national painting prize for a canvas entitled *Violencia*, which depicted a pregnant woman lying dead, with her breast and womb cut open. Sociologists at the National University in Bogotá embarked on an entirely new field of study, which they termed 'violontology'. Gonzalo Sánchez Gómez highlighted the 'ceremonial display of murder, which is expressed in an almost studied perversion, like cutting out the tongues (the words of others), goring pregnant women (eliminating the possibility of the other reproducing), crucifixion, castration and many other things that are directed not only at eliminating 200,000 people . . . but at leaving an indelible mark on the millions of Colombians who remained'.†

What was this 'indelible mark'? Clearly, the upshot of the violence was a terrible and inescapable fearfulness, but to what end? First, to show that anyone who crossed local politicians could expect to be shut up for good. Second, that despite the façade of democracy, neither the police, the judges nor Congress could be relied on to do anything to defend their victims.

The Liberal guerrillas responded by declaring their withdrawal from the conflict in 1964. From then on they considered themselves citizens of an independent Republic of Marquetalia,

---

* Hylton, *Evil Hour in Colombia*, p. 52.
† Gonzalo Sánchez Gómez, *Pasado y presente de la violencia en Colombia*, cited in Steven Dudley, *Walking Ghosts: Murder and Guerrilla Politics in Colombia* (Routledge, 2004), p. 7.

the village in the department of Caldas where they had their base. This wasn't the first time that Colombia's warring parties had taken a separatist turn. In the nineteenth century the departments of Antioquia and Santander both toyed with the idea of declaring themselves independent of Bogotá. At one point the Colombian government even made overtures to Washington, DC in the hope that Colombia might become one of the United States of America.

But in the Cold War years an independent peasant republic, particularly one led by communists, was unconscionable. The Army attacked Marquetalia from the air and sent in 16,000 soldiers to capture their encampments. They found them abandoned. Forty-three guerrillas fled to seek refuge in the mountains of Cauca in the southwest, and later that year founded the FARC.

The FARC were not alone in committing themselves to an armed overthrow of the state. Inspired by the Cuban Revolution of 1959, a generation of young Colombians headed into the mountains to take up arms. In 1963 a strike by oil workers in the river town of Barrancabermeja led to the formation of a second guerrilla force, the Ejército de Liberación Nacional – the National Liberation Army. For the next ten years, the ELN was no more than a tiny band of argumentative young men, living in great hardship in the mountain jungles of Santander and Antioquia and only occasionally making the news when they shot up some back-of-beyond police station. The organization was dominated by the Vásquez brothers. Like Manuel Marulanda of the FARC, they were largely driven by a desire to avenge the death of their father, who had been killed by Conservative hit squads. Gradually, they built an irregular army of *campesino* volunteers, who they ruled over with messianic brutality.

Over the course of the 1960s the Liberal Party tried to address the concerns of the poor peasants, all too aware that to ignore them would only add to the guerrillas' appeal. In 1970 President Carlos Lleras Restrepo created the Asociación Nacional de Usuarios Campesinos (ANUC) – the National Association of Peasant Farmers – to mobilize for land reform. Although plenty of high-ranking politicians backed ANUC, the president's land-reform policies proved to be ill-conceived, partial and half-hearted. Besides, the politicians in Bogotá didn't have enough sway to impose land reform on the powerful cliques that governed village life. Perhaps the factory owners and industrialists did, but they dropped their backing for reform when they realized that a steady stream of *campesinos* fleeing the countryside kept wages down in the cities. Ten years after the laws promising land reform were passed, only 1 per cent of the lands earmarked had been appropriated, let alone distributed.

But ANUC kept on growing. By 1972 it had 750,000 members, far in excess of any of the country's trade unions. Inevitably, it soon split into pro- and anti-government factions. The latter had had enough of waiting on vacillating, ultimately treacherous politicians. On the Atlantic Coast, ANUC members invaded the large haciendas and began distributing the land among themselves. The landowners, backed by the region's political bosses, responded with public and private force. They succeeded in recovering much of their land, but their belligerence only fed the ranks of the armed insurgency in the mountains.

In 1970 the country went to the polls to elect a new president. Victory looked certain to be won by ANAPO, the party of the former dictator Gustavo Rojas Pinilla, who had borrowed some of the populist rhetoric of the martyred Jorge Eliécer Gaitán. But the National Front wasn't prepared to cede power to an outsider. Television coverage of the returning ballots was suspended that night. The following morning, Colombians woke to find that the National Front had orchestrated a fraudulent victory for the Conservative Party candidate, Misael Pastrana.

The stolen election of 19 May spawned yet another guerrilla army, which called itself the M-19. Unlike the FARC and the ELN, the M-19 drew its support from the growing numbers of students, teachers and factory workers in the cities. Their rhetoric was vague – nationalistic, revolutionary, anti-US and anti-National Front – but effective. The M-19 became the focal point for a generation of young patriots inspired by the myth of Simón Bolívar, the Liberator supposedly undone by a corrupt and selfish oligarchy. The M-19's first action was typically brazen. Their guerrillas stole Bolívar's sword from the Quinta de Bolívar, the national museum that had once been the Liberator's home in Bogotá, pledging to return it only when his ideals had been realized.

The ever-smiling Misael Pastrana didn't flinch. He pressed on with a raft of measures that aimed to sweep away all barriers to investment in the countryside. But this only led to more land passing into fewer hands. Small-scale peasant producers became still less able to compete with wealthier farmers, and many were forced to sell up. Some joined the bands of itinerant farmhands wandering the countryside in search of the next harvest. Others threw in their lot with both organized and spontaneous invasions of rural properties, which only prompted more crackdowns from local honchos.

The poorest farmers had no choice but to move into less populated parts of the country, where they began clearing virgin land. Many of these frontier settlements lay in remote jungles and mountain valleys where the FARC constituted the only authority. They, not the government, banded the *campesinos* together to build the schools and roads that were needed. Between 1970 and 1978, the FARC went from being a community of 500 people to a small army of 3,000, with a centralized military hierarchy, training school and political programme. As if that weren't enough, the government also had to contend with the guerrillas of the ELN, the M-19, the Maoist EPL* and the indigenous guerrillas of Quintin Lame, who were based in the southern mountains of Cauca. Never had so many Colombians from so many walks of life seemed so convinced that their government had to be overthrown. The stage was set for the great National Civic Strike of 1977. If ever there was a revolutionary moment in Colombian history, this was it.

And yet, as it had in 1948, the moment came and went. Though still the oldest constitutional government in Latin America, the National Front was happy to ditch the less convenient aspects of democratic rule when pressed. They already had the press and television stations in their pockets, and were practised in the intimidation, coercion and repression of those who asserted their right to freedom of speech and assembly. They could also count on the millions of Colombians who regarded the government's critics as little more than hooligans.

In 1978 Julio Cesar Turbay was elected president, vowing to defend the established order from the rising tide of dissenters. Turbay ushered in the most drastic curtailment of civil liberties the country had seen since the days of the dictator Rojas Pinilla. Thirty-three military detention centres were built across the country, within whose confines the Army devised fifty distinct forms of torture. Selective assassinations and disappearances became routine practice. Gradually, the government wrested the initiative from their opponents and some order was imposed on the country.

*

*Esperanza Paz y Libertad (EPL) means 'Hope, Peace and Freedom'.

But the Colombian government's response to the guerrilla threat has never been constant. As presidents have been voted in and out of office, it has continually shifted between fear and hope; coercion and concession; violence and appeasement. In 1982, Belisario Betancur became president. He dropped Turbay's repressive policies and instead suggested that the FARC convert their military force into a political party. The FARC High Command welcomed his overtures. In 1984, the guerrillas renounced kidnapping, and both sides agreed to a ceasefire.

The site of their peace talks was La Casa Verde – in reality, not a house but a tiny mountain hut – which became the symbol of the tentative peace process. Unfortunately, shortly after negotiations got under way, guerrillas from the M-19 seized the Palace of Justice building in Bogotá. It was a spectacularly audacious move, as was the Army's counter-attack, which was called 'the 26-hour coup'. Over 100 people, including several Supreme Court judges, were killed. It was a disaster for all sides. It confirmed that President Betancur had lost control over the Army and that the military was incompetent. It also showed the guerrillas to be as inept and bloodthirsty as either of their adversaries. Although the FARC had played no part in the debacle, they were quickly tarred with the same brush.

The peace talks continued, but in an atmosphere of mutual recrimination. And yet, in spite of the impatience of the generals, progress seemed to be made towards an end to the armed struggle. Negotiations led to the formation of the Unión Patriótica (UP) – the Patriotic Union – a new political party, affiliated to the FARC and the Colombian Communist Party, which offered the left a peaceful, legal route to power. The UP campaigned in the elections of 1986, and gained significant parliamentary representation.

The new president was the Liberal Virgilio Barco. Barco had come to the conclusion that the power-sharing deal struck by

Liberal and Conservative leaders back in 1957 had only convinced many on the left that peaceful participation in politics
was a waste of time. So Barco dissolved the National Front,
making his the first one-party administration Colombia had
seen in almost thirty years. He offered the FARC 'an out-
stretched but firm hand'. If the guerrillas turned in their
weapons, the government would guarantee the safety of their
allies in the Unión Patriótica.

This was easier said than done. The generals might have been
barred from fighting the guerrillas while peace talks were
ongoing, but they were more than happy to provide covert support to the paramilitary forces that were massing to take on the
guerrillas. At the time, these so-called 'self-defence' groups
were legal. A law of 1968 had stipulated that the Army could
arm civilians 'when it was deemed appropriate, as in the defence
of private property'.

In the first half of the 1980s, the FARC were stepping up their
extortion and kidnapping of landowners, businessmen and
town councillors across the country. The Army seemed unable
to defend them, so they went looking for wealthier patrons.
The guerrillas had also been targeting those who had started to
make serious money from smuggling cocaine into the United
States. In 1981, M-19 guerrillas had kidnapped Martha Nieves
Ochoa, the sister of cocaine trafficker Fabio Ochoa. In response,
Ochoa and other members of the Medellín cartel set up Muerte
a Secuestradores (MAS) – Death to Kidnappers.

This nefarious alliance of landowners and newly-minted
cocaine barons was determined to do what the government
would not: to wipe out 'communism', in all its guises. MAS
rarely engaged the guerrillas in armed confrontation, which
they would in all likelihood have lost. Instead, they attacked the
weakest link in the guerrillas' chain of command: their sup-

porters. In their eyes, that meant anyone in the UP, the trade unions or community organizations.

In 1987, MAS planned and paid for a series of massacres of unionized banana workers in Urabá. MAS had no scruples about killing government employees either: when the government sent a judicial commission to investigate the rising number of massacres in the Magdalena Medio, the fertile delta region where much of the country's best farmland is to be found, their convoy of jeeps was attacked and all twelve passengers killed. M-19 backed down. They released Don Fabio's sister and agreed never to kidnap drug traffickers or their families again.

By now, President Barco was at war with Pablo Escobar and the other barons of the Medellín cartel. He could see that the legal self-defence groups had morphed into private armies at the service of the traffickers and their allies, so in 1989 he banned them. But the government's writ carried little weight in the field and the Magdalena Medio soon became the epicentre of para-militarism in Colombia.

As the self-defence groups became more aggressive and better organized, many in the Army felt that they deserved their back-ing. It was a trend that was to recur whenever the generals felt that the government was being soft on the insurgents. They had spent years playing cat and mouse with the guerrillas, who always seemed to know the terrain better than the young con-scripts who made up the regular army. During the Turbay years, the Army had targeted the urban militia on which the guerrillas depended for funding and recruits, but torturing student radi-cals had provoked criticism from abroad. By contracting out the job of counter-insurgency to these private armies, the generals hoped that they could undermine the guerrillas, while avoiding scrutiny from foreign critics.

Encouraged by the success of MAS and with the covert support of senior Army officers, a new generation of landowners moved from self-defence to a more offensive strategy. The Israeli mercenary Yair Klein was brought in to teach the farmers' sons of the Magdalena Medio the rules of counter-insurgency. Ivan Roberto Duque, the head of the local ranchers and farmers association, was unapologetic: 'If fascism implies defending private property and the family with vigour and energy, defending the state, defending democracy and shaking off the dangerous spectre of communist totalitarianism, then let them call us fascists.'

With financial backing from Pablo Escobar, MAS began decimating the UP with impunity. Jaime Pardo Leal, the UP's candidate for president, became the target of repeated death threats, which he did his best to make light of. 'If they shoot me in the head, they'll miss because of my tic. And if they shoot at my balls, that's not a problem either, because I'm so scared that my balls are in my throat.'

Members of the UP needed a gallows sense of humour. The Unión Patriótica was a FARC initiative, part of what Jacobo Arenas, its ideological leader, called *'la combinacion de todas formas de lucha* – the combination of all forms of struggle' to bring Colombia to revolution, whether at the ballot box or by force of arms. It seemed a comprehensive and coherent strategy; in fact, it was a recipe for disaster for UP supporters.

Since its foundation, the UP had encouraged the formation of community groups, known as Juntas Patrióticas. They were a great success in areas where local people had long been excluded from any say in decision-making, and within two years there were 4,000 of them. But the rise of a legal left-wing party that still enjoyed the backing of an illegal, armed insurgency unnerved traditionalists in the Liberal and Conservative parties. By 1986 the FARC had doubled in size, adding fourteen new fronts, many in UP strongholds. Rumours began circulating that municipal funds were being used to finance the rebels' expansion. The FARC were accused of 'armed campaigning' – in other words, scaring people into voting for the UP.

The UP began to look like an agent of, rather than an alternative to, the armed struggle. Despite their experiment in parliamentary politics, most of the FARC high command was still committed to taking power by force of arms. At their Seventh Conference in 1982, Jacobo Arenas had proposed building an army of 28,000 soldiers by 1990, which would then slowly encircle the cities. Even UP leaders knew that the high command had created the new party to serve as a façade, behind which they could build their army while using peace talks with President Barco to buy time.

Obviously, this undermined the UP's credibility. Alberto Rojas Puyo, representing the 'social democrat' wing of the UP, wrote to Jacobo Arenas with his objections. 'What the government and virtually everyone else thinks, including me, is that you can't campaign with guns in your hands. If you're going to accept peace, the guns should disappear, even if you don't hand them in.'

Relations between the UP and the FARC grew strained. Braulio Herrera, one of the leading lights of the new party, became known for carrying a pendulum with him to judge whether his food had been poisoned. Looking back on the rise of the UP twenty years after the party was decimated by paramilitaries, its head of communications acknowledged that many UP activists had been slow to see the dangerous contradiction inherent in the '*combinacion de todas formas de lucha*'. 'Every war needs some sacrificial lambs. Jacobo Arenas knew this. We knew this. We were the disposable ones.'*

And yet, despite the growing unease of senior figures in the UP,

---

* Álvaro Salazar, UP propaganda chief, cited in Dudley, *Walking Ghosts*, p. 95.

their party was making great strides. Jaime Pardo Leal had won 326,000 votes in the presidential elections of 1986. It was less than a tenth of the tally polled by president Virgilio Barco, but it was still judged a triumph in a country that had never had a democratic left-wing party. Braulio Herrera and Iván Márquez became UP congressmen, making them the FARC's first and only democratically elected representatives. Herrera called it a 'profound "yes" to peace and the politics of the democratic opening'. Colombia finally had a popular alternative to the traditional parties – albeit one with a powerful armed wing.

Liberal and Conservative politicians started to take the UP (and the FARC) much more seriously. The generals grew increasingly suspicious of where peace talks might lead. On being told that 'every day someone from the UP is being killed by paramilitaries,' the Minister of Defence was reported to have said that 'at that rate they'll never get the job done'.[*]

In October 1987 paramilitaries assassinated the UP leader, Jaime Pardo Leal. The brave man who stepped into his shoes was Bernardo Jaramillo. He got the government to offer better protection for his party's members – which was grimly ironic, since the UP's bodyguards received their training from the DAS intelligence service and their weapons from the Army, in spite of both agencies' involvement in the murders of UP members.

The government seemed torn between democratic good order, an Army-led counter-insurgency strategy and the paramilitaries' dirty war against the left. When the FARC ambushed and killed a further twenty-seven soldiers, Barco's interior minister said, 'If the FARC do not disarm and dissolve, the only

---

[*] The remark was made by the Minister of Defence, General Samudio, to a presidential advisor, Carlos Ossa Escobar; see 'Former Presidential Advisor: Army Worked with Paramilitaries to Exterminate Opposition Party', *Justice for Colombia* newsletter, 5 June 2011.

option left for the government is to wipe them out militarily, no matter how much that might cost.' Anticipating a renewed assault from the paramilitaries, the UP asserted that it was independent of the FARC, but to no avail. Braulio Herrera and Iván Márquez – the UP's only representatives in Congress – gave up their seats and returned to the mountains to rejoin the FARC.

Bernardo Jaramillo stayed at the helm of his party, steering it towards what generations of unarmed leftists in Colombia have come to call 'the deadly middle'. The UP president was growing increasingly tired of the FARC's strategy of kidnapping, extortion and executions, to say nothing of the never ending, unwinnable war they were bent on fighting. Not long after making a pro-FARC speech at Jaime Pardo Leal's graveside, Jaramillo laid into the guerrillas in a speech to party activists.

The FARC's political leader, Jacobo Arenas, didn't like the line Jaramillo was pursuing. The UP's commitment to parliamentary democracy might have offered Colombians the surest route to peace, but it undermined the FARC's *raison d'être*. Bitter and jealous, in 1989 Jacobo Arenas chastised the former UP congressman Braulio Herrera before sending him off to do the impossible: retake the Magdalena Medio from the paramilitaries. Once there, Herrera's paranoic pendulum turned on his own soldiers. He had 100 of them killed before he was forced to flee the country.

Bernardo Jaramillo's move towards the centre ground did nothing to reassure the UP's enemies on the right either. The Autodefensas Unidas de Colombia (AUC) the United Self-Defence Forces of Colombia – was an umbrella group covering all of the paramilitary armies that sprang up across Colombia in the course of the nineties. From the point of view of its commander-in-chief, Carlos Castaño, the UP was still a tool of the FARC. 'Anything that came from the left, and anything that was communist, was for us the same thing, including the trade

unions.' Bernardo Jaramillo seemed to know that this spelt his
end. He wrote in his diary, 'When the things that we fight for
and believe in dissolve into the reality of our world, men seem
to find, almost happily, death.'

In later years Castaño would call destruction of the UP the
AUC'S 'biggest mistake . . . If we had had the slightest education that taught us at least what the democratic left was, what
the radical left was . . . We wouldn't have made so many
mistakes.'* This failure to distinguish between a legal political
party and an illegal terrorist organization was at the heart of the
conflict. The UP was the one organization that might have
tempted the FARC's guerrillas out of the mountains and into
Congress. Its decimation by AUC paramilitaries could only lead
to the entrenchment of the FARC's hardliners.

Carlos Castaño's turn to paramilitarism had begun in 1987,
when the FARC kidnapped his father Jesús Castaño in the gold-
mining town of Segovia, Antioquia. The Castaño brothers paid
their father's ransom twice, but when his kidnappers demanded
a third payment, they refused. In response, the guerrillas killed
their father. Fidel, Carlos and Vicente set out to avenge his
death. They led an attack on the people of Segovia, burying
them alive, hanging them from meat hooks and mutilating their
bodies with chainsaws. By the time the Castaño brothers left the
town, they had killed forty-three people.

'The Germans have a word for what the Castaños did –
schrecklichkeit, or frightfulness,' Robin Kirk writes in *More
Terrible Than Death*, her account of the rise of the AUC. 'It was
applied in their invasion of Belgium and France, to circumvent
the civilian resistance. It was not homicidal mania, but deliberate,

---

* Dudley, *Walking Ghosts*, p. 202.

part of the plan.'* Looking back on the early days of the AUC, Fidel Castaño offered a more circumspect account. 'At that time, the border between justice and vengeance was very difficult to decipher, very vague . . . We killed a lot of civilians.'†

During the late nineties, paramilitary alliances of landowners, Army generals, local politicians and cocaine traffickers seized control of the most important regions in the north of the country. They wiped out the union representing workers in the banana plantations of Urabá, replacing it with a stooge union of their own. On the border with Panama, they pushed the FARC into the deepest jungles and began running cocaine through hidden bays on the Caribbean coast. In the Montes de María, a region near Cartagena that has long been dominated by huge estates, they forced entire communities to flee. With smallholders out of the way, they planted the deserted fields with huge plantations of West African oil palm, which still supply much of the biofuel that the United States is so keen to encourage.

For years, urban Colombians chose to turn a blind eye to paramilitarism. For many of them, the Castaño brothers' campaign of terror was justified, even noble, and Fidel Castaño was able to move freely in the circles of high society. Scarcely an eyebrow was raised when he bought up dozens of Fernando Botero's paintings, had his photograph taken with Salvador Dali and bought an apartment in Paris. As Steven Dudley noted, 'one could imagine him splitting someone's head open with a machete one night and drinking a nice Chianti the next.'‡

Rather like the National Socialists in Germany, the AUC's relationship with the elite was ambiguous. Some paramilitaries

---

* Robin Kirk, *More Terrible than Death: Drugs, Violence, and America's War in Colombia* (Public Affairs, 2004), p. 144.

† Dudley, *Walking Ghosts*, p. 146.

‡ Ibid., p. 148.

were essentially traditionalists, who claimed only to be doing what the government could not. Others called themselves 'right-wing guerrillas', and argued that their 'self-defence groups' should be recognized as the third actor in the conflict. The Army's attitude to the AUC was similarly opaque, perhaps best summed up by a retired colonel, who said that the relationship between the armed forces and the paramilitaries was akin to that between a married man and his mistress. 'You can't take her home, but you have to have her.'*

By 1990 Colombia was polarized between competing illegal groups – guerrillas, paramilitaries and the cocaine cartels – united only by their faith in violence and their increasing willingness to target the unarmed. The last days of Virgilio Barco's government were especially violent. Gunmen assassinated several presidential candidates, including Carlos Pizarro of the M-19 (which had just turned in their arms) and Bernardo Jaramillo, the doomed leader of the UP. The paramilitaries even killed Luis Carlos Galán, a Liberal Party politician who had looked certain to win the presidency. Among his election promises had been a commitment to crack down on the cocaine cartels.

---

* 'Official Report Illustrates Uribe Carnage', *Justice for Colombia* newsletter, 27 January 2011.

6. Downriver to Mompós

To find out what happened next – what might be called the end
of the beginning of the Colombian saga – I'd arranged to travel
to the delta town of Mompós to meet two former FARC guerrillas: James and Nicolás. From San Gil I travelled back to
Bucaramanga and then west, down from the easternmost range
of the Andes and onto the floodplain of the Magdalena. From
Barrancabermeja I could catch a boat that would take me downriver through the Magdalena Medio to Mompós.

I made it to the wharf with an hour to spare before the boat
was due to leave. A doughty-looking woman was selling *empanadas* from a table set up under a beach umbrella. As I stood there
munching, she gestured at the skinny kid who had been begging
me for change a moment before, and now stood with his back to
us looking out over the river. He was one of the *desechables* –the
disposables– she said; a good-for-nothing and a thief. Be that as
it may, when he drifted back to her stall, she handed him an
empanada and a glass of guava juice without a word, as if putting
her thoughts into words had troubled her conscience.

The radio news reported that in some of the coastal cities 500
times more rain had fallen than was normal. The whole country
seemed to be under water. November was usually a dry month,
but in Bogotá, the average rainfall for the month had fallen in a
single day. As the rain saturated the land, hillsides collapsed,
bridges and roads were swept away by mudslides, and crops rot-
ted before they had a chance to ripen. The weatherman blamed
La Niña, a seasonal cooling of the Pacific. This year, the ocean
had cooled a degree lower than usual. La Niña was 'maturing',

he warned, building towards its 'maximum expression'. He spoke of the rain going on until May; that was seven months away.

Looking out over the river, I wondered if the Magdalena was as wide here as the Thames was at Waterloo. It was hard to compare such different rivers, but it looked about right, though the Magdalena was full and the milky brown water looked deeper and faster than the Thames.

The boat we boarded at Barrancabermeja was surely too small for such a big river; it looked like something you'd find on the Serpentine in Hyde Park. It was made of fibreglass, with wooden benches for about fifteen people and a low roof that sagged under the weight of the sacks of rice, flour and plantain that the porters had strapped to it. The captain and his assistant wore pressed white shirts with strips of black felt on the shoulders to approximate naval epaulets. Once we were all aboard, the captain's assistant cranked up the outboard motor. The boat raised its prow out of the water and tipped us backwards into our seats, and this was how we travelled for the next seven hours.

Not long into the journey, we hit one of the many trees that were floating downriver with the floodwater, a collision that sent the boat careening off towards the riverbank. The captain eased off the throttle and the vessel glided to a halt just short of the reeds. The passengers looked at one another, wondering how close we had come to disaster. 'Such things often happen,' the captain said nonchalantly, and off we went again.

Apart from the occasional fisherman's cabin, there were few settlements on the banks of the Magdalena. From the river to the distant mauve hills in the east and west, the floodplain was covered with dense, emerald-green woods. Every few miles we passed a solitary white heron looking out over the river. Once, I saw a pelican fly overhead. As we travelled further downstream, the temperature began to climb and the *costeño* accents got thicker.* The passengers got darker as black, indigenous and multifarious *zambo* mixes of the two took the seats that had been occupied by the paler people upriver. The old woman in front of me felt compelled to talk, about what I couldn't tell. I did as the locals did: gave her a nod of acknowledgement and proceeded to ignore her.

Every hour or so, we'd pull up at a riverside wharf. As the roar of the outboard motor died down and the captain eased his boat to shore, I could hear music from the mobile phone that the woman behind me had pressed to her ear, as if it were wrong to be in company without music, or even a tinny facsimile of music. 'Puerto Wilches,' the captain announced. I recognized many of the names he called out that day as sites of paramilitary massacres or guerrilla attacks on Army patrols.

Until recently, few outsiders dared venture into the Magdalena Medio. Although apparently peaceful, its river towns still carried an air of menace. When I had told him that I was planning to go to Barrancabermeja, Carlos had warned me to be careful who I spoke to and what I said. It was hot, in both senses of the word, as I knew all too well. I'd been there before, when I accompanied a delegation of British trade unionists back in 2005. I remembered a teenager, not long out of high school, who was working for one of the women's groups in the town. I'd promised to send her a souvenir from England, but time and distance had helped me give my conscience the slip. Now that I was back in her hometown, I felt a twinge of guilt.

I still have a copy of a letter that she showed to me before I left the town. It was from the local paramilitaries, who called themselves the United Social Cleansing Squad.

---

* In Colombia, *a costeño* is somebody from the Caribbean coast, though 'the coast' refers to the departments which border the Caribbean, which may extend up to a hundred miles inland.

All these so-called displaced people's organizations, human rights defenders, trade unions, NGOs and a whole political party of sons of bitches who think they're untouchable are guerrillas. We will wipe out anyone opposed to the development and security of this country. We will not allow you to carry on spreading your stupid little ideas that belong in the past. Fucking bastards, you're going to regret the day you were born. We will destroy you. Traitors to the fatherland – get out or die. Peace in Colombia – and in your graves, you fucking grasses.

We reached the town of El Banco just before four o'clock. I'd been told to expect more harassment there than just about anywhere in Colombia, but with the heat, the warnings seemed to have evaporated from my head. When I disembarked, my only thought was for a cigarette and the need to stretch my numb behind. I was quickly surrounded by ten men, all offering to take me to Mompós by motorbike.

'There is no bus to Mompós and there's no boat either,' one of them said. 'The rain, you see,' said another, gesturing at the bruised clouds overhead. After seven hours of passive observation, suddenly all eyes were on me, demanding a response I didn't have the means or inclination to give. I scowled and sighed and told them to come back after I'd had a smoke. 'No problem,' they agreed, nodding among themselves – and then came back a second later with the same demanding looks.

A few young Army conscripts were milling around the wharf, most armed with rifles. One had a grenade-launcher slung over his shoulder. He looked as dazed as I felt, so I asked him if there was a bus to Mompós, in the hope that he wouldn't have the wherewithal to lie. But like the others, he said that the only way out was by motorbike. So I relented; one of the bikers took my rucksack from my back and strapped it to the pillion of his bike.

With my precious camera and laptop perched on the petrol tank, I stopped worrying and got on the back.

Off we went, too fast for my liking, under the jacaranda trees that shrouded the wharf and onto the elevated road that cut through the sluggish marshes. For the first few miles, the road was paved. Then we spent a mile or two on gravel before the pavement started again. Stranded cattle stood in the road, looking out over the flooded pastures on either side. A straggling band of mules and donkeys cantered past in the opposite direction. We passed families that had moved from their flooded homes up onto the road, where they had built lean-tos between the trees and rigged up power from the overhead line. They sat watching TV in the twilight; their skinny dogs sprawled in the road, barely looking up as we raced past.

Half an hour later, my driver was forced to stop by the flood water from the fields to our right, which had washed the road into the fields further inland. It looked to be impassable, but then we heard somebody whistle from the shade cast by an oak tree and saw that some of the locals had dugout canoes ready for us. While one of them wheeled the bike aboard the *chalupa*, their children came out to show me the baby parrots they had balanced on their fingers.

Once aboard, we were punted in silence through submerged gateways, where we had to duck into the boat to avoid the strands of barbed wire, into drowned fields where nothing stirred. We came to an abandoned village, where a stranded kitten on a doorstep meowed as we drifted past. A man stood stock-still in the water, watching us float by with a demented look in his eye. We were travelling at the same speed as the smoke that rose from the cigarette he held in his crippled fingers.

Only after half an hour of hallucinatory drifting did we hit higher ground. My driver pushed his bike down a hastily laid gangplank, I climbed on the back and we sped on. Three times, the land disappeared under the water and we had to cast our eyes around for the boatmen in the shade. By the time we boarded our last *chalupa*, the sky was growing dark, making silhouettes of the trees and reflecting shades of dark blue in the still, chrome water. The frogs started croaking. The boatmen's voices grew lower and then died away.

In the days when Colombia was a colony of Spain, boatmen used to row foreign goods upriver from Cartagena to Mompós, and then on to Honda, where they would be loaded onto mules for the long climb through the mountains to Bogotá. As they rowed upriver, they would sing: '*Que triste está la noche; la noche que triste está; no veo en el cielo una estrella; rema y rema y rema* – How sad is the night; the night, how sad it is; I see no star in the sky; row and row and row.'

The boatmen would probably have blamed the flooding on El Mohán, the mythical guardian of the Magdalena who upended *chalupas* and dragged fishermen to the bottom of the river whenever he saw small fish in their nets. On stormy nights, he could be heard laughing at the destruction he wrought. The only way to placate him was by making him an offering of salt and tobacco. It was a colourful myth, but until well into the twentieth century El Mohán was quite real to many fishermen. They would see him in the marketplaces – a short, muscular man who came into town to buy tobacco and *aguardiente* and chat up the local women.

We made it to Mompós an hour after the last of the light had left the sky. The Army had mounted a checkpoint on the approach into town. Under a solitary street light clouded by thick swarms of mosquitoes, a conscript asked me for a cigarette. 'And one for my friend too?' he asked, gesturing at a wordless soldier in the hot gloom.

My driver told me that the Casa Amarilla was under water, but I asked that we go there anyway. The owner was an English journalist and I'd been looking forward to meeting him. His guesthouse was at the far end of a small muddy square, down one side of which ran what would have been a narrow riverfront park, had it not been swallowed up by the swollen Magdalena. Sandbags protected the high front door from the floodwaters. The housekeeper ushered me into a beautiful colonial house, with floors of thick terracotta tiles, rooms the size of hay barns and high ceilings of dried and blackened sugar cane. Carmen told me that the owner was in Bogotá, so I dropped off my things and went out to look for something to eat. At the first restaurant I came to, I found the waiter asleep at an outside table. He raised his head only to say that it was too late for dinner.

Standing in front of the Casa Amarilla to smoke a cigarette the next morning, I watched a monkey clamber from tree to telegraph wire to rooftop. For once, the only music to be heard on the street was the muffled piping of an oboe from the music teacher's house next door. An iguana was inching its way up a rotten branch, which soon snapped, sending the lizard scuttling away into the floodwaters. I thought of the Louisiana bayou and the Mississippi emptying into its vast delta of swamps and lakes, like a reflection of the Magdalena on the far shore of the Caribbean, a thousand miles to the north.

Although few visitors make it as far as the steamy towns of the Magdalena delta, Carmen had told me, without any indication of her own feelings, that Momposinos didn't like foreigners. They had shown a haughty lack of interest in the foreign film crew that came to the town in 2006 to shoot *Love in a Time of Cholera*. Behind every sophisticated, culturally sensitive foreigner, Carmen seemed to suggest, lurked a *libertino* – a 'narco-tourist' – who was only there for the cheap cocaine.

In colonial days Mompós had been a prosperous town, made rich by the waterborn traders who plied the Magdalena between

Cartagena and Honda. But it was left a backwater when shipping was diverted onto the other branch of the river at the end of the nineteenth century. Since then, Momposinos had grown accustomed to being overlooked by more vibrant towns. This imperviousness had become the default stance from which they regarded the outside world. They had weathered their town's decline by embracing hand-me-down memories of better days.

I had some time to kill before I was due to meet James and Nicolás, the two demobilized FARC guerrillas who I hoped would explain the longevity of the army they had once served in, so I wandered over to the small church that ran down one side of the square. It had an unusual tower: squat and six-sided, with a wooden balcony that ran around its girth.

'The church of Santa Bárbara,' I heard a voice say. I turned to find myself face to face with the town's only tourist guide. 'Founded in 1633. It is the only church in Colombia to have Moorish influences. And look – the roof is in the shape of the crown of martyrdom.' José nodded encouragingly, and carried on speaking slowly and clearly, rather as one might to a simpleton. 'Santa Bárbara represents storms and artillery. People still mark a cross in ashes on the road when storms hit Mompós, in the hope that Santa Bárbara will lift the tempest.'* José paused and gave me a quizzical look. 'But you Europeans don't much like looking around churches, do you?' he asked politely. 'You always say, "Please, not so many churches – we've already seen two."'

In colonial days, the church of Santa Bárbara would have been reserved for the notables of the town, but to one side they had built a chapel for their slaves. José pushed open its great

---

* Many of the religious customs and local legends mentioned in this chapter are taken from Luís Eduardo Cabrales Jiménez, *Mitos, leyendas y relatos del Río Magdalena comentados otra vez* (Jiménez Editorial Lealon, 2009).

wooden door and we stepped into the cool, musty interior. It was bare, except for an especially bloody figure of Christ, who was bleeding from countless lashes of the whip and the crown of thorns on his head. The iconography of Catholicism seemed to grow bloodier as I neared the Caribbean. The masochism reached its pinnacle with San Pedro de Claver, the patron saint of slaves, who was said to have bound his fingers with horsehair in an attempt to share in the suffering of his slaving parishioners.

Mompós had been one of the first towns in Colombia to free its slaves, shortly after it rose up against the Spanish in 1810. I'd assumed that the darker skinned people of the town owed their colour to the Africans who were shipped to the New World to work its mines and plantations, but in fact the slave population left for Cartagena and Chocó soon after independence. It seemed that the mix here was of Spaniards and the Quimbay, an indigenous people from the alluvial fan of swamps and islands that lies between Mompós and the Caribbean. I thanked José for the impromptu tour and made my way back to the Casa Amarilla.

I found James and Nicolás sipping coffee in the courtyard. James was a big, light-skinned black man, calm and taciturn, with a ready smile. Nicolás, who had the *mestizo* features I recognized from the hill towns around Bogotá, called him '*negrito*'. It wasn't meant to be patronizing. Everywhere I went, people described each other by skin tone and body shape. I was the *mono* (white) and Nicolás was *flaco* (skinny).

I started by asking them about the Constitution of 1991. For the first few months of that year, the country had been glued to news from Bogotá's Hotel Tequendama, where the National Constituent Assembly was thrashing out the new rules of the political game. The Soviet Union had collapsed, and across Latin America guerrilla armies were handing in their weapons.

Public opinion baptized it the 'peace constitution'. It seemed a promising start, so why had the new constitution failed to bring an end to the conflict?

'Some of the bricks that fell with the Berlin Wall certainly landed on Colombian heads,' Nicolás told me with a laugh. 'But Colombia's guerrilla armies were offered only six of the seventy seats in the National Constituent Assembly.' This small guerrilla representation had been the condition on which the Army's generals agreed to the rewriting of the Constitution.

As negotiations got under way, representatives of the country's business associations were aghast that they should have to justify the government's economic policies to a group of 'gangsters'. The guerrillas had not ended their attacks on the country's oil pipelines, nor had there been any let-up in their kidnappings, seizures of villages or attacks on police stations. With great reluctance, the capitalists explained to the communists how things stood vis-à-vis the new globalized economy, of which Colombia was but a small part. Free trade and privatization were sacrosanct, as was their alliance with the Americans. Poverty alleviation, job creation and educational reforms, they assured them, would come in time.

The guerrillas emerged from the talks divided. The FARC and the ELN chose to play no further part in the Constituent Assembly. But other guerrilla movements – such as the M-19 and the EPL – handed in their weapons, and vowed to reinsert themselves into mainstream politics. Thanks to the presence of these demobilized guerrillas, the Constituent Assembly looked like a determined effort to include all parties. It was the first time that Conservative and Liberal party politicians had sat with former guerrillas and representatives of the indigenous and Afro-Colombian communities.

The upshot was a document of 400 articles, to this day widely admired by foreign observers as a model of reasonability and inclusiveness. For the first time, the collective land rights of the indigenous and Afro-Colombian communities were recognized and new institutions of state were set up to ensure that those rights were respected.

I had seen cheap photocopies of the constitution being hawked at Sunday flea markets. In a country so accustomed to the absence of law bringers, the Constitution of 1991 is precious. It is often the only defence the weak have against the strong. To know the constitution is to know the appeals you can and cannot make when the arbitrariness of raw power falls on your head. Wherever bribery, corruption and intimidation are the norm, the weak find that the constitution is the only authority they can appeal to.

Formally, the Constitution of 1991 addressed many of the underlying problems that were driving the conflict, as the politicians tried to strike a balance between the regions and the capital, the Church and the universities, the tax authorities and income earners. But the formal face of Colombia is like a doll's house – a pristine replica of a much larger building that has long been abandoned to the elements. As a result, despite living under laws that carry little weight on the ground, most Colombians still believe that life under siege is an exception to the norm – the norm being the stable, peaceful democracy promised by the constitution, which is always just a step away.

'At the same time that the delegates to the National Constituent Assembly were sitting down, the Army was bombing the FARC's camps,' Nicolás told me. 'On the one hand, they were talking about a Colombia for all, but at the same time they were trying to make sure that the armed opposition had no say in things.' The unarmed opposition was given no say either. The Unión Patriótica was still suffering what the Inter-American Court of Human Rights judged to be a 'genocidal persecution'. UP senators, congressmen, mayors and councillors were being killed off as soon as they were voted into office. 'Some of us thought that we could build socialism in Colombia,' said Nicolás. 'But there was no way to organize around those kinds of politics. The only way to save our lives was to take up arms.'

Nicolás had been an undergraduate at the National University in Bogotá in 1991. Hungry for change, he soon realized that the new constitution was not going to deliver it. 'When I was at university, I got involved in community politics, trying to sort out the drainage, the power supply and childcare. But I soon saw that there was no way to sort out the problems of the city or the country. You might solve a lad's hunger for a day, only for him to go hungry again the next. It was going to take a radical transformation of the power structures. And for that you need a revolution.'

So in 1991, just as the rest of the world was celebrating the collapse of communism, Nicolás headed for Sumapaz, where he joined the 52nd front of the FARC. His *comandante* was Marco Aurelio Buendía, a pseudonym chosen in honour of the man who founded Macondo in *One Hundred Years of Solitude*. 'I got to know another way of life up there. Sumapaz is actually part of the capital district, but it had been abandoned by the state. The people had been influenced by Bakunin, and had an anarchistic way of going about things.

The highland moors that look down on the capital are the world's largest. Their dense mists provide cover for Andean bears and tapirs, as they once did for guerrillas, who easily evaded the Army's helicopters. 'In the fifties, after the dictator Rojas Pinilla outlawed the Communist Party, the party held a historic conference in Sumapaz. That was when the Communist Party decided to become a guerrilla force. So it became a place very close to the hearts of the FARC. I spent four years up there and became a different kind of fighter, one that did work in the community. We took over the land and launched a land-reform programme.'

James's story was different. He was from a village near Cartagena, on the Caribbean coast. 'It was – and still is – poor,' he told me. 'The whole region has been abandoned by the state. There are no proper roads, no health clinics and only one school. Everyone lives on cassava and a lot of the children are malnourished.' But unlike Nicolás, as a young man James had no interest in joining the 'army of the people'.

'One day, a commission from the FARC showed up. They asked me to show them the way to San Cristóbal. I said, "Just walk straight up the path. You can't miss it." They said, "No, we want you to show us the way." Once I agreed to help them, they became a lot less threatening. I spent the whole night walking with them and didn't get home until seven in the morning. The next day, they came to find me again. By then, people knew that I'd been helping them and I was scared that they would either capture me or just kill me. It could be an Army patrol that had been tipped off about where I lived, or at an Army checkpoint the next time I went to Cartagena. I joined up because I couldn't see a way out. That was 1987. I was eighteen years old.'

After joining the FARC, James spent a year moving between the departments of the Caribbean coast. 'I hadn't joined the FARC of my own free will, but once inside, I was committed to the process. I thought that we could make real changes. There was no sign of the Army or the police in those places. We *were* the local authorities. In time, a lot of officials in the municipalities came round to our way of thinking,' he told me.

I couldn't help but smile at his phrasing. Surely they didn't have much choice in the matter? 'Well, very often, they collaborated with us out of fear,' James admitted. But in those days, he thought that the fear that the 'army of the people' inspired was a necessary evil. By force of arms, they were breaching the

invisible walls that had kept the poor in their place for generations. Only by muscling their way into the mayors' offices could
they tackle the endemic corruption that had condemned the
countryside to backwardness. 'Once we got our hands on copies
of the budgets and showed them to the people, they could see
that they were being robbed. "Why should we pay taxes to a
government that gives us nothing?" they would ask. The FARC
seemed to be the only ones who might change anything.'

In 1994, Colombians elected a new president. Ernesto Samper
came to office with a promising programme of social reforms
and rapprochement with the guerrillas. Just a few days after his
inauguration, the FARC spelt out the conditions on which they
were prepared to resume peace talks. They demanded that the
paramilitary groups lay down their weapons, and that the Army
withdraw from the FARC-dominated municipality of La Uribe
in the department of Meta.

Samper gave the order for the Army to withdraw. But just as
the new president built one bridge, another seemed to collapse
behind him. The previous year, Pablo Escobar had been gunned
down on a Medellín rooftop, after the most intense manhunt in
the country's history. In the process of bringing down the
Medellín cartel, the government had grown increasingly close
to Escobar's rivals in the Cali cartel. President Samper's term in
office was stymied by accusations that he had received campaign
contributions from the *capos* of Cali. It dealt a terrible blow to
Samper's credibility, which his overtures to the FARC did nothing to restore. The US ambassador, retired military officers and
the business associations were outraged. General Bedoya, the
commander of the armed forces, threatened Samper with a military coup if he was ordered to pull out of La Uribe. The
president, his room for manoeuvre already sharply limited,
backed down. Peace talks were once again off the table.

This was a huge setback for Samper, but not for the FARC. By the mid-1990s, Colombia's revolutionaries were in the ascendency. They were making $200 million a year from kidnapping, and $180 million a year from 'taxes' on the cocaine business.* Flush with booty, they were confident that they could defeat the Army on the battlefield.

'We had a strong programme and a bright future,' James told me. 'The days in which a FARC unit meant eight soldiers were gone. We were going out in units fifty strong. Between 1994 and 1999, we were getting stronger by the day.'

President Samper was paralysed. Public trust in his government was ebbing away. The FARC made several demands as a prerequisite for more peace talks, but the president felt that he had no choice but to go on the offensive once again. The Army mounted an ambitious series of military operations that produced absolutely no results. The generals floundered, the morale of their troops sank, and the Army became ever more dependent on the paramilitaries to deliver results.

'In Sucre, the local paramilitaries were led by Rodrigo Mercado Peluffo, who they called "Cadena",' James said. Ironically, many of Cadena's best fighters were former guerrillas. All of Colombia's guerrilla armies were sticklers for discipline, and there was a steady stream of deserters. 'As fugitives, they were always in danger from the group they'd deserted from, as well as the Army and the police. So when the local cattle ranchers started organizing self-defence groups, those fugitives approached them, offering to help.'

A casual observer of the political scene in 1998 could have been forgiven for thinking that the traditional oligarchy was still in control. Yet it was a façade, another trick of the one-way

* Alfredo Schulte-Bockholt, *The Politics of Organized Crime and the Organized Crime of Politics: A Study*, (Lexington Books, 2006), p. 133.

mirror dividing Colombia, and the political class knew it. The country was coming apart at the seams, under the combined pressure of drug traffickers, guerrillas and paramilitaries, none of whom had any official representation in Bogotá. The leading candidates in the presidential elections of 1998 began to court the insurgents once more. Both the Conservative Andrés Pastrana and the Liberal Horacio Serpa promised to withdraw the Army from five FARC-dominated municipalities in the department of Caquetá as a precondition for full and frank negotiations with the ageing FARC commander-in-chief, Manuel Marulanda.

Despite furious opposition from the Army and their champions on the right, Andrés Pastrana won the presidency by a narrow margin. He kept his word and met with Marulanda. Pastrana talked about dismantling the paramilitary groups; Marulanda wanted to see the decriminalization of popular protest; both men welcomed the participation of the international community. And yet ultimately, the protracted talks came to nothing. The Army had lost patience. When Pastrana announced that he was pulling out of the negotiations, it was only a matter of hours before Air Force planes were bombing the FARC's encampment.

Why did the peace talks fail? Perhaps because those doing the talking didn't understand one another. It was said that President Pastrana had never been to Caquetá until he went there to meet the leader of the FARC. Manuel Marulanda had in turn never been to Bogotá. After almost forty years of prolonged guerrilla warfare, they and the parties they represented had grown up in what might as well have been different countries. The only thing they shared was their experience of post-traumatic stress, which practically seemed a requirement for anyone seeking a high-ranking post, be it in government, the insurgency or the paramilitaries. Conservative party death squads had killed

Manuel Marulanda's parents while he was still a boy. Andrés Pastrana had been kidnapped by the Medellín cartel. And the FARC had killed Jesús Castaño, father of AUC head Carlos, who had in turn gone on to kill literally thousands of innocent *campesinos*. The entire country seemed caught in the cogs of some nefarious machine, driven by an insatiable desire for revenge.

By 1999, 65 per cent of Colombians were in favour of intervention by the international community, even if it meant sending in US troops.* The Americans were well aware of the danger facing their friends in Bogotá. The FARC were alarmingly close to the capital. Seen through American eyes, the need to stem the growing power of Colombia's guerrillas was part and parcel of the 'war on drugs'. Although the country's insurgents and its cocaine traffickers were quite distinct entities – indeed, they had spent much of the past ten years at war with one another – President Pastrana was happy to go along with the notion that 'narco-guerrillas' were responsible for the crack cocaine epidemic ravaging North American cities.

Shortly after coming to office in 1998, Pastrana had gone to Washington with a rough sketch of what he called 'Plan Colombia', an ambitious proposal to address both coca cultivation and the under-development of the countryside that fuelled it. Bill Clinton's government had taken Pastrana's pitch and rewritten it, with much more stick and much less carrot. Rather than tackle rural poverty, the Americans would fumigate the coca fields from the air and supply the training and funds needed to put the Colombian police and Army on a firmer footing. The document that President Pastrana took back to Bogotá was a done deal – it had even been written in English, and had to be

---

* James Zackrison, 'Colombia', in Yonah Alexander, ed., *Combating Terrorism: Strategies of Ten Countries* (University of Michigan Press, 2002), p. 127.

translated into Spanish before Colombia's Congress could approve it.

Since stepping down as president, Pastrana has often been derided for allowing the FARC to stall him in fatuous talk of peace. Manuel Marulanda never intended to lay down his arms, argue his critics. The wily old guerrilla was just biding his time, waiting to deliver a decisive blow to the Army.

But Pastrana was no fool himself. The plan he agreed with Washington ensured that there would be no need for more peace talks, at least not until the FARC were in a much weaker bargaining position. Over the next eight years, the Colombian government – or at least, its Army – would receive little short of $1 billion a year from Washington. Unfortunately for Pastrana, his term of office came to a close before the funding came on stream, so the plaudits for the fight back would go to his successor.

After the collapse of negotiations with the FARC, peace became a dirty word among many Colombians, used only by those who failed to appreciate the enormity of the struggle that lay ahead. An American author's analysis was prescient: 'The fact that the government changes its policy under pressure gives the terrorists hope that their objectives can be met and encourages more terrorism. The only way to escape this cycle is to find an effective leader capable of withstanding the pressure long enough to develop a coherent and stable policy and then demonstrate the strength to implement it.'* In his campaign for the presidency, Álvaro Uribe made it clear that he was that leader. He had no interest in talking to the FARC. Instead, he promised 'a big heart and a hard hand'. Over the next eight years, most Colombians were to see a lot more of the latter than the former.

* Ibid., p. 130.

Uribe's election campaign benefited from the near disappearance of the two traditional parties. The Conservative Party supported him in return for the posts that allowed them to buy and control votes and keep their party machine ticking over. The Liberals splintered, with much of the right wing of the party falling in behind him. With the backing of the bulk of the political and business class and the media, Uribe was confident of carrying the urban vote.

In the countryside, the paramilitaries regarded Álvaro Uribe as their man. Uribe was himself a landowner and friend of many of the biggest landowners in Antioquia. As governor of the department in the late 1990s, he had created an association of 'private rural security agencies', known as Convivir, to counter the rising threat of kidnap by the FARC. The Convivir were widely regarded as forerunners of the paramilitary armies that had gone on to over-run the northern departments. In villages across the country, the paramilitaries set about mobilizing the rural vote, pressuring rival candidates to stand down and buying lunch and *aguardiente* for those who voted for *el patrón*.

The abstention rate in the presidential elections of 2002 ran at 54 per cent, but still Álvaro Uribe's victory was greeted as a landslide. The White House backed Uribe throughout his term of office, despite their being all too aware of his background. CIA reports going back as far as 1994 recognized that the White House's Colombian allies 'employ death squad tactics in their counter-insurgency campaign' and have 'a history of assassinating leftwing civilians in guerrilla areas, cooperating with narcotics-related paramilitary groups in attacks against suspected guerrilla sympathizers, and killing captured combatants'.*

* According to declassified documents prepared by the CIA and released by the National Security Archive in Washington, DC in January 2010; see 'Body Count Mentalities: Colombia's False Positives Scandal', *National Security Archive Electronic Briefing Book No. 266*, 7 January 2009.

But the Americans needed Uribe to counter the rising influence of left-wing leaders like Lula da Silva in Brazil and Hugo Chávez in Venezuela. Not that there was much prospect of Colombia following the continent's swing to the left. Thanks to the paramilitaries, the FARC had been pushed out of regions they had held for decades. After the extermination of the UP, the unarmed left was articulated through victims' groups, indigenous organizations and rural community groups, but they too had been practically annihilated by the paramilitaries. Colombians had learnt to keep their heads down.

This put the FARC in a tight spot: President Uribe had the support of wide swathes of the electorate, a huge budget for his army and no intention of negotiating. For the FARC's hardliners, the situation confirmed what they had been saying since the early 1980s: that only armed struggle would secure peace and social justice in Colombia.

'In the 1990s, the leadership was only thinking about how to build an army,' James told me. 'Drug traffickers would often move their merchandise through areas controlled by the FARC. It used to be that the FARC just charged the *gramaje* levy. They didn't like the drugs trade, but they also knew that to spurn it entirely would only give the paramilitaries more clout. "OK, let's negotiate something here," they said. "Bring us this many guns, and we'll let you through." Eventually they became partners with the traffickers and now the FARC have their own cocaine-producing laboratories in the south of Bolívar.'

'With the drugs came a lot more money,' said Nicolás. 'But the drugs business has no sense of ethics or politics, and that business permeated the FARC. The *comandantes* used to be happy to have a watch. Now they wanted one with a hundred and fifty memories, and a calendar for I don't know what.'

'I'd spent a lot of time fighting corruption in the municipalities,' said James, 'making sure that money destined for such-and-such little village got there and wasn't siphoned off into someone's pocket. But now some of the *comandantes* were making deals with mayors, saying, "Let's send ten per cent of what was allotted to the job and split the rest between us." That corruption was our greatest enemy. It was a bigger threat to the FARC than the Army or the police ever were. But by the time we realized the extent of the rot, the organization was completely riddled with it.'

'The FARC's strength depends on its relation to the people,' said Nicolás. 'It has to be laudable, altruistic and noble. Before, we had no money, so we focused on loving the people so that they would support us, feed us and provide us with the intelligence that we needed. But now we bought everything.'

'The lads slowly lost interest in their political education,' said James. 'The sacrifices that inspire people, the idea of organizing the peasants to build the roads and the schools that they needed – all that went out the window.' Of course, the FARC still had committed socialists in its ranks, many of whom had been fighting their revolutionary war since they were teenagers. But the unwavering focus on building an army, combined with high unemployment and biting poverty in the countryside, meant that they were soon outnumbered by jobless farmhands who were just looking for a steady wage.

'Imagine a peasant, growing up in a little village, living the life of a mule,' James went on. 'He's eighteen and can barely read or write. He joins the FARC without being able to explain why, just because that's what his friends are doing. When he joins the FARC, he gains people's respect. He becomes relevant. But when he runs up against the reality of life in a guerrilla army, he soon starts thinking about how he can escape. By then, he's surrounded by enemies. The organization regards him as a traitor. The Army and police just see him as a member of an illegal armed group, so there's no way he can join either of them.

So he ends up joining the self-defence groups, who are always on the lookout for recruits with combat experience. This war is not about political convictions. It's about military interests.'

The FARC's militarism also explains their longstanding reliance on kidnapping wealthy businessmen and politicians for ransom. But kidnapping has become a public relations disaster. In the eyes of the public, it turned faceless, corrupt politicians into prisoners of war. For the first time, Colombia's oligarchs were regarded as victims, like so many others. And as soon as Uribe declared that he would not negotiate with the FARC, whatever purpose the hostages might have served as bargaining counters evaporated.

The need to guard their captives also reduced the guerrillas' mobility. As the Army gradually learned more about the jungle, they became adept at breaking the guerrillas' lines of communication. Increasingly, the generals could count on the support of country shopkeepers and small business owners who regarded the 'war tax' the FARC demanded of them as little more than extortion. And as the cash nexus corrupted the guerrillas' ranks, the Army found no shortage of deserters ready to collaborate in counter-insurgency operations in return for a cash reward. The guided missile that had killed Mono Jojoy in his bunker shortly after I arrived in Bogotá was the last move in an operation that began when an ordinary *guerrillero* accepted a bribe and agreed to betray his *comandante*.*

As the Army closed in, FARC *comandantes* spent ever more time trying to root out suspected informers, collaborators and spies. 'Now everything in the village had to go through the FARC for approval,' James told me. 'No one was allowed to be neutral. "You're either with us or against us," they'd say.'

Yet most *campesinos* had little choice in which army they

---

* Boris Salazar, 'Jojoy y la guerra perversa de Colombia', *Razón Pública*, 27 September 2010.

ended up fighting for. The conflict was effectively being fought by forced conscripts. 'The guerrillas and the government's soldiers are all the children of poor people,' James said. The conflict was coming to resemble the interminable wars of the nineteenth century. Beset by deserters and heavy losses sustained in combat with the Army, by 2005 the FARC's *comandantes* were pulling complete novices into their ranks. Villagers watched helplessly as they frogmarched their children into the mountains. With both guerrillas and paramilitaries hellbent on draining the pond of the other side's fish, *campesinos* found themselves caught in a vice. 'You can't stay here. You've got twenty-four hours to get out,' the *comandantes* would say. 'So a family that has spent all their lives working their little plot, loses everything overnight.' Those who tried to reason with or resist the FARC were often shot.

Trafficking in drugs, kidnapping business owners, extorting money from shopkeepers, shooting innocent villagers, recruiting children and forcing *campesinos* to grow coca was no way to run an 'army of the people'. The FARC high command had become no less venal than those they professed to fight. 'It was absurd and I didn't agree with it,' said James. 'So I took my concerns to my *comandante*. "Whose side are you on?" he asked me. "The side of reality, or the side of the dreamers?" In the end I had to leave just to save my own skin.'

Nicolás nodded forlornly. 'It's hard to leave your family. That's what the FARC had become for me. In the twelve years I was in the organization, I lost all of my best friends in combat. My only enemies were armed. For the rest I felt only deep love – political and ideological love – between people fighting for a better country.'

The FARC might have been born of the most high-minded ideals, but they seem not to have noticed the tide of public opinion turning against them. They still believe that some day their cadres will be marching down Avenida Séptima in Bogotá. Such a precious ideal demands ever more vigilant protection the further it slips from reality. 'I'm still in danger,' James told me. 'The organization never forgets and it never forgives. If I were ever sent to jail, the FARC would get someone on the inside to kill me.

'It's not easy being a former combatant. After spending fourteen years in the guerrillas, you don't have much work experience to speak of. And if an employer finds out you've spent time with the FARC, they worry that you're sizing them up to be kidnapped.'

I asked Nicolás how his political views had changed since leaving the organization. 'I still think that socialism is the hope of the poor. But everything changes – you can't put your foot in the same river twice, right? When I joined the FARC, if you bought the Communist Party newspaper, you were marked out for assassination. If you were campaigning for the UP, you had to go out in disguise. But these days you can go out campaigning anywhere in the city. The mayor of Bogotá, the second most powerful man in the country, is from the left and he came to power without firing a single shot. We don't have to go the painful way – of armed struggle – any more.

'When I was up in Sumapaz, I used to look south and think about the new governments of Latin America. Many of the FARC's ideals are being put into practice by Rafael Correa in Ecuador, Hugo Chávez in Venezuela and Christina Rouloff in Brazil.' The grim irony is that after almost fifty years of guerrilla warfare, whether the cause is public healthcare, the right to a free education or slapping taxes on multinational companies, no country is further from realizing the cherished ideals of the Latin American left than Colombia. This might appear to be the inevitable result of centuries of rule by an oligarchy, but in the process of building an 'army of the people', the FARC has only succeeded in consolidating their country's less than democratic political traditions.

'But I'm pretty optimistic that this country can find a political solution to the war,' said Nicolás. 'I don't think that the Colombian people are capable of putting up with fifty years of war. Some people say that if the government could kill ten thousand guerrillas on the battlefield, it would put an end to Colombia's problems. But I don't think so. We have to negotiate – not tactical negotiations, in which both sides are trying to get the best deal. We have to sit down at the table and build a Colombia in which there is room for all of us.'

After five nights in Mompós, the flood waters had receded. The streets that had been under water when I arrived were now dry, the mud already baked hard by the sun and sandbags outside the Casa Amarilla had been broken up. I was ready to get the taxi, boat and bus that would take me out of the Magdalena Medio.

By now I was the only guest left at the Casa Amarilla. On my last night I sat in my room watching the leader of the ELN guerrillas address his public via YouTube. I could hear the cicadas whirring from the bushes of whatever mountain camp he was speaking from. Reading down the line of his nose, through the glasses perched at its end, *Comandante* Nicolás 'Gambino' Rodríguez had the fastidious manner you might expect of a schoolteacher trying to talk over a class of rowdy children; of a man determined to be resolute but inclined to shrillness.

Comandante Nicolás joined the Ejército de Liberación Nacional at its inception in 1964. He was fourteen then, and has led the clandestine, persecuted life of a Colombian guerrilla for the past forty-six years. Twenty years ago, the ELN made some headway in the slums of Medellín, but the city's paramilitaries pushed their urban militia out of the *comunas*. Today their fighters have little presence beyond the sparsely inhabited mountains

in the south of the department of Bolívar. Brutality and isolation are only to be expected, but the lack of interest in what
the armed left has to say is unprecedented. The guerrillas are
unable to get their message off the internet and onto the streets,
much less organize or agitate. They have even lost credibility on
campus. Despite their claim to be 'armies of the people', neither
the FARC nor the ELN represents anybody but themselves.

The intransigence of the elite might have provided the
spark, but the conflagration that has raged for the past fifty years
has done nothing to resolve the contradictions of Colombian
society. Some have gone further, imagining that the war is, by
some diabolical pact, the very thing that both sides wanted all
along. It has become both the bread and the circus for a poor
and frustrated nation and the *raison d'être* for many of its institutions. It has made the Colombian Army richer and more
powerful than ever, while the chaos of war provides perfect
cover for drug traffickers. The arms manufacturers that supply
all sides with their weapons aren't exactly lobbying for peace
either.

The FARC and the ELN still talk of taking power by force of
arms, but that is a fantasy. The Colombian Army currently has
336,000 military personnel.* The FARC has about 10,000; the
ELN, less than half that number. As the prospect of seizing
power recedes, the guerrillas have gone back to raiding the
coffers of isolated backcountry mayoralties, launching lightning
attacks on Army patrols and engaging in what one writer has
called 'armed lobbying for pet causes'.† The causes are often
worthwhile. The guerrillas have long argued for job-creation
programmes and investment in the machinery, storage facilities

---

* See http://www.nationmaster.com/country/co-colombia/mil-military
† David Bushnell, *The Making of Modern Colombia: A Nation in Spite of Itself*
(University of California Press, 1993), p. 256.

and roads that might create viable farming economies in remote departments like Casanare and Arauca. Under threat of kidnap and sabotage, companies such as British Petroleum have ceded some ground and funded schools and local farming projects.*

But armed campaigning has borne bitter fruit. The oilmen were among the chief backers of Plan Colombia, and by 2005 Casanare and Arauca were swarming with soldiers, trained and equipped by the US military. The guerrillas got the government to spend money on the countryside in the end. They'd wanted bridges and roads; what they got was Black Hawks and fumigation planes.

The eternal guerrilla threat conjured up by the Army's press releases and propagated by *El Tiempo* flatters the insurgents. Perhaps the reality of this war is the opposite of the words and images used to describe it. Perhaps the guerrillas know that their moment has been and gone. Perhaps they know that from now on, their priority will be to survive the selective assassinations that await them as and when they lay down their arms. Perhaps they are scared.

Something else occurred to me as I lay in bed in the Casa Amarilla that night, musing on the time I had spent with Nicolás and James. When all your heroes are soldiers, perhaps war is inevitable. Doesn't Colombia's creation myth – of the Liberator Simón Bolívar and his valiant struggle for independence – ensure that the armed defence of sacred principles will always be a favourite posture? No sooner had Bolívar declared independence from Spain than his followers were at each others' throats. Armed struggle was practically state policy until both sides agreed to a National Front in the 1950s. Even then, the party grandees could only put an end to the strife by excluding from

---

* Forrest Hylton, *Evil Hour in Colombia* (Verso, 2006), p. 91.

power anyone who wasn't in one of the two parties. Naturally, the excluded took up arms.

Latin American revolutionaries have been celebrating the sanctity of armed resistance to oppression for half a century. They are the lost saviours, sustained by memories of the subjugation imposed on their kind since the days of the colony, and the need to honour those memories in a wilfully forgetful country.* The FARC, the Army and the politicians all claim Bolívar as their own. Indeed, listening to their high-flown rhetoric, I was often hard pressed to tell them apart.

---

*Mauricio Puello Bedoya, ' "Jojoy", una cara de Colombia', *Razón Pública*, 27 September 2010.

7. Going Back to San Carlos

I was standing at a bus stop at the bottom of a very high waterfall. Tropical verdure crowded overhead, parrots shrieked from the trees, and the sound of crashing water was making it hard to concentrate on the bus map. I was trying to work out how to get a bus to Camden Town.

I woke up and tried to get my bearings. I was lying in bed in a windowless room, lit by a fluorescent strip on the ceiling. Oh yes . . . San Carlos, a small town tucked into one of the countless folds of the mountains of Antioquia, a few hours west of the River Magdalena. The climate was no longer steamy enough to make cold water welcome, so I got out of bed and walked onto the balcony at the front of the hotel to have a cigarette before braving the shower.

I had felt some trepidation in coming to this town — it had been the setting for some of the most brutal violence of the conflict — but it fell away at the sight of the yellow and purple flowering trees that crowded the square and the mountains rising into the sky behind it. The warm morning air had sent the mist that enveloped the town at nightfall creeping back up the mountainside, leaving just a few stray wisps to drift around the squat tower of the church on the far side of the square. It wasn't a beautiful church — it was new and box-shaped, like a picture of a church that a child might draw, with red bricks separated by bands of mortar that a careful hand had painted white. From a corner of the square, I could hear dogs fighting and the voices of the men who had gathered to cheer them on.

A television was on downstairs; children's voices were singing something familiar – 'Look inside the eye of your mind . . . ' But the words of the Oasis song had been doctored for the new Coca-Cola jingle. Travelling Colombia by bus had given me plentiful chances to listen to the radio and I already knew the words off by heart. 'Every day, more and more people come back to Colombia, to find a country where there are more smiles than there is bad news. A country of music that you can't help but dance to. A country with the happiest people in the world.' It was saccharine stuff, but it was almost true. According to the Happy Planet Index, Colombia ranks as the third happiest country in the world.

It might have been happier still if there weren't so many towns like San Carlos. I had come here because it seemed to offer a microcosm of the countrywide effort to come to terms with the conflict, which for most Colombians was coming to an end. Somewhere between the eternal spring of the mountains of Antioquia and the harvest of terror and death that its people had reaped lay the essence of Colombia and its fratricidal feuds. Isolated from the cities, the dirty war the people of San Carlos had endured was little known by the outside world. It had once been a busy market town of 33,000, but between 1998 and 2004 *sancarlinos* had been pummelled by the illegal armies battling for control of Antioquia. Most of them had fled for Medellín, until only 4,000 people remained.

In 2005, President Uribe sent a beefed-up Army and police force back into San Carlos. An incredible peace came over the town, as it did over much of the country. Journalists who had once found the countryside too dangerous to report from, now found themselves able to travel freely. They were in the enviable position of having more stories than their editors could run. Gradually, the people of San Carlos began coming back to the houses and plots they had left behind. The town now had almost 19,000 inhabitants.*

I'd arrived on a Saturday afternoon after a four-hour bus ride from Medellín. The journey had taken us along the *autopista* for two hours, before we turned off towards Granada. From there, the asphalt road turned to gravel, and we wound our way along the contours of meandering valleys, many so narrow that you could have thrown a stone from the wooded crest of one side to the other. Trees, laden with flowers of two distinct shades of pink, lined the road. Then we would pass over a hill into the next valley, where the same tree produced only purple flowers.

The land on the lush valley floor had been given over to cattle raising, though there never seemed to be many cows in the fields. The local farmers could be seen further up the steep sides of the valleys, hoeing their carefully tended fields of coffee bushes, plantain and cassava. The bonsai landscape they had fashioned was dotted with one-storey adobe farmhouses that reclined in the shade cast by towering groves of bamboo. Their verandas were decorated with still more flowers that cascaded from old vegetable-oil cans. On the balcony of one of the older houses I caught a glimpse of a young boy who was watching tropical fish twitch and turn in a tank.

As the bus approached San Carlos, we passed properties with 'for sale' signs hammered to their walls. The Army wouldn't let prospective buyers in until they were satisfied that there were no landmines planted in the houses. San Carlos is still the second most heavily mined municipality in the second most heavily mined country in the world. Other properties were being slowly

* According to Iván Darío Alzate Martínez, the director of UCAD (Unidad Coordinadora de Atención y Orientación a la Población Desplazada), which was set up to help returnees to San Carlos.

colonized by weeds. On one little house somebody had painted the words 'death to paramilitary grasses', probably a parting shot from the FARC before they pulled out of the area in the early 2000s.

I had a cold shower, got dressed, and went downstairs to have breakfast at the bakery under the hotel. A passing couple caught my eye – she had Sophia Loren's eyes; he was wearing a fake Armani tee shirt. They could both have been modelling for the real thing. They got on the back of what should have been a Vespa, but was actually a spluttering Indian moped, and trundled off across the square.

I found Fernando Pamplona waiting for me with two cups of coffee in his hands. He was one of the few indigenous people I'd seen in Antioquia and one of the 4,000 people who had chosen to stay in San Carlos for the duration of the conflict. We found a table next to a glass cabinet of cakes iced in dayglo orange and green that was slowly revolving in the corner of the bakery. Fernando worked for an organization called Acción Contra Minas. He showed me the scars on his leg. He had been making his way up to his little plot, an hour's walk into the mountains, when he had trodden on a mine. The scars didn't look too bad; he'd been lucky.

I asked him if he knew who had planted the mine, but he spoke only of 'the armed groups'. His vagueness was probably deliberate. I'd often found that victims of guerrilla or paramilitary violence didn't like to distinguish between them for fear of being seen to be taking sides. When I pushed Fernando for details, he lowered his voice and told me that AUC paramilitaries had planted 1,800 landmines around San Carlos. But the guerrillas had planted mines too, he said, mainly to protect their coca fields. And even the Army planted mines to protect their bases.

'Landmines are the perfect soldiers,' Fernando said. 'They don't need to eat or sleep, they don't need supplies and they don't get demoralized.' But they were less discriminating than real soldiers. A demobilized FARC recruit had told Fernando about the twenty-four mines that he had planted along a path as his unit beat its retreat. His *comandante* had told him to go back and make sure they had been set properly. He checked each of them in turn but trod on the twenty-fourth, which blew his leg off. Soldiers on all sides knew just how much it demoralized a young recruit when he saw one of his friends lose a limb.

Since the mid-seventies the Ninth Front of the FARC had occupied everything to the west of San Carlos, all the way back to Granada. Since the mid-nineties, the AUC had occupied everything to the east, from the village of Jordán, where they had a base, down to the River Magdalena, where they had their strongholds. As the paramilitaries gained the upper hand, the FARC were forced to retreat into the mountains. They planted landmines so they wouldn't be followed.

Fernando had just come back from a meeting of landmine victims in Medellín. What had most struck him was that the vast majority of them had lost a left foot. 'Why the left foot and not the right?' Fernando asked with a puzzled smile. It was good to hear him find humour in the situation. He showed no outward signs of suffering or trauma. If I hadn't seen his leg, I'd have taken him to be a typical citizen of 'the third happiest country in the world'. But despite his cheeriness, Fernando admitted that he was always thinking about the unexploded mines that still lie under the paths leading from the town into the surrounding mountains. In San Carlos alone, 109 people have been killed or injured by landmines. Some of the survivors have prosthetic limbs but most don't, and few have been able to find work. Some don't even want to work – anyone who has lost a limb to a landmine is prone to depression, Fernando told me. I asked him what he thought of those who'd planted the mines. He said he felt a helpless rage.

★

Pastor Mira García was sitting at the café under the flowering trees in the square. She was watching a pick-up truck, heavily laden with wardrobes, mattresses and dressing tables, inch its way into a parking space in front of the church. It was another family of returning *sancarlinos*. Like Fernando, the *pastora* was one of the hardy few that had stayed in San Carlos for the duration of the conflict. I liked her straight away: she was fifty or so, straight-talking, engaging and impatient. She smoked a lot, unlike just about every Colombian I'd ever met, who if tempted, seemed content to buy a single cigarette for a couple of hundred pesos. She drank a lot of coffee too and talked nineteen to the dozen, so it was an effort to keep up with her as she pointed this way and that around the square, telling me who had died, where they had been shot and by whom; even what their families had said at their funerals.

Mira had been living with the violence all her life. She still remembered the day a neighbour had called at her house and pushed her away with the barrel of his gun before training it on her father. The neighbour was a *chulavita*, affiliated to the Conservative Party; her father was a life-long Liberal. She was five years old at the time. 'The first job I ever had was in a place right next to the house where the man who killed my dad lived. I wanted to tear his eyes out. But what do you learn if you just perpetuate the evil that's been done to you? So I started helping him out. His kids were having a hard time of things, so I used to dress them and take them to school. I felt something very positive inside when I was able to do good.'

The inter-party feuding that followed the assassination of the populist leader Jorge Eliécer Gaitán in 1948 had wracked many of the small towns of Colombia, including San Carlos. For most of the sixties, however, Mira's hometown had been relatively peaceful. 'When the guerrillas first came here, relations were good. The Army and police were nowhere to be seen, and the guerrillas came in proposing that they take their place. There were selective killings, but the problems only really started in the late seventies, when the guerrillas began extorting money from the local cattle farmers. Then they started kidnapping them and stealing their herds. The government didn't do much about it, so the farmers began recruiting local boys to help them defend themselves.'

Mira was keen to show me the town's Centro de Acercamiento, Reconciliación y Reparación (CARE) – the Centre for Reconciliation and Reparation – that she had helped to found after the paramilitaries of the AUC demobilized in 2005. So we finished our coffees and walked down the hill, past the town's heavily barricaded police station, to the CARE office.

'Between 2002 and 2004, this building was one of the paramilitaries' command posts,' Mira said. 'When we first moved in, there were still bloody handprints all over the walls.' She made us some more coffee, while I had a look at the children's drawings that had taken the place of the bloody handprints. One of them was of what looked like a tall house, surrounded by armed men.

'That's the hydroelectric dam that they built at San Rafael,' Mira said, handing me my coffee. Heavy rainfall, steep-sided valleys and mighty rivers ensure that Colombia gets 70 per cent of its power from hydroelectricity. The mountains of Antioquia were a prime location for expansion and the dam at San Rafael had been a huge undertaking, requiring considerable investment. It had aroused a lot of opposition from local people; the guerrillas, who considered themselves a buffer between the poor and the politicians, had backed them. 'That's when things started to get really bad,' said Mira.

It was a grim irony that in Colombia, these outward signs of economic progress were invariably accompanied by an upswing in violence, as the guerrillas sought to sabotage the country's dams, gas-fields and oil pipelines, and the paramilitaries tried to protect them.

By the mid-1990s paramilitaries from the river towns of the Magdalena Medio had linked up with 'self-defence' groups in the banana-growing department of Urabá to form a chain to block the guerrillas' path. The AUC had promised to 'wipe out anyone opposed to the development and security of this country', which included opponents of the dam at San Rafael. They came up from the river into the hills around San Carlos, looking for recruits. They considered anyone who shied away from the fight to be on the side of the guerrillas and were liable to 'disappear' them.

Paramilitarism might have been born in the Magdalena Medio, but in the late 1990s and early 2000s it flourished in Antioquia as nowhere else. Almost two thirds of the victims of paramilitary violence in Colombia are *antioqueños*. In each of the 120 municipalities that cover its rugged mountains, an average of 200 people have been killed in the past twenty-five years, mainly by paramilitaries. Antioquia might be the most dynamic, modern and efficient department in the country, but it also has all the conditions needed for paramilitarism to thrive. Much of its farmland is in the hands of big landowners, who depend on the labour of poor *campesinos*, who have long had to struggle just to survive. Its politics are clientelistic, in that people are accustomed to voting for the candidate who pays best, whatever their provenance. Despite their reputation for being fiercely independent, come polling day many *campesinos* are no less servile than their feudal ancestors. Ask a paramilitary soldier who he works for, and he will nod towards the big house and say '*el patrón*', just like generations of rural labourers before him.

Many Army officers backed the landowners when they began organizing private armies to defend themselves against the FARC. Their rabid anti-communism was deemed sufficient justification for waging terror on the civilian population. Lastly, Antioquia and its capital, Medellín, were crawling with cocaine traffickers, who had the will and the means to turn the AUC into a well-disciplined and heavily armed force of 18,000 men.[*]

Looking back on the early years of the AUC, the former paramilitary commander Ernesto Báez insisted that their terror campaign had the near-unanimous backing of local elites. 'I can't understand how a politician who is campaigning in areas infested with paramilitaries or guerrillas can say that he had nothing to do with those who run the region – that he won the election fair and square. That's just not possible. When I first arrived in Puerto Boyacá, all the authorities were there: the DAS [intelligence service], the Bárbula battalion of the Army, the police, the Attorney General's office and the mayoralty. But nothing happened without the say-so of Henry Pérez, who was the commander of the self-defence forces at the time.'[†]

Back in 2001, when the conflict was still raging in San Carlos, Mira would spend her days tending the tomato and broccoli crop that she and a group of local women raised in polytunnels on the outskirts of the village. But at night, they'd talk about how they could find their missing relatives. Such was the generalized state of fear among the people of San Carlos that two thirds of disappearances went unreported, even by the victims' families. The mothers of the disappeared lived in suspense, never knowing whether their husbands, uncles, sons and daughters were alive or dead.

As the years went by, they came to fear the worst, but always held out the hope that somebody might tell them where their loved ones were buried. Mira's neighbours were too frightened

---

[*] 'Origen del paramilitarismo en Antioquia', as explained by then-Senator Gustavo Petro, is available to view on YouTube.

[†] '35.000 no éramos los miembros de las autodefensas, ¡jamás!', *Semana*, 9 February 2011.

to talk openly about what they'd seen or overheard, so she and her friends would slip photocopied maps of the area under their doors, asking them to mark any gravesites they knew of. The following night they would come back to collect the pages. Invariably, they had been left untouched.

The mothers of the disappeared only began to make progress in 2005, when the government put its weight behind the Justice and Peace laws. 'President Uribe was looking to be re-elected and saw that he needed to clean up the image of the state,' Mira told me. 'Human rights abuses had rocketed and the United States wanted the government to put a stop to the killings. They called it a peace process, but really it was about getting their tigers back in their cages.'

Mira led me into an adjoining room to show me a pin-board that had been covered with paper flowers. 'Don't forget me. I deserve a tomb,' said the title at the top of the board. 'We only stop existing when people stop remembering us,' Mira told me. 'But the disappeared are never forgotten, because there's always someone waiting for them.' Each of the flowers had been labelled with the name of somebody who had been 'disappeared' from San Carlos. 'There are two hundred and forty-seven of them,' Mira said.

Sometimes, a body would be found. I noticed that instead of a flower, the name 'Johana' had been pinned to a dragonfly. Johana was fifteen when she was abducted. Her body was found buried in the backyard of the CARE building in 2005. 'The dragonfly represents freedom – for her body as well as for her family.'

'And here's my daughter Sandra,' Mira said, pointing to another dragonfly. 'The paramilitaries held her for six months before they killed her. She was buried near Jordán for seven and a half years. Finding her was like putting together a jigsaw puzzle, but we got her back in the end, in July 2009.'

Mira told me that the paramilitaries of San Carlos had also kidnapped and tortured her teenage son Jorge. In a break from his torture, one of the younger paramilitaries, who was just a teenager himself, had started talking to him. He wanted to demobilize; he'd had enough of terrorizing people who had been his classmates only a year before. But he was frightened of what his bosses might do to him if they knew his true feelings. Jorge told the young fighter to go and talk to the *pastora*. Days later, the boy showed up at Mira's house. She knew Jorge was dead when she realized that the young man standing at her front door was wearing her son's clothes.

Just weeks after his death, the Justice and Peace laws came into effect. In return for lenient prison sentences, paramilitary fighters were required to admit their crimes and identify their victims, including the location of their graves. Thanks to these generous terms, only two paramilitaries have had to stand trial for murder. Eduardo Cobo Téllez, better known as 'Diego Vecino', and Uber Bánquez, alias 'Juancho Dique', were found guilty of the forced disappearance of 1,194 people in and around Mampuján, a tiny village in the northern department of Bolívar. The local police suspected their involvement in 6,000 other crimes, but under the terms of the Justice and Peace laws, the maximum sentence the judge could give them was eight years.

Judges often asked members of the press to leave the hearings before former combatants revealed the names of the politicians and Army officers who had given them the green light to kill somebody. Proponents of the Justice and Peace laws insisted that leniency for the accused, and impunity for those who paid them, was the only way to bring the paramilitaries' reign of terror to an end.

One by one 31,000 paramilitaries from the forty-three blocks that the AUC had established all over Colombia handed over their weapons and turned themselves in to the authorities.

As demobilized paramilitaries gave their testimonies, Colombians were forced to acknowledge the extent of the savagery that the AUC had visited on their country. By May 2011, the government had identified the remains of over 10,000 people disinterred from unmarked graves, while acknowledging that at least that many again had yet to be identified.* In San Carlos, hundreds of people had been killed or disappeared, and thousands had been forced to flee their homes. As bodies were pulled from mass graves in the hills around the town, Mira was able to add a few more dragonflies to her pin-board.

'It's not a bad thing to have feelings of hatred or to want revenge,' Mira told me. 'The question is: what do you do with those feelings? An eye for an eye is the worst thing you can do. That just means that everyone becomes blind. Committing yourself to non-violence doesn't just mean that you don't throw the stone. It means convincing the man with the stone in his hand not to throw it. If we can just exercise some self-control, we can build ourselves a house with those stones. We can start building a different kind of country.'

In 2006, Mira and the other mothers of the disappeared banded together with those who had lost limbs to landmines and concerned officials from the mayor's office and set up the Centre for Reconciliation and Reparation. She told me about a demonstration that CARE had organized in 2009. Their placards were all blank except for one, which asked 'Who will take responsibility for what happened in this town?' One by one, people came forward to take the microphone. Some simply told the crowd what had happened to them. Others tried to justify what had been done, saying that it had been the only way to get the guerrillas out of the town.

---

* 'Colombia Identifies Almost 10,000 Bodies in Unmarked Graves', *Guardian*, 27 May 2011.

I asked Mira if any former paramilitaries had come forward to take part in the reconciliation process. She mentioned a local man who had been one of the band that had come up to San Carlos from Jordán, where the local paramilitaries had had their base. He hadn't said much, but he had written something in the CARE visitors' book, which Mira pulled out to show me. She turned page after page, much of it written in the sprawling hand of local children, until she found his words: 'Believe in me and I'll believe in you' was all it said.

'When you actually sit down and talk to ex-combatants, you find that a lot of them come from really violent family backgrounds. It's amazing how much abuse of children there is here,' Mira told me. 'But macho culture says that men don't cry, so a lot of the men who have been affected by the violence turn to drink to blot things out and end up neglecting their homes. People say, "OK, so send the dad to jail." But it's not as simple as that. Sending the dad to jail just leaves his wife to raise their kids by herself.

'I know a man called Miguel whose brother was disappeared. Their mother lives in Jordán and I've spoken to her about what happened. But Miguel? Never. He's never let any of us into his world.' I wondered if I might meet him. Mira told me that he was running for a seat on the district council. He'd probably be at the mayor's office.

Mira had a parting shot for me before I left. 'These aren't problems that the government can solve by decree. If San Carlos is peaceful today, it's not because of any help we've had from the mayor or from Medellín. It's down to what we did ourselves. The war won't come back here. We won't *let* it come back!' She hit the table with her fist and the coffee cup jumped in its saucer.

Polling day was seven months away, but campaigning for the local elections had already begun. Since the candidates no longer had to cut deals with one or other of the armed groups, there was a good chance of a clean contest. When I first arrived in San Carlos, I had seen yellow banners strung across the street and naively thought that they signalled the rebirth of the Unión Patriótica in Antioquia. Yellow had been their colour; it had marked them out from the red and the blue of the Liberal and Conservative parties. But the UP and over 3,000 of its most active members really were dead and buried. The banners were for Sylvia Ramírez, a local woman who was running for mayor.

I found Miguel Ángel Giraldo at the town hall, where he was deep in conversation with two women from the committee that had been set up to help those who had recently returned to San Carlos. The first thing I noticed about him was the scar on his face. It was unavoidable: a white line that ran along his hairline from one ear to the other. He had a second scar in the corner of his mouth, where it looked as if he'd been stabbed with a broken bottle.

I introduced myself and told him that I was there to find out more about the days when the guerrillas and the paramilitaries were vying for control of the town. Miguel seemed more than happy to talk. He was planning to go to Jordán that afternoon – he wanted to hear what the villagers expected from their council representatives. He had hired a motorbike; if I covered the cost of the hire, he'd be more than happy to show me around. 'There'll be plenty of people with stories to tell in Jordán,' he said. 'It was one of the paramilitaries' biggest regional bases. Carlos Castaño used to land there in his helicopter.'

It was hard to hear what Miguel was saying as we sped towards Jordán. A mile or two outside the village, we came to the River San Carlos. Not so long ago, the paramilitaries had thrown their victims from the bridge; they used to cut open their guts and weigh their bodies down with stones so they wouldn't float. Once over the river and past the Army checkpoint, the road turned to gravel and we snaked our way through dense forest bordered by neatly trimmed laurel hedges. We passed two young men at the wheel of a bulldozer, which was clearing the road of the topsoil brought down by the winter rains. Their girlfriends were chatting on a nearby log.

Not far from Jordán, the chain slipped off our motorbike for the second time. Miguel decided that we'd be better off leaving it by the side of the road and getting a ride with the bus that we'd just passed. It was a *chiva*, a converted American school bus, open-sided and decorated with folk paintings of posies. We clambered aboard and the bus strained its way higher into the forest, roaring and groaning as it went. The driver's bench had room for seven. The girl who was the driver's slightly-too-young girlfriend had a beguiling mix of European and Asian features. She would probably spend the rest of her life in the mountains of eastern Antioquia, but if ever she made it to Japan, she'd be an instant hit among manga fans.

A lot of the people of eastern Antioquia were strikingly beautiful. The faces kept coming: the boy with dark eyes set in a slender, olive-skinned face, who leaned into the driver's seat to fill the bus with petrol when we pulled into Jordán, might have been Sephardic Jewish. I'd heard more than one proud *antioqueño* put the region's famous work ethic down to the Jews who came to this part of Colombia after their expulsion from Spain at the close of the fifteenth century.

Once off the bus, Miguel asked a young man on a motorbike, who looked like Prince's better-looking brother, if he might ferry us from the bus stop to the hamlet. He was happy to help, so we trundled down the hill for a mile or two, until we came to a bar, set on a switchback in the sandy road leading down yet another hillside. Some local boys were playing pool; plaintive *vallenato* ballads boomed out across the treetops. Alongside was a thatched hut, where people from the outlying smallholdings had gathered to put their concerns to their prospective councillor.

While Miguel drummed up support for his election campaign, I sat on a grassy bank looking out over the valley. One by one, the locals came over to tell me their stories. Humberto Martínez had left Jordán for Medellín in 2001. 'We couldn't stand it any more,' he told me. 'They were killing a lot of people – good people who'd done nothing wrong.' On his return to Jordán in August 2009, Humberto found the plot of land where he had once grown plantain and cassava overgrown with weeds. His house was in ruins. Inside, the bath, toilet and sink had been ransacked – even the electrical fittings had been stolen. The surrounding roads were in a terrible state and there were no public services. Most of the teachers of eastern Antioquia, who to this day are routinely branded guerrilla sympathizers, had fled. The doctors had run away too, for fear of being cajoled into treating the injured of one armed group or the other, which only made them targets for reprisals from the other side.

The return of thousands of displaced *sancarlinos* had put the mayor's office under great strain. Humberto had gone to the mayor's office to ask for help, but all they could offer him were roof tiles, 'and they only gave me them after a lot of arguing'. Councillors were usually able to give returnees small sums of money for the seed, fertilizer and calves they needed to get their little farms up and running again. But they couldn't guarantee them food, shelter or work.

'A lot of people who came back to San Carlos are worse off now than they were before they were displaced,' Humberto told me. 'It's a miracle some of them survive at all. There's no work, no food and no productive enterprises at all. We just hope that all the improvements in security aren't blotted out if we're forced out again by hunger.'

Miguel and I had to cadge another lift back up the hill to

Jordán, but his scant resources never dampened his spirits. Everywhere we went in the village he was pressing flesh and kissing babies. Everyone was his *amigito* – his little friend. He was getting farmers to sign up to a scheme he had launched with the department government in Medellín. The governor would cover the costs of the seeds, fertilizer and tools; all the local farmers had to do was contribute their labour. '*Amigito*,' he asked each man, 'avocadoes, cocoa, fattening poultry or fisheries?' It sounded like a good deal, though judging by the wary looks on the farmers' faces, they were long accustomed to seeing politicians' promises go unfulfilled. Still, they signed up, gave Miguel their mobile phone numbers and watched as he dashed off to find another would-be supporter.

Only at the end of the day, when we were sitting in a café, drinking the sweet hot water that passes for coffee in the Colombian countryside, did Miguel tell me how he got the awful scars on his face. The paramilitaries had tried to kill him eight times. At their last attempt, they'd beaten him with iron bars and left him for dead. 'You know what an egg shell looks like after you've cracked it open and thrown it in the rubbish?' he asked me. 'That's what they did to my head.' Considering what he'd been through, his wounds had healed remarkably well. He had titanium plates holding his forehead, cheeks and nose together. 'My face is pioneering,' he said proudly.

Remembering what Mira had told me, I asked him if he ever felt anger towards his persecutors. 'Of course I do. But I never let it show.' And he didn't. In the course of the day, I saw none of the telltale signs of anger or bitterness. No scowl, sneer or frown marked his face. 'Thanks to God,' he kept saying.

By now it was past eight o'clock and there was still no sign of the bus that might take us from Jordán back to San Carlos. Luckily, Sylvia Ramírez also happened to be campaigning in the village that day, so Miguel asked the mayoral candidate if we might load his stricken motorbike onto the back of her pick-up. She was happy to help, so we followed her to her Toyota 4x4. It was a machine of rare beauty in those parts, and was emblazoned with her campaign posters. Her husband Álvaro took the wheel and Sylvia struggled to get her bulk into the passenger seat.

She wasn't an immediately appealing candidate. She had fake eyelashes and the immobile, doll-like expression common to those who have had too much plastic surgery. But her girl-friends/advisors – two well-fed middle-aged women with too much make-up – deferred to her in a way that suggested she wasn't to be messed with. I made a mental note to tread care-fully. Colombia's landowning class always gives me the creeps.

I daresay the feeling was mutual. European journalists are widely regarded as troublemakers. Any Colombian with an interest in politics knows that behind the Europeans' objections to Colombia's human rights record lurks a cabal of lily-livered, know-it-all do-gooders. Thanks to them, when President Uribe asked for the European Union's support for his war against the terrorists of the FARC, its parliamentarians blanched, leaving the Americans to pick up the bill for equipping and training the Colombian Army.

Sylvia told me a little about her campaign, but was quick with questions of her own. Who did I work for? What did I think of Colombia? Did I like the former president and the wonderful things he had done for his country? I kept my answers short and sweet and so did she. As the few street lights of Jordán receded into the distance, she fell quiet, so it was left to her friend Liliana to explain her friend's plans for San Carlos. 'The environment is at the heart of Sylvia's campaign,' she told me. 'Sylvia is very keen to protect the forests, to make this region's development sustainable and to encourage organic production.' This wasn't what I had expected to hear at all: it sounded eminently laudable.

'The old way of doing politics is on the way out,' Liliana

went on. This could only be a good thing: I had heard that two former mayors of San Carlos had been killed while in office. Another two were in prison, having been convicted of colluding with paramilitaries. 'The new breed has closer contacts with the people and is committed to them and their interests.' What did she think of the current mayor, I asked. She thought for a moment, trying to find a diplomatic way of explaining herself. 'He's a good person, but he's too provincial. He has the heart of a melon, so he doesn't have the right contacts. Plus, he's surrounded by unqualified and inexperienced advisors, who have driven his budget into the red.'

Sylvia, on the other hand, was wealthy and had travelled the world, so she didn't need to go pilfering the municipal coffers for the price of a car or house. This struck me as a pretty watertight argument for rule by the rich, but I didn't say a word. Neither did Miguel, who was looking out of the open window at the fireflies blinking in the black fields. He could have used a car of his own – but I suppose he didn't have the right contacts either. 'Sylvia isn't a professional politician,' her friend stressed, 'but she knows politicians and that is very important if we're to attract the international, national and departmental funds that San Carlos needs.'

It must have been close to midnight by the time we got back to San Carlos. Sylvia and her team were sorry not to be able to talk more, but they had to be back in Medellín for a meeting with the governor of Antioquia the following morning. If they set off now, they could be there by dawn. Miguel and I watched them go, their taillights receding into the distance. The side streets were empty and near silent, but as we walked towards the town square, the sound of *vallenato* came booming out from bars on all sides. Only when the music was loud enough to cover his voice did Miguel tell me that Sylvia Ramírez was a *testaferro* – the business partner and legal front for a well-known Medellín cocaine trafficker. She had also been found guilty of fraudulently selling national park property to cattle ranchers, which had led to the clearance of hundreds of hectares of virgin forest. So much for her 'eminently laudable' green credentials.

Back in my room in the hotel above the bakery, I lay in bed, listening to the windows reverberate in time with the bass line. It was like trying to sleep inside a loudspeaker. The music seemed to be a fire, keeping the people of San Carlos warm. As I waited for sleep to come over me, I set to thinking about the stories I had heard.

A labyrinthine geography that hindered communications; proud and isolated communities founded by pioneering *colonos*, who resisted laws drawn up in Bogotá as a matter of principle; a hidebound elite of landowners, listening out for the word of God, and accustomed to near-feudal relations with the peasants who worked their land; a guerrilla insurgency, rising in power and falling in popularity; and a backlash against them and anyone who looked remotely like them, largely funded by cocaine traffickers, often backed by the Army and put into practice by death squads.

I thought too about all the people who have been forced to flee the fighting over the last thirty years. Colombia has more internal refugees than any other country in the world. There are 4 million of them, which means that one in ten Colombians has been displaced from their homes. Among the rural population this figure rises to three in ten.[*]

Most of them have come to whatever rest they can find on the peripheral shanties of Medellín, Cali and Bogotá. I remembered

---

[*] As cited by the economist Luís Jorge Garay: see 'El proyecto de Ley de Víctimas aprobado en la Cámara tiene rasgos de inconstitucionalidad', *La Silla Vacía*, 8 January 2011.

being in the capital in 2007, when '*Bogotá sin Indiferencia* – Bogotá without Indifference' – was the mayor's watchword for the city. It was part of a campaign to get *bogotanos* to address the anti-social habits and general indifference with which many of them viewed their city. Having come to the capital from all over the country, in great numbers and over quite a short period of time, many of the displaced found themselves living in the unplanned, chaotic hillside neighbourhoods in the south of the city. Most of them were unaccustomed to city living; there was no room to grow cassava or plantain, and they found themselves living amongst equally poor and traumatized people.

I'd been to those treeless *barrios* a handful of times. They were forlorn, windswept places, whose only blessing was the spectacular views they offered over the more settled neighbourhoods below them. There were only three textures to be seen: concrete, cement and the steel bars that protected doors and windows from the neighbourhood's burglars.

I also remembered a trip I made to the Pacific city of Buenaventura back in 2002. Colombia's largest port was an obvious way out for those who chose to keep running. The port authorities had built high fences around the wharf and employed security guards to patrol it, but under cover of night plenty of young men swam out into the harbour and clambered aboard ships bound for San Francisco, Long Beach or the ports east of the Panama Canal.

Eduardo was one such stowaway I met there. At the age of fifteen he and some friends had hidden in the hull of a ship bound for New Orleans. They had left home with the bare minimum – a bag of white cheese and another of *panela* sugar water. They had spent day after day at sea, living with the ship's groans and the stench of their own diarrhoea, before the ship finally stopped moving and they were able to creep out onto the dock. They wandered the streets for a few days, three teenage Afro-Colombians in shorts and bare feet with only a handful of

English words between them, before they were picked up by the local police and sent back to Colombia on the next ship.

For many Colombians, running away has been their defining experience of nationhood. During *La Violencia*, they ran away from Liberal lynch mobs or gangs of vengeful Conservatives. Since the 1980s, they'd been fleeing guerrillas and drug traffickers. But in the last fifteen years, far and away the biggest villains of the piece have been the paramilitaries. Often working in collusion with local Army brigadiers, they would threaten local people. If necessary, they would kill the most prominent ones. This wasn't just because they were suspected of being FARC supporters. That might have been the justification given, but the weeks I had spent on the road, travelling first to Villavicencio, then San José del Guaviare, Bucaramanga, Barrancabermeja, Mompós and now San Carlos, had shown me that the roots of the crisis ran deeper than that.

Perhaps, at some point in the conflict, a group of wise men had gathered in the back room of some police station, Army barracks or government ministry, and decided that the millions of little plots, farmed by millions of little Colombians, were unsustainable. After all, many of those plots lay at the end of terrible roads, miles from city markets. Who could muster the will to invest in the infrastructure needed to turn things around? The farmers' sympathies would never lie with a government that couldn't or wouldn't supply the healthcare, schooling and legal protection that they needed. In the future, with the help of their eminences at the Ministry of Agriculture and the World Bank, the *campesinos'* fields would have to make way for the 'megaprojects'. Talk was of West African oil palm plantations, oil wells, coalmines and gas-fields. These projects needed little input from the local population; indeed, they were only likely to be jeopardized by the locals. Perhaps, it had been decided, it would be better if they simply left.

8.   'NN': No Name

While we had been hiking the Canyon Chicamocha, Carlos had described for me the mental sketch he'd made of his second novel. It was set in another imaginary Colombian town, whose mayor forbids its residents to leave. Since nobody comes through the town, nothing ever happens. Over time, people's lives stagnate and they become profoundly bored. One day, a newcomer arrives in town: a dead man, found floating in the river. More bodies appear. The townspeople pull them from the river and bury them in the cemetery. Nobody knows who they are or why they died.

Being bored, the people of the town start to make up stories about the lives the dead once led. They give them names and talk about the families and careers they left behind. As these stories become more elaborate, the characters in the town's drama begin to mingle; one story overlaps with another; lives entwine and then become entangled. The townspeople start arguing about what one dead man might or might not have done to another dead man. Before long, they are at war with one another to defend the honour of their imaginary friends. The fighting goes on for years, passed down from parents to their children, who inherit these sacred causes without ever really understanding what they mean or how they started.

Carlos told me that the story was inspired by the time he spent in Puerto Berrío, a town on the Magdalena four hours east of San Carlos. In the mid-eighties, he had completed his military service there. Puerto Berrío was in the paramilitary heartland of the country. I knew that the fighting had been no less fierce there than it had in San Carlos, and wanted to find out more about the town and the modern-day parable it had inspired.

I arrived on a Saturday afternoon, with the mercury nudging 38 degrees. From the bus station, I followed the abandoned railway tracks that led over the river into the town. It was over 300 miles from Puerto Berrío to the Caribbean, but the Magdalena was already over a mile wide. The railway had been built in the mid-nineteenth century to carry British machine tools from the coast to the textile factories then being built in Medellín.

From the bridge that carried the tracks over the Magdalena, I could see a group of men sifting sand on the banks of the river below me. A truck laden with sandbags was lumbering along the rutted lane that ran under the bridge, bound for the cement factory upriver. Carlos had told me that the sandbaggers had often lent a hand when the Army recruits arrived to pull bodies from the river. They had grown used to the sight of bloated corpses drifting with the current.

The Magdalena wasn't the only Colombian river to have borne the dead to a watery grave. In the early 1990s, when Cali's cocaine-trafficking cartel was at its height, their *sicarios* (hitmen) would often throw their victims into the River Cauca, which flows north through Cali. Their bodies would float downstream for many miles, until they came to a bend in the river at the town of Marsella, where many of them got caught in the trees or were washed up on the sandbanks.

Local fishermen would heave the bodies from the river and take them to the town morgue. Special buses were laid on from Cali so that the families of the disappeared could go to Marsella to see if their sons and husbands were among the dead. Often, the bodies were so badly disfigured that relatives could only recognize them by the shoes they wore. When a body went unclaimed, it would be taken from the morgue to the cemetery, where the gravedigger would remove the corpse's shoes before burial. His grave would be marked 'NN' (*ningun nombre* – no name). His shoes would be lined up outside the cemetery wall, waiting for the day when a relative might recognize them.

In the days when cocaine trafficking was in the hands of colourful killers like Pablo Escobar, stories like these regularly made their way into the newspapers of distant countries. Over the past twenty years, however, Colombia's once-famous cocaine cartels have been broken up. These days, the real money is made by the Mexican cartels, while the Colombian end of the business has splintered into hundreds of mini-cartels. Cocaine production and smuggling is still a lucrative enterprise, but those who stepped into Escobar's shoes have learnt the value of discretion. Killings are rarer than they were and no longer make the headlines, even of *El Tiempo*.

The bodies pulled from the Magdalena and buried as 'NN' in the cemetery in Puerto Berrío might have been those of rival traffickers. Or perhaps they were spies for the guerrillas, informants for the Army, whistle-blowers, gossips, or any of the thousands deemed to know too much. In truth, nobody knew who they were, since they'd been pulled from the river with no trace of identification. If they showed up shortly after a local person went missing, there was a chance that a relative might be found and the corpse identified. But most of the NN that the sandbaggers of Puerto Berrío dragged out of the river were not local men. They could have been pitched into the Magdalena anywhere downriver of the rapids at Honda, northwest of Bogotá.

The head of the local association for the disappeared was Teresa Castrillón, a middle-aged woman with deep-set eyes, who I met at the town cemetery the following morning. She wore rosary beads and a small, worn wooden cross around her wrist. Over the past twenty-five years, Teresa's mother, uncles and nephews had all been killed or disappeared. Her father and brother had been killed together. She read out their names from the list of the murdered and disappeared that had been painted on the wall of the cemetery. 'Julio Sierra Taborda, killed on 13 February 1985. Jesús Sierra Taborda, killed on 12 December 1985. María Ovidia Taborda, killed on 10 November 1988 . . . '

The list had been painted in a mock-parchment style in shades of brown, complete with cracks in the margins of a curling scroll. I tried counting the names, but there were too many. I did a rough calculation: there were thirty names in the first column and seven columns, which meant that over 210 people had been murdered or disappeared in Puerto Berrío since 1985. The population of the town was 6,000 – perhaps 8,000 if you included the outlying farms.

Most of Teresa's family were cattle farmers. Perhaps they had been targeted because they owned land coveted by other landowners? But why would anyone have wanted to kill her husband? He had worked in the local bank – perhaps he'd been killed because he was a member of the bank workers' union? Or perhaps he'd turned down somebody's application for a bank loan? His killer's motive was as much a mystery as the location of her husband's grave. Teresa was resigned to the fact that she would probably never find answers to any of her questions.

What was beyond dispute was that her dead relatives were not the 'collateral damage' of Colombia's 'war on terror'. The last guerrillas in the Magdalena Medio had been driven out in the early eighties. The last of the critical journalists, teachers and trade unionists who might have been suspected of collaborating with them had either left or been killed a long time ago too. In these parts, at least, Colombia's dirty war was over. But the tactics devised to fight that war had since been adapted for day-to-day business practice. They might be used to secure a building contract, drive down the asking price for a farm, or extort money from the owner of a supermarket. Terror had become a last resort in all kinds of disputes.

I asked Teresa if she knew who was responsible for killing her relatives. 'I see them all the time,' she said. 'They were the men in sunglasses that you saw lounging outside the café earlier today. They're the ones on the big motorbikes that always get waved through the Army's checkpoints on their way back from the *finca* at Quebrada El Suán. Everyone knows that it's a paramilitary base.'

There was little trace of indignation in her voice. Although Teresa had long since given up hope of seeing the killers brought to justice, when President Uribe passed the Justice and Peace laws in 2005, she thought that the demobilization of the paramilitaries would at least bring some peace to Puerto Berrío. The first signs were promising. The fighters of the local AUC front turned in their weapons and prepared to be 're-inserted' into civil society. The government paid them a monthly stipend to tide them over while they looked for legal work. Some signed up for courses in computer science, catering or bricklaying. Others owned and drove most of the taxis in Puerto Berrío.

But the law of supply and demand ensured that the killings went on. On the second of the three days that I spent in the town, a teenager was shot and killed by local vigilantes for selling marijuana. Teresa told me that for a week of the previous month, bodies had been showing up on a daily basis. People whispered about the new paramilitary groups that had risen from the ashes of the old, under the relatively innocuous name of *bandas criminales* – criminal groups.

A friend of Teresa was on her way out of the cemetery. She'd been laying flowers on her husband's grave. 'If God wants it, you have to go,' she said languidly. She and Teresa walked slowly away into the midday sun, leaving me alone to have a look around. On a wall of the porch over the main entrance was a sign that read '*Aqui todos somos iguales* – we are all the same here'. The avenue that led up to the little chapel at the top of the cemetery was lined with gravestones, most of marble and all well tended. Beyond them ran a wall that was covered in plaques, behind each of which was a small chamber for the bones of the dead.

The sunlight glancing off the whitewashed tombs was blinding, so I walked up the avenue in the hope of finding some shade. The *panteón militar* was a wall of plaques commemorating the soldiers of Puerto Berrío who had died fighting the guerrillas in the early eighties. A middle-aged woman was carefully scrubbing the black metal grill in front of a plaque. I could see an airbrushed photo of a fallen soldier. He looked to have been in his twenties, a blond-haired, blue-eyed face surrounded by clouds and framed by the beams of a setting sun.

Most of the plaques carried the names of men who had died young. One of them read: 'So destiny has separated us without giving us the opportunity to love one another as we dreamed we might.' Another bore the words: 'Lord, in the light of your splendour, everything looks different: life, pain and death.' The language of the faithful was foreign to me, but even I could see that without their faith in the divine it would be hard to bear so little earthly justice or protection.

Every Monday, a special mass was held for the children of Puerto Berrío. The priest's words crackled over the loudspeakers that were dotted around the cemetery. The faithful sat or stood all over the cemetery, listening attentively. When an old woman took to the microphone and began to sing a plaintive folk song, they sang along.

Wandering the tombs, their singing drifting in and out of earshot, I found the NN of Puerto Berrío behind the multi-storey vaults, hidden from the avenue that led up to the chapel. Their tombs had been blackened by the rain and then bleached by the sun, and the whitewash was flaking away. Black birds with thick beaks hopped from the path into the dry grass as I walked the length of the walls.

On the slab that enclosed one tomb was scrawled a question, 'This is not David. Is it Luna?' The disappeared of Puerto Berrío were names without bodies; the NN were bodies without names. It was only natural that the bereaved should try to put them together, in an attempt at normalizing the abnormal. The people of the town believed that by adopting an NN they might curry favour with God. If an innocent had been killed, he was sure to be in Heaven. By tending his grave, a woman – the adopters all seemed to be women – might have celestial favour bestowed upon her.

Nearly all of the NN tombs had been 'adopted' by someone in the town and most of their plaques had been engraved with the words 'Thank you for the favour received – a devotee.' Many of the NN had been given names by their adoptive families. One read, 'Though unknown, you will always have a friend.' In some cases, the adoptive family hadn't had the money to pay for a plaque for their NN, so the gravedigger had simply marked the concrete slab covering the hole in the wall with an inky finger. In some cases, he had just written 'Escogido – Chosen' – by whom and for what, we were not to know.

I watched a woman walk ahead of me. She tapped three times on each of the tombs. 'It's a custom in Antioquia,' she said. She smiled, but not for long. 'You knock three times on the tomb of the deceased and say a quick prayer for the person inside.' She had adopted her NN a week ago. 'My husband was a paramilitary. He demobilized in 2005, but they disappeared him not long after that. They were worried that he would talk. His body still hasn't been found, so the wife of the cemetery keeper told me to choose an NN. I liked this one,' she said, pointing to a small marble plaque. 'I cleaned it up – it was very dirty before.

I imagine it's a man – most of them are. I call him my little friend.' I asked her if she had made a wish when she adopted her NN. She nodded. 'But it's a secret. If I tell you, it won't come true.'

When I'd checked into the Hotel Golondrinas, I'd asked the receptionist why the hotel was named after swallows. 'You'll find out later,' she'd said. As the light faded at the cemetery, I watched the swallows dart out from behind the cracked slab covering a tomb. One after another, they dashed up into the reddening sky. When I got back to the hotel, I fell asleep, convinced that I had sunstroke. I woke up at nine o'clock that evening, still exhausted, and looked out of the window. The swallows were massing in their hundreds on the telegraph wires overhead and the balconies of the block opposite. As I fell back to sleep, I could hear them outside my window, chattering and tapping at the air-conditioning unit. I couldn't help but imagine that they were carrying the hundreds of fevered stories the dead would never get to tell.

Mention the word 'disappearance' in Latin America and most people think of Chile under General Pinochet, where 3,000 people were killed or disappeared after the military coup of 1973. Others remember Argentina, where 30,000 people were disappeared by the generals in the 'dirty war' that they waged against the left in the late 1970s. In the 1980s the practice was taken up in Central America when civil wars engulfed Guatemala, El Salvador and Nicaragua. In the eyes of the world, Latin America became synonymous with fratricidal mania.

And yet somehow Colombia's dirty war seems to have gone barely noticed, subsumed as it has been by sensational stories of its cocaine traffickers and guerrilla armies. Between the late 1990s and 2005, Colombia's paramilitaries waged a war of terror, though it was barely mentioned in the British press. Perhaps we had simply grown bored of hearing bad news from Colombia.

Perhaps Bogotá's foreign correspondents took their lead from Colombian friends, many of whom were just glad to see somebody do something to counter the rising power of the guerrillas. Or perhaps, post 9/11, we have come to believe that wars fought by pseudo-Marxists and crypto-fascists are just rather passé.

Only now, as the threat of the FARC recedes, are Colombians themselves beginning to discern the grim outline of the paramilitaries' brutality. When I was here in 2005, Colombia's associations of families of the disappeared had spoken of there being 15,000 cases of forced disappearance. At the time, they were accused of exaggerating the numbers. By 2010, it was clear that in fact they had vastly underestimated the scope of the terror. A report from the Colombian Attorney General's Office calculated that over the last twenty-five years, the paramilitaries have been responsible for 173,000 homicides and 34,000 forced disappearances, during which time they also committed 1,600 massacres.[*]

The killings haven't stopped. Though you'd never know it from reading a Colombian newspaper, let alone a British one, every day of the year a community activist or trade unionist goes missing in Colombia.[†] Well, that's not strictly true: three times as many people are disappeared during the week than at weekends. Disappearing people is a job and nobody likes to work weekends.

The following day, I met Teresa Castrillón again. This time, we walked out to Portón de la Vega. She told me that for as long as

[*] 'Fiscalía tiene documentados 173.183 homicidios cometidos por "paras"', *El Espectador*, 13 January 2011; also see *Breaking the Silence: In Search of Colombia's Disappeared* (Latin America Working Group Education Fund and the US Office on Colombia, 2010).
[†] 'Varias ONG piden a la UE condenar las desapariciones forzadas en Colombia', *Semana*, 8 April 2011.

anyone could remember, it had been no more than a cocoa field, set among cattle pastures on the outskirts of the town. Then rumours began circulating, of hundreds of bodies buried under the cocoa trees. In no time, the owner of the field cleared the trees and built a new neighbourhood on what was reputed to be the town's biggest mass grave.

The two-storey houses had concrete stairs that looked as if they'd been cast from a jelly mould. Some kids were playing in a paddling pool on a patch of burnt grass in the middle of the estate. Men dressed only in shorts lounged in the shadows, staring forlornly into space. One of them was quietly singing along to a melancholy *vallenato* song that was playing on the radio.

Teresa introduced me to a friend of hers called María Inés Gómez, a woman with blonde hair and skin that had been deeply tanned by the sun. She had a gossipy, maternal air about her. When Teresa told her that I was in Puerto Berrío to hear more about the NN of the town, María said that she was amazed that I was there at all. Most journalists steered clear of the town. I was a *verraco* – a brave man – she said. It was the last thing I wanted to hear. I looked around me and the men in the shadows returned my gaze sullenly. María invited me into her house to talk and sent her daughters out to buy a bottle of Cola, a pink, apple-flavoured drink.

It was good to be out of the sun. A small poster that read 'Love is the force behind this family' had been tacked onto one of the bare breezeblock walls of the living room. 'My husband disappeared on 26 February 1989,' María told me. 'He'd taken photos of some of the bodies that washed up on the river bank. He was going to take them to the mayor's office. He thought they might be able to use them as evidence.' His killers came for him the night after he had picked up the photos. Fearing that they might come back for her, María packed all that she owned into a couple of suitcases and left Puerto Berrío with her children a few days later.

Her two children rushed back into the house. They were both about ten. One of them poured me a welcome drink while the other gawped open-mouthed at their foreign visitor. María had only returned to Puerto Berrío in 2005, she told me, shortly after President Uribe signed the Justice and Peace laws. Officially at least, paramilitarism was brought to an end, and María was relieved to see the local paramilitary commanders pushed out of the mayor's office. The mayor, however, was nowhere to be found – he went about in a bulletproof jeep, guarded by armed escorts, she said. He had no contact with the people, much less the poor people living in neighbourhoods like Portón de la Vega.

The People's Defender of Puerto Berrío, whose father had been killed by paramilitaries, encouraged people to come forward with the stories they had long been too scared to tell. There was also a lone colonel at the battalion in town, who was at least willing to listen to María's story. But he had no idea who the people in her husband's photographs were, or what had happened to their bodies. María told me that he had seemed relieved to find that there was no case to prosecute.

Under the Justice and Peace laws, fifty people in the town received compensation for the losses they had suffered. Teresa Castrillón was given about £17,000. It was some recompense for the loss of the main breadwinner in the family, but anyone wanting to know where the dead had been buried, or when their killers might stand trial for their crimes, was left in the dark. Requests for more information were ignored or passed to other ministries, government bodies or judicial bodies, which passed them back, on or up, in what seemed a concerted effort to hush up all that had happened over the past twenty-five years.

Since then, Teresa and María had taken part in silent marches through the town, but their wordless reproach was the only protest they were prepared to make. As for the photos that María's husband had taken, she thought it unlikely they would make any difference. The authorities didn't want to know about the bodies that kept washing up in the town and most of the witnesses were too frightened to speak out. 'NGOs and human rights people come through asking questions from time to time,' María said. 'But nothing seems to change.'

The families of the disappeared are deeply stigmatized in Colombia. The bereaved are often threatened or forced to leave by people who regard their relative's death as proof that they had some involvement with the guerrillas, and therefore deserved their fate. This is in marked contrast to attitudes towards the families of those who have been kidnapped by the guerrillas. In a country as polarized as Colombia, it should come as little surprise to learn that the victims' associations too are split between 'them' and 'us', depending on who fell victim to whom.

Critics have long argued that the Justice and Peace laws are a half-hearted attempt to put a stop to paramilitarism. Around 7,000 members of the private armies didn't go through the demobilization process at all, and are still at large. And since 2005, many of those who did demobilize have returned to lives of crime. Most are former AUC commanders, the ones with the contacts in the cocaine business, who are determined to keep control of the territories and smuggling corridors they held before 2005.*

The government, however, has drawn a line under paramilitarism. Ministers admit that there are *bandas criminales*, but insist that they should not be credited with having any political moti-

---

* 'Las Bacrim tendrán unos seis mil hombres, en seis estructuras', interview with Álvaro Villaraga, co-ordinator of the organization DDR (Demobilization, Disarmament and Reintegration), *Semana*, 18 January 2011.

vation. To do otherwise would be to acknowledge that the corruption and collusion that the paramilitaries depended on for their spectacular rise to power are as virulent as ever. This has led to situations as gruesome as they are absurd. In June 2010, a group of thirty uniformed paramilitaries showed up in an isolated village in the northern department of Córdoba, telling the people that they were from the Águilas Negras – the Black Eagles – before shooting a handful of local men and driving away. When the authorities eventually showed up, the villagers were told that the perpetrators couldn't have been from the Águilas Negras, because the group didn't exist.[*]

Only in late 2010 were city dwellers forced to sit up and take notice of the *bandas criminales*, when they killed two young students from the elite Universidad de los Andes in Bogotá. Mateo Matamala and Margarita Gómez had been camping in a fishing village called Boca de Tinajones, in Córdoba. Prior to 2005 the Caribbean departments were notorious for the outright corruption of their politicians and their frequent collusion with paramilitaries. But tourists had never been given cause for alarm – or at least not until the two students pitched their tent on a key cocaine-smuggling route on the night a large consignment of cocaine was being carried to the coast.

News of their deaths quickly reached Bogotá. It seemed to be the first time that Colombia's urban middle class had been hit by violence from the right. Suddenly, everyone was talking about the *bandas criminales*. Forced to admit the scale of the problem, the police acknowledged that in the last two years the police and Army had engaged in more hostilities with the '*bacrim*' than they had with the FARC. The head of the police, General Óscar Naranjo, called them 'the biggest threat to national security'.

Who are these organized crime groups that have displaced

[*] 'La seguridad, en entredicho', *La Verdad Abierta*, 3 May 2011.

the FARC at the top of Colombia's list of public enemies? A fifth of the *bacrim* are dedicated cocaine-trafficking organizations, prominent in the coastal departments, the lower Cauca, the south of Bolívar, Meta, Guaviare and Medellín – all regions important to the traffickers. But half of the *bacrim* gangs are also engaged in illegal mining and expropriating land. They include the Rastrojos (who have 2,500 members), the ERPAC (1,400 members) and the Paisas (800 members).

The third grouping of *bacrim* is more akin to the old AUC. The days when paramilitaries controlled entire departments might be gone, but the new generation is still capable of intimidating voters and funding candidates. They still have military structures, territories that they control, and strong links with local Army and police units, not to mention politicians. They are in the business of driving people off their land, killing community leaders, fighting the guerrillas and controlling communities – all of which give them a distinctly political profile. They include outfits such as the Águilas Negras and the Nueva Generación – the New Generation.* These were the names whispered under cover of the *vallenato* ballads that boomed from the cafés and bars of Puerto Berrío.

Back at my hotel, the woman at reception asked me, not for the first time, why I had come to the town. After all, there were no sights to see. When she'd first asked, I had told her that I was there to visit friends. This time, against my better judgement, I told her that I'd come to find out more about the disappeared of Puerto Berrío. 'Talk to the river,' she said with a strange smile. The river couldn't talk; despite the much-celebrated demobilization of the paramilitaries, neither could anyone else. Once in

---

* According to a report by the NGO Corporación Nuevo Arco Iris, the *bandas criminales* have about 6,000 members, in six main structures, though membership is fluid and constantly changing. '¿Y ahora quién responde por las víctimas de las bandas criminales?', *La Silla Vacía,* 8 February 2011.

my room, I wrote up my notes on my laptop and then tore the originals into tiny pieces.

The following morning was my last in Puerto Berrío. Teresa had suggested I talk to a friend of hers called Mary, so I called her and we arranged to meet outside the Hotel Golondrinas. While I was waiting for her to show up, I watched two men on horseback drive a herd of young heifers through the main street of the town. The pavements were crowded with farmers and their families, who had come into town to buy storage tanks, plastic buckets and bags of fertilizer. A man walked past me hawking bootleg DVDs. I had been told to be watchful of the DVD sellers: they were often *sicarios*, who held the latest Hollywood titles in one hand, only to distract their victim's attention from the pistol in the other hand.

Mary was indigenous, with dark copper skin and long black hair that she wore plaited down her back. She told me that she was seventy, but she had the upright gait of a much younger woman. We walked out of town, along the same country road that had taken Teresa and me to Portón de la Vega the previous day. The sky was overcast, so the walking was easier than it had been the day before, but the air was humid and the dew still wet on the grass come ten o'clock. Overhead were the power cables, running between enormous pylons, that I guessed to be carrying hydroelectricity from the dam at San Rafael across the Magdalena to Bucaramanga.

Long-eared Brahman cows watched us walk the dusty road with the dumb curiosity of cows everywhere. Mary asked me about the price of a pound of meat in England. I thought of the packets of mince I used to buy in Tesco, what seemed a very long time ago. I must have paid about £3.99 for 500 grams – how much of a pound was that?

Two farmers astride quad bikes greeted us and asked where

we were going. They seemed excessively polite, as if protesting their innocence. 'Nowhere, just walking,' Mary told them. They smiled and rode away. A mile or so beyond Portón de la Vega, we came to a creek. Mary picked me a guava fruit from a tree that was hanging over the track. 'It's good for babies. It gets their appetites going. Makes them grow up big and strong.'

We sat on the bank of the creek and Mary told me her story. 'I have seven children, but they killed two of them. Jacinto Alberto was twenty-one. We used to call him *Cuerpopan* – Bread Body – because he was big and chubby. A friend of his told me that a white van had pulled up at the football field. The men in the van had a list of names of local boys and Jacinto's was at the top of it. At first, the boys thought that the men were looking for farm workers. But when they dragged them into the van, they realized that they were paramilitaries.

'They took them to a nearby farm. They said they wanted to recruit them. They made all kinds of promises, but Jacinto didn't want to join them. Then they accused him of being a grass, and put a revolver to his head. They took him outside. They had a grave ready. His friend told me that before he died, Jacinto said, "I want to talk to my mum." They kicked him into the hole and then a man they called El Cabo shot him.

'By chance, I saw El Cabo five days later, as I was walking back into town. He was with some of his men. He knew my name. I didn't know how or why. "Why's this old woman still moaning on about her son?" he said. "Do me a favour – make sure I never see you again. And don't ask me about your son. I don't know where he is."'

Jacinto's friend chose to join the paramilitaries, but was killed before Mary found out where her son had been buried. 'I always hope that my son will come back. But I know that he can't, that he's buried out there somewhere. But where? I pray to God that he'll tell me where he is. I even have dreams where I'm asking the same question. Not so long ago, I saw a man on a street corner and thought it was Jacinto. I rushed up to him, but of course it wasn't him.

'One day, I was at the cemetery with my friend Emilse. Bodies were being brought in in bags. Nobody knew who they were. "Why don't we adopt two of these NNs?" Emilse asked me. "One for you and one for me?" I felt very strange. I don't really believe in those things, but I went along with it and we did the nine-day wake for two of the NNs. Emilse bought herself a lottery ticket and a few days later she won a million pesos. To keep our side of the deal, we went back to the cemetery to bury her NN. When the gravedigger uncovered the body, we saw that it was a young woman. She had been cut up with knives and her forehead had been crushed.'

A mule was braying in a field that ran alongside the river; a terrible, hopeless cry that I had often heard, but could never get used to. It was time to go. We crossed the metal bridge over the creek and watched two fishermen cast their nets into the still water. '*Cómo son las historias de aqui: bonitas o feas?* – What are the stories like around here: nice or nasty?' Mary asked.

'Both,' said one of the men, as he pulled his empty net from the river.

9. From Valledupar to the Cape

After Puerto Berrío, I decided to put away my Dictaphone and laptop. I had heard enough – or at least, enough to know why so many Colombians felt so let down, not just by the government and the law courts, but by the guerrillas who had proposed to take their place. I needed some time to digest the heavy meal that had been put before me, as well as to see the country, which was after all my original reason for coming back.

So I took a flight to Leticia, the Amazonian town where Colombia meets Peru and Brazil, then another to Popayán in the southern Andes, from where I bussed my way to the pre-Columbian burial sites at Tierradentro and the Desierto de la Tatacoa. I took a boat up the River Atrato, from the steamy border with Panama to Quibdó, the capital of the department of Chocó. From there, I went to Manizales, sixty miles away as the crow flies, though by bus and with the western Andes to climb, the journey took over twelve hours. I went to Pereira, Palenque and Pamplona, by bus, taxi, plane and boat, through rainforests, cloud forests and highland *páramo*. I never did make it to Playboy (or Balmoral or Berlín), but I got my fill of Colombia's bounty and met with nothing more threatening than idle curiosity.

Then, on the first day of December, I had an email from Lucho. I hadn't seen him since the morning we'd walked down Calle 19 in Bogotá, when the newspapers had been celebrating the death of Mono Jojoy. He was planning to fly to Valledupar the following day to hear testimonies from a group of local people who were commemorating the paramilitary massacres that had taken place on the coast. By chance, I was a bus ride away from Valledupar, so I emailed him back, and he suggested that I join him and his friends for a drink at the Café de la Plaza.

The following evening was a hot and close one. People were sitting outside their houses, chatting with friends under the low trees. Valledupar had seemed very orderly, at least as seen from the bus. There were none of the low shacks teetering on the edge of a fetid swamp that are the usual sign that you're about to enter one of Colombia's coastal cities. This was a prosperous place, built on cattle raising, though I guessed that the *bonanza marimbera* had played its part too. That was what *costeños* called the marijuana boom of the 1970s, when a generation of North Americans had latched on to smoking Santa Marta Gold.

Valledupar's main plaza was named after Alfonso López Michelsen, the state governor who had gone on to become president in 1974. It was dominated by an outsize sculpture in concrete and bronze, a pile-up of what looked like three conjoined lipsticks, thrusting skyward at a cock-like angle and carrying an over-muscled male torso and a second female figure, whose contours were lost in what I supposed to be buffets of silk. The sculpture was dedicated to La Revolución en Marcha, a grandiose, top-down development programme launched by Michelsen's father, Alfonso López Pumarejo, when he was president in the 1940s.

I found Lucho sitting at a table outside the café, where a thickset, dark-skinned man with a short neck poking out of a Hawaiian shirt was holding forth on the corruption of the governor's office. The transport budget allocated by Bogotá had gone missing. It had been pilfered, he said, by the 'cartel' that was running the neighbouring town of Manaure. The six other local men at the table nodded in agreement with their friend's assessment.

The man sitting next to me introduced himself as Rodolfo. He had been born in Valledupar but lived in Bogotá, where he was a university professor and leading member of the Green Party (so named not for their environmentalist credentials, but for being the latest attempt to build a legal alternative to the old blue and red colours of the Conservative and Liberal parties).

When Rodolfo went to the bar to order more drinks, Lucho told me in a whisper that he had been a childhood friend of Simón Trinidad, perhaps Colombia's best-known 'traitor to his class'. Trinidad had been born into one of the noble first families of Valledupar and studied at Harvard University for a time before becoming manager of the city's branch of the Banco Popular. One day in 1987, under cover of a strike that filled Valledupar's plaza with angry peasant farmers, Trinidad went to work and stole £10,000 from the vaults of his bank. He then made his escape to the mountains, where he joined the FARC. He took with him the account details of several of his former banking associates and family acquaintances, which, in the years that followed, the FARC used to extort large sums of money from some of Valledupar's most powerful businessmen and landowners.

By 2004, when he was arrested in Ecuador and speedily deported to Colombia to face charges of extortion and kidnapping, Simón Trinidad had become the FARC's 'foreign secretary' and a leading member of its Secretariat. At the end of that year he was extradited to the United States to stand trial for the kidnapping of three American military contractors, and is currently serving a sixty-year sentence at the 'Supermax' prison in Florence, Colorado.

In 2008, the man known as Jorge 40, the most powerful paramilitary chieftain on the coast, and by chance a childhood friend of Simón Trinidad, was also extradited to the United States, in his case on charges of cocaine smuggling. Jorge 40 had been implicated in more than 500 murders on the Caribbean coast, including twenty-one in the town of Aracataca, the town Gabriel García Márquez has acknowledged as being the inspiration for Macondo, the imaginary settlement immortalized in *One Hundred Years of Solitude*. Once classmates, Simón Trinidad and Jorge 40 had both taken up arms, one to fight for revolution, the other to organize what he called 'the resistance'. Now they stood indicted by the same foreign justice.*

I would have liked to ask Rodolfo what Simón Trinidad had been like as a child, but he was midway through giving the table his thoughts on a speech that Juan Manuel Santos had just given to Congress. The president had been outlining his Victims Law. Whether they were victims of the guerrillas, the paramilitaries or the Army, plaintiffs in any case since 1985 would now be entitled to compensation for what they had lost. If the Victims Law made it through Congress, the number of claims would in all likelihood run into the millions. It marked a huge step forward from the line taken by former president Uribe, who had always denied that there were any victims of state violence in Colombia.

President Santos was also pushing for approval of a Land Law, which would put the onus on landowners to prove that they had legal title to their land. If passed, this too would have momentous consequences. In the late 1990s, paramilitaries had stolen land on a vast scale. In some cases, they simply helped themselves to the fields, houses and livestock left behind when their owners fled the fighting between the Army, guerrillas and paramilitaries. In other cases, they made the owner an offer he couldn't refuse. Many *campesinos* had left for the city after accepting a paltry sum for their life's labour. Once the paramilitaries had drawn up fake ownership papers, they would then sell the land, often to cocaine traffickers.

* I recommend Spanish-speaking readers interested to know more about the story of Simón Trinidad and Jorge 40 to read *Líbranos del Bien*, a fictionalized account written by Alonso Sánchez Baute and published by Alfaguara in 2008.

There has been a lot of speculation about just how much land the displaced have left behind over the past thirty years. Lower estimates are of 2 million hectares; upper estimates are closer to 5 million. According to the most recent, and most credible, calculations, 6.6 million hectares – 25,482 square miles – is nearer the mark. That's an area the size of Ireland.* Such was the scale of the land grab, it has been said that half of Colombia's productive land has been acquired illegally. Not that it is very productive any more: more than half of those displaced from their land believe that their fields have simply been left to grow weeds. This in turn suggests that the land was bought not for farming, but as a quick and easy way of laundering the cocaine traffickers' ill-gotten US dollars for Colombian pesos.

'Get that,' Rodolfo said with a stab of a stubby finger, 'America's staunchest ally in the war on drugs has done nothing to stop drug traffickers buying up half the country! Well, if the president is finally making noises about returning that land to its rightful owners, all to the good. But I'll believe it when I see it!'

Returning fallow land to its rightful owners should be relatively straightforward. But in the many cases in which the land is being farmed, the process is going to be more difficult. If the Land Law is to reverse the rural counter-revolution that the AUC oversaw, and achieve justice for the millions of smallholding farmers who have been forced off their lands, Santos will have to take on the cocaine traffickers, as well as the stubborn remnants of the paramilitaries.

Unlike his predecessor Álvaro Uribe, Juan Manuel Santos isn't a landowner. Prior to becoming a politician, he worked as a journalist and then as a businessman. He is from one of the

---

* According to a survey conducted by the Comisión de Seguimiento a la Política Pública sobre Desplazamiento Forzado and reported in '*El Botín de las Tierras*', *Semana*, 11 December 2010. Ireland covers an area of approximately 27,000 square miles.

most illustrious families of the *bogotano* elite. I had seen photos
of a young Juan Manuel with a beard, posing by his Alfa Romeo
in the mid-1970s, before he set off on a road trip around Europe.
He didn't put the wind up me like Uribe once did; by default, I
liked him. So did millions of Colombians – in the presidential
election of 2010, he won more votes than any candidate in the
country's history. Santos has admitted that Colombia is 'a very
unequal country', adding, 'if we don't correct that we will never
really have a solid democracy.'* He says that he wants to make
his government transparent, effective and responsible, and has
vowed to root out corruption, create a million and a half jobs
and build a quarter of a million new homes – what isn't to like
about Juan Manuel Santos?

So why was he challenging the *narcos*? I asked. Contrary to
received opinion, they aren't exactly pariahs in Colombia: a
third of those with seats in the last Congress were thought to
have struck deals with cocaine traffickers, paramilitaries or both.
'It's a populist move,' said the man in the Hawaiian shirt. 'He's
just trying to curry favour with the voters.'

Lucho wasn't so sure. 'Santos knows that agriculture has to be
modernized,' he chipped in. 'Most of the *narcos* are only interested in raising cattle – the rightful owners would put it to better
use.' It was a neat answer, but a little too neat for my liking.
While cocaine traffickers have left much of their land fallow,
they have also invested in huge plantations of West African oil
palms for biofuels, as well as many other crops that are exactly
what the globalized food business is looking for. Far from holding back the progress of Colombian farming, some of the *narcos*
are at the forefront of modernization.

In fact, it is the poor *campesinos* who are most at odds with

---

* 'Juan Manuel Santos: "It is time to think again about the war on drugs"',
Guardian, 12 November 2011.

Santos, the technocrats at the Ministry of Agriculture and their World Bank advisors. Remembering the conversation I had with Humberto Martínez in Jordán, it struck me that even if the peasants did get their land back, they were going to have to grapple with the familiar problems of rural poverty. They needed access to markets and easy credit. The studies to determine what was and what wasn't a viable crop had yet to be written.

Be that as it may, in the last months of 2010, bureaucrats from Incoder* – the Colombian Institute for Rural Development – set about distributing token amounts of land. Although most of it had long been left fallow, official ceremonies in departments like Putumayo, Meta and Chocó showed that there was real political will behind the president's campaign.

But attempts to kick-start land reform in the villages around Valledupar weren't going well. Prior to his arrest and eventual extradition, the paramilitary chieftain Jorge 40 had forced out hundreds of *campesinos*. What he didn't keep for himself, he parcelled out to his friends in the mayor's office, killing seventeen people in the process. 'Incoder was due to hand over one hundred and seventy-two properties in December,' said Rodolfo, 'but the head of the local branch had to resign after they found out that even he had had a hand in the paramilitaries' land grab. Plenty of local lawyers, mayors and police officers were in on it too. They've been making fraudulent deals in land around here for the past twenty years. Lots of the landowners around Valledupar are *testaferros* – fronts for cocaine traffickers. The local authorities have got used to negotiating with corrupt businesspeople and corporations.'

Rodolfo was not optimistic for President Santos' Land Law. 'Look what happened up in Apartadó,' he went on. In the closing months of 2010, attempts to return land to its rightful owners in the banana-growing lowlands near the border with Panama

---

* Instituto Colombiano para el Desarrollo Rural.

had also failed. Local farmers had stood in line for hours, clutch-ing weathered photocopies of the deeds to their properties, patiently waiting for the officials from Incoder to show up. If their title were acknowledged, the years of humiliation would be over. The landless and the displaced would become true citi-zens, with rights recognized and respected by the state. 'They showed up on the Friday and before Monday morning, the president of their co-operative was dead,' said Rodolfo. Every-one assumed that he had been killed by *sicarios* from one of the *bandas criminales* still active on the coast. 'It was a brutal way of saying "over our dead bodies . . . and if we have any say in it, yours".'*

President Santos' attempt to address the longstanding griev-ances of those forced to flee their lands is a laudable one. But even if every displaced farmer gets his land back, the govern-ment faces a steep uphill struggle if it wants to secure peace in the Colombian countryside. Ever since independence, its land-owning families have ruled huge haciendas, particularly in the coastal departments and the eastern plains. These *antioqueño* and *costeño* families enjoy the kinds of privileges last enjoyed by the feudal lords of medieval Europe. As Alfonso Cano, the late leader of the FARC, once pointed out, only one in every two hundred farms in Colombia covers more than 500 hectares, but those estates cover over 60 per cent of the country's farmland.† In Cauca, the southern department whose fertile soils are ideal for growing sugar cane, pineapples and all manner of tropical crops, one can travel for hours without leaving the property of one man. Huge swathes of land are given over to raising cattle, which generates few jobs and little food. Much of this land is

---

* 'Historia de una cruzada', *Semana*, 15 January 2011.
† He was citing a report prepared by the Agustín Codazzi Geographical Insti-tute in 2001; see 'Mensaje de Alfonso Caño', January 2011, at http://horadecambios2006.blogspot.com

under-used because while owning land is a sign of wealth, keeping it unused is a sign of great wealth.

Colombia's biggest landowners have jealously guarded the status quo for generations. Direct taxes on property, land or income, which would have a disproportionate impact on the rich, contribute a much smaller proportion of the government's income than they do in richer countries.[*] That is because the landed rich have long had more political clout than other interest groups. That clout only grew bigger when they joined forces with Colombia's paramilitaries and drug traffickers. In defending their interests, they've colluded in some of the worst atrocities and become still more reactionary, belligerent and uncompromising. Mindful of atrocities to come, President Santos has made it clear that his Victims Law will accept compensation claims until 2021.[†]

The next morning I was woken by the sound of a man singing at the top of his lungs, in a hoarse voice that veered from lament to reproach. Then I heard what I took to be an exotic bird; in fact it was the sound of his cackle. He seemed to fall asleep after that. Moments later, the students of the music school around the corner from the Hostal Provincia struck up the national anthem on their drums, trumpets and triangles.

On the list of things to see and do around Valledupar, the owner of the hostel had mentioned the spot where Jorge 40 and 2,000 of his men had demobilized in 2005. Only a few years before, the people of Valledupar would have been too scared to mention his name. Now, with the local *patrón* behind bars in

---

[*] 'Desigualdad extrema', *Semana*, 12 March 2011.
[†] 'Armed Conflict in Colombia: A Concession to Reality', *The Economist*, 26 May 2011.

Miami, they were encouraging the tourists to come and have a look for themselves.

I'd arrived in the low season. The Hostal Provincia was only a couple of years old and was still having teething troubles. A carpenter was taking a plane to the edge of the bathroom door, which had been sticking in its jamb. The landlord and a couple of high-school apprentices looked on expectantly. This was the city's first foray into hostel tourism and the owner was hopeful that it would attract young backpackers, both Colombian and foreign, to his city. Valledupar, he told me, was the obvious jumping-off point for a trip into the Sierra Nevada de Santa Marta, the highest coastal mountain range in the world. Pico Cristóbal Colón is 5,775 metres high, but only 25 miles from the idyllic beaches of the Caribbean.

Over dinner at 'Nandoburgers', I found myself sitting opposite a cattle-ranching family, who were all wearing cowboy hats. The head of the family looked as prosperous and paunchy as a bull, as he sullenly chewed a steak that looked like boot leather. I ordered the meatballs. 'They've had the last of them,' the waitress told me, pointing with her lips at the family slurping their way through plate-loads of cassava, plantain, rice and beans. I ordered the chicken – again. The colour of green vegetables glowed in my memory like emeralds, so long had it been since I last ate one.

After dinner, I took a stroll around the town. One house I passed seemed to be getting ready for a party. Twelve or so plastic chairs had been set up around the little front garden, all facing a sound system that must have scared the birds out of the trees hours ago. But apart from two teenage girls, the seats were empty, and since the *vallenato* was too loud to make conversation, they just stared into space. Everywhere I'd been in Colombia, I'd heard the sounds of *vallenato*. A couple of tunes had stuck in my head, but for the most part, I found its shrivelled vocabulary of boy-meets-girl, set to an umpah-lumpah rhythm, to be uninspiring stuff. I was looking forward to getting back to Bogotá, where salsa was king and *vallenato* was the country cousin.

So when I returned to the hostel to find the courtyard crowded with musicians tuning their accordions and guitars, getting ready for a *vallenato* session, I gave an inward groan. But the music they played that evening was worlds apart from what I'd heard on the radio. They sang about local people that everyone seemed to know and their songs were accompanied by loud laughter and cheering.

During a break in play, they invited me to sit in and a fresh bottle of rum was cracked open. The accordionist told me that they were in town for the same commemoration of the paramilitary massacres of the nineties that Lucho had attended earlier that day. I asked him why the *vallenato* he was playing sounded so much better than the generic fare I'd heard booming from bars, buses and isolated Army checkpoints up and down the country.

'The *vallenato* that they play on the radio is popular, but it's no longer *folk* music,' the accordionist said. 'Folk songs can be inspired by anything, you know? The birds singing in the trees, how the river has risen, a friend who's had a mishap . . . The good, the bad – everything.' *Vallenato* had been the dominant sound in the coastal departments for generations, he told me, but it was only in the last ten years that it had become popular outside the region. Now there was only one kind of *vallenato*. The sounds of *merengue*, *puya*, *paseo* and *son* were gone, as were the stories they illustrated. 'These days, all they sing about is love. It's a shame, but it's the record label that decides what is recorded and all they want to know is whether the song will sell or not,' the accordionist said, as he helped himself to more rum.

Tomás, a wiry and quick-witted man of fifty, had been listening to our conversation and chimed in. 'The music they make now sounds like *ranchera*,' he said, dismissing the Mexicans' cowboy music with a wave of the hand. '*Vallenato* is no longer a music that identifies the people who make it.' Like many Colombians, Tomás was a keen and gifted raconteur. Real *vallenato* had evolved over hundreds of years, he assured me. The music-makers of the Caribbean coast had composed *merengue-vallenatos* to pay tribute to Simón Bolívar during the war of independence. Eighty years later, Felipe Yepes had written *vallenato* songs for his fellow soldiers during the War of a Thousand Days, before dying on the battlefield in 1901. But to understand the roots of *vallenato*, Tomás told me, I had to know something about the history of Valledupar.

Not for the first time, I found that a question about the present quickly led me to an answer from the distant past. Tomás topped up our plastic cups, took a thespian pause for breath and began to tell me the story of his hometown. 'Valledupar lies between the Sierra Nevada to the north and the tail end of the Andes further south. To the west is the River Magdalena; to the east, the desert of the Guajira . . .'

The city was originally called *la valle de Upar*, Upar being the chief of the Chimilas, the people indigenous to this part of Colombia. In 1531 the German Ambrosius Dalfinger became the first European to reach Upar's valley. One of the members of his expedition kept a journal, in which he described the natives' farms and fields, as well as their trade route inland, where they traded their sea salt for gold. This pass opened to the south and was an obvious avenue for Dalfinger's quest to reach the South Sea. The natives were 'a very numerous and spirited people', the journal keeper wrote, and 'from what we saw and learned . . . a truthful people'. Moving up the pass, Dalfinger's men met another peaceful people, the Pacabueyes, who invited them to stay in one of their villages, which had over 1,000 huts. Dalfinger's journal keeper wrote that 'all the Indians of this town of

Tomara work gold. On some days, we obtained, by gifts or by trading, over 20,000 *castellanos* (91 kilos) of gold.'

However, the free-trading idyll described by Dalfinger's man is flatly contradicted by the account of a Captain Salguero, who wrote that 'Dalfinger came through the Upar valley, destroying and ravaging with bloodthirsty fury, and even burning chiefs . . . After ranging across the lands of Upar and collecting a small mountain of gold, he moved on to the savannahs of Guatapurí and Garupare, putting many Indians to the sword. He annihilated the Pacabueyes.'*

2010 saw the 200th anniversary of Colombian independence, one that prompted many to stoke the old debate over the motives of the priests and soldiers of Imperial Spain. The contradiction inherent in missions led by men who held a Bible in one hand and a sword of Toledan steel in the other was no less apparent to the conquistadores than it is to their descendants. In 1536 Gonzalo Jiménez de Quesada, the man who would found Bogotá six months later, also passed through the Valle de Upar on his way south from Santa Marta. The governor of Santa Marta had told him to 'take every care to make the peoples by which you pass peaceful, giving good treatment to the Indians. As soon as you are at peace you will ask them for gold.' But if the tribe refused to part with its treasure, Jiménez was to read them 'the Requirement' – and if that failed, 'wage a war of fire and blood on them'.

The Chimilas soon learned to be wary of these strange new arrivals. Near the Valle de Upar, Jiménez' men were attacked by Chimilas carrying the only native weapon that the Europeans had cause to fear: poison arrows. One of those on the receiving end of that attack wrote that if the arrow drew blood 'it causes

---

* I have embellished Tomás' account with material from John Hemming, *The Search for El Dorado* (Michael Joseph, 1978), pp. 32–5.

trembling and convulsions of the body, and loss of reason that makes men say bold, terrible things of dubious faith for dying men.' Some soldiers tried to protect themselves from the Chimilas' arrows by covering their bodies and their horses in quilted cotton padding. 'A man seated on a horse, protected by such armour, looks like the most deformed and monstrous thing you could imagine,' a Spaniard wrote. 'It turns a trooper into a tower, a misshapen object that fills Indians with great terror.'[*]

The Chimilas were eventually defeated, and the Spanish went on to found some of their first American settlements in the Valle de Upar. The early resistance and eventual capitulation of the Chimilas became part of their tribal lore, which they would sing to the sound of two sticks being hit together, as a way of teaching the tribe's history to people who couldn't read or write. It was only after the arrival of enslaved Africans that the Chimilas learnt to compose music for two flutes, drums and the *guacharaca*, the friction instrument that looks like a cheese grater, which is still a key part of the *vallenato* sound. They also took to playing a 'female' flute, which was in time supplanted by the accordion, and a 'male' flute, which supplied the bass line. The Spanish settlers contributed their tradition of organizing verses into quartets and choruses. Over the years, the hybrid genre became something like a travelling newspaper, carrying news from village to village along the Caribbean coast. Therein, said Tomás with a flourish, lie the true origins of *vallenato* music.

The accordion, the instrument synonymous with *vallenato*, only arrived later. Some say that it was a copy of the *sheng*, a kind of panpipe brought to Panama from Hong Kong by a Chinese sailor at the end of the nineteenth century. But when I put this idea to Tomás, he scowled and shook his head vigorously.

[*] Ibid., p. 70.

'The first accordion was brought to Valledupar by a German called Kildemian in 1929.'

That year the businessmen of Bogotá and Medellín were celebrating a boom in world prices for coffee and bananas, building textile factories and railways on the proceeds and enjoying an era of prosperity that they called 'the Dance of the Millions'. Colombia's cities were being swept into the modern era, but as ever, these outward signs of progress were only apparent to a lucky few. The countryside, home to isolated communities that hadn't changed in centuries, still abounded with all kinds of legendary monsters and fabulous creatures, strange hybrids of indigenous, Spanish and African beliefs.

'People were very credulous back then,' said Tomás. 'The best drummers used to carry the head of a woodpecker in their pockets as a charm to help them play better. Some of them would make their drums from the hide of a black dog because they thought it had magical powers.'

Such was the world that the most famous of all *vallenato* accordionists, Francisco Moscote, later known as Francisco el Hombre, was born into. It was a name I had heard before, since he makes several appearances in *One Hundred Years of Solitude*. 'They say that one dark night, Francisco el Hombre was riding his donkey home, playing his accordion, when, from under a big tree at the side of the road, he heard the sound of another accordion. As Francisco got closer, he saw that it was the Devil himself, playing like a virtuoso. The Devil challenged Francisco to a duel and they set to playing. After a while, the Devil looked like winning. Afraid of what the Devil might do to him if he won, Francisco had no choice but to get down on his knees and pray. Hearing the Lord's Prayer, the Devil fled back down to Hell.

Anyone from the developed world unconsciously guards the boundary between fact and fiction, myth and reality. But Tomás, an educated and erudite *costeño*, was more circumspect. 'My father knew Francisco el Hombre,' he said. 'He met him in Atanques in about 1925. People were still telling the story of his duel with the Devil even after he died in 1945, by which time he was over one hundred years of age.'

Robert Johnson, the Mississippi guitarist credited with pioneering the blues, is also said to have duelled with the Devil. But when Johnson realized that he was being outplayed, he didn't recite the Lord's Prayer. He sold his soul in exchange for the Devil's talent. Blues was the music of lost souls: the Devil's music. But *vallenato*'s best-known practitioners never claimed to have sold out to the Devil. They admitted defeat, kept their souls intact and contented themselves with their less than diabolical talents.

Given the choice between the Devil's music and that of the good Christians of Valledupar, I preferred the blues. It might have been wretched, but it was also raw, whereas *vallenato* – or at least its modern incarnation – had always struck me as being worryingly wholesome, like the music played on American radio stations before people cottoned on to the dirty rhythms of rock 'n' roll. It was upstanding, defiantly old-fashioned, and reassuringly Colombian.

But just when I was ready to write off Francisco el Hombre as a chicken-hearted goody-two-shoes, I stumbled on a second, less upstanding version of his story. By this account, Francisco wasn't just a master of the accordion, but also its discoverer, having found a squeezebox in the treasure chest of a ship that had sunk off the Caribbean coast. This accordion gave him the power to bring the dead back to life. Every man wanted to drink with him and every woman was driven mad with longing by his songs. When Francisco moved on to the next village, those left behind would swear that they had seen him at the crossroads at midnight, exchanging his soul with the Devil.

My favourite version of the story however was an amalgam of the good and bad Franciscos, according to which no deal was ever struck. The Devil had indeed tried to drag Francisco to Hell, but he had saved himself by offering Old Nick a swig from the bottle of rum he was carrying. The Devil knocked off the bottle in one go, and staggered back to Hell, drunk and alone, never to return.

Aside from the remnants of magic and myth, something else that had struck me about *vallenato* was the absence of female voices. It wasn't just that women were barred from taking to the microphone. Having commandeered the stage, the man on vocals seemed to spend much of his time singing about the treachery of women and the stoic resignation of the men they left behind. *Vallenato* delighted in the expression of male heart-break. When I first heard them, *vallenato* lyrics had seemed the epitome of noble selflessness, but in time, they came to seem a front for self-pity, and even faintly menacing.

'*Vallenato* is pretty masculine,' Tomás said with a sagacious nod of the head. 'Men have always dominated Latino culture. Traditionally, women were for bearing and raising children, and they were expected to be submissive. But there have been some good female accordionists. Rita Fernández played the accordion well. And of course, at the turn of the twentieth century Armina Vásquez was up there with the best of them.'

Tomás caught himself and smiled. We had finished the rum and he was getting lost in lore. It was time for bed. I'll say one thing for *vallenato*, though. While it was often sad and always sentimental, it had no room for existential angst. The *juglares del vallenato* didn't allow their despair to stray from the province of love. Colombia's music, like its people, was never hopeless, which was a sentiment that had quickly come to seem a western luxury.

Recalling the exploits of the conquistadores, as well as those who resisted them, it seems fair to say that resilience has always been a Colombian trait. For sheer endurance, miles walked, and tribes, hills and rivers discovered, the feats of those early pioneers far exceed the more famous travels of the nineteenth-century explorers of Africa. The men who chose to join the first transatlantic ventures were not mercenaries and received no pay from the expedition's leaders. Nor did they have the wives, families and religious convictions that sustained the English Pilgrims who boarded the *Mayflower* in 1620, bound for the Thirteen Colonies of North America. Most of those who headed for South America were simply adventurers, who took passage in the hope of making their fortunes.

Gonzalo Fernández de Oviedo, who settled on Santo Domingo, the Caribbean island that is today divided between Haiti and the Dominican Republic, watched many of the early adventurers set sail for the Spanish Main. 'They are the sort of men who have no intention of converting the Indians to Christianity or of settling and remaining in this land. They come only until they have some gold or wealth in whatever form they can obtain it. They subordinate honour, morality and honesty to this end, and apply themselves to any fraud or homicide and commit innumerable crimes.' Oviedo also noted that although most of their leaders were Spanish, 'no language from any part of the Christian world is lacking here. They come from Italy, Germany, Scotland and England, and include Frenchmen, Hungarians, Poles, Greeks and Portuguese.'

The first Europeans to explore the New World were driven by desperation as much as by greed. In 1492, when Christopher Columbus 'discovered' America, parts of Spain were among the most densely populated in Europe. Castile alone had a population of 7 million. Seville, with 150,000 people, was one of the biggest cities in the world. So there was considerable demographic pressure for colonial expansion, which was only heightened by the extreme aridity of much of Spain and the country's appalling social inequality. The aristocracy, nobility and knightly classes made up just 2 per cent of the population, but they and the Church owned 98 per cent of the land. It was said that the Marquis of Villena enjoyed annual rents of 100,000 ducats, while the average day labourer got by on just 17 ducats a year. To anyone accustomed to such hardship and with so little to lose, the Americas must have been a potent lure.

The Crown contributed nothing to the costs of these trips. Everything had to be raised or borrowed, and loans for trips to the Americas were expensive. To make matters worse, the King decreed that adventurers could only voyage west under the command of a governor, who had to apply for a licence to conquer and settle the lands of the New World. In return for this licence, the Crown demanded that a fifth of any riches brought back to Spain be delivered to the royal coffers. Many licence holders were impoverished noblemen, desperate to keep up appearances even if they owned little more than their cape and sword. To be a gambler, visionary or tyrant was probably a bonus.

Arrogance and cruelty weren't confined to the nobility. The anti-colonial campaigner Bartolomé de las Casas complained that even men born into servility shunned any manual labour as soon as they set foot in the Americas and expected to be 'elevated with a staff in their hands, to be persecutors of the tame and humble Indians, and to command!'*

Whatever the humble origins of the men who ventured into the New World, they suffered no lack of ambition. Spaniards of their generation had already made discoveries beyond the dreams of their fathers. They had encountered and then defeated the Incas, Aztecs and Mayas. Nothing in history rivalled the sheer tonnage of silver, gold and jewels looted from those civilizations.

To desperation, arrogance and greed was added credulity.

---

* Ibid., pp. 35–9.

Most of the conquistadores were ignorant, uneducated men. Intoxicated by dreams of wealth, they nourished themselves on rumours, which flourished until, 'by repetition and wishful thinking, they gained the stature of truth'. When Walter Raleigh, who did more than anyone to popularize the myth of El Dorado, described his encounter with the Ewaipanoma, a tribe in Guiana 'whose heads appeare not above their shoulders', who would have doubted him? In a continent of armadillos, sloths, tapirs, manatees, peccaries and llamas, who was to say that the fantastic creatures of medieval and classical legend would not also be found in South America? Perhaps the Ewaipanoma really did 'have their eyes in their shoulders and their mouthes in the middle of their breasts'.*

Before flying back to Bogotá, I wanted to visit Cabo de la Vela, a fishing village at the tip of La Guajira, the desert peninsula that juts out into the Caribbean. La Guajira is the northernmost point of the Latin American continent and its desert sunsets are said to be among the most beautiful sights in Colombia. Cabo de la Vela was also the first landing point for those who crossed the Atlantic from Europe at the close of the fifteenth century. A trip to where it all began seemed a fitting way to bring my travels around the Colombian countryside to an end.

On Sunday morning I got up at five, ready to catch a north-bound bus at six. The bus turned out to be a shared car; with my arrival it was full, so off we went, skirting the eastern foothills of the Sierra Nevada, heading north towards the desert. Since none of the passengers seemed in the mood to chat and the driver seemed allergic to silence, he played the same *vallenato* CD endlessly. We drove about sixty miles per loop, along empty roads that led through rich cattle pastures dotted with oak trees.

* Ibid., p. 173.

After a couple of hours, we came to El Cerrejón – South America's biggest coalmine. From the entrance to the mine, the road ran parallel with the railway tracks that carried the coal to the wharf at the tip of La Guajira. Being Sunday, there wasn't much traffic on the rails. A single convoy of black wagons rumbled past us on its way north, each filled to a uniform line with coal. Thanks to the mine, Colombia is the fifth biggest coal exporter in the world, and many of Britain's power stations run on fuel hewn from El Cerrejón.

It was close to midday by the time the driver dropped me off at Cuatro Vías. There was nothing there bar what the name suggested: a crossroads, where the road between Riochacha and Maicao crossed the one running north from Valledupar into the desert. I waited in the shade of a thorn tree for the next car to fill up. Someone had left a goat, minus its innards, at the side of the road, like the forgotten victim of a '*chupacabra*'. The goat-sucker has become a modern-day legend in the Caribbean: from Mexico to Puerto Rico, farmers speak of finding their goats and sheep sucked dry of flesh, blood and bone, yet with their skins unbroken. Some say that the culprit is a man with the head of a coyote; others, that the *chupacabra* comes from outer space.

It was very hot, so I wandered over to a battered roadside kiosk for a drink. The woman inside was talking to a friend about the *langosta*. One night, while waiting for a bus to Maicao in the summer of 1999, I had watched a man do battle with one of these flying lobsters with a baseball bat. I say lobster, as the locals did, but in fact, this *langosta* was more akin to a giant locust, which some evolutionary quirk had swollen to the size of a seagull. Luckily, it was the wrong time of year for *langosta*.

After half an hour, a pick-up truck pulled into Cuatro Vías. I squeezed onto one of the wooden benches in the back, with twelve Wayúu men and women, plus a couple of little kids who sat on the bags of cement in the middle. Bags of rice and cut chicken were squeezed under the benches; drums of petrol were strapped onto the roof, and off we went. There are 200,000 Wayúu, making them the biggest indigenous tribe in Colombia. It was comforting to hear them speak their own language. It meant that I was under no pressure to understand anything and could drift away with my own thoughts for a while.

I wasn't adrift for long. No sooner had we crossed the coal company's railway tracks than we faced the worst mud bath I had ever seen. The road was at least two feet deep in yellow clay. An articulated lorry, carrying who knew what to who knew where, was stranded in the mire, its length blocking what would have been both carriageways, if the road had had such things. Ahead of us, two more lorries were revving furiously, their back wheels spinning in the mud. Several passenger loads had gathered on the bank to watch this traffic jam in the desert, so we joined them under the blazing sun. A boy passed us with a goat on his back. Its legs were tied together and it bleated with a sound I'd last heard when I was playing *bola* in Villanueva with Carlos: that of a goat that knows what it has coming.

After a while, a bulldozer showed up and we watched a security guard and a man from the coal company argue about whether they were allowed to use it to clear mud. They each spoke to Don Manuel at HQ, and then carried on arguing, the company man issuing more *hijos de puta* ('son of a bitch') as his powerlessness became clear. When he'd run out of curses, he turned on his heel and walked into the desert. The bulldozer issued a slow, deep roar and pulled itself up onto the road, where it began pushing the mud to one side, leaving a dry and relatively smooth road in its train. We clambered aboard our pick-up and set off again.

Fortunately, the mud only lasted for a few hundred yards, after which we followed a dry road that ran parallel to the railway tracks for four bumpy hours. All afternoon we rode in silence. Since the tarpaulin had been pulled down the pick-up's sides to shield us from the rain, the only distraction was the young Wayúu woman sitting nearest the tailgate. With her was a clever-looking girl of five or so, who I took to be her sister. Like all the Wayúu women, the older girl wore a loose-fitting dress that reached to her ankles. She had high cheekbones, a wide Asiatic face and beautiful, open brown eyes. I watched the glistening skin on her jaw as she turned to look at the way we'd come, her slender neck and the outline of her breast where the afternoon light passed through her dress.

I tried not to stare but there was nothing else to do. The other passengers were watching her too: some older women, with deep creases in their faces and long black hair, who looked like Red Indians; two younger men of thirty or so, with the build of hard workers and the same steady gaze as the women; and a jowled old man who looked like a frog. I wondered if it was me – the stranger – that made them watchful of her. Perhaps they were half protecting, half chastising the prettiest one aboard.

When I did steal a peep from under the tarp, the landscape was as it had been for hours. The yellow clay of the desert was covered with a webbing of thorn trees that crouched close to the land as if sheltering from the wind. Come late afternoon, the same coal wagons that I'd seen leaving the mine at El Cerrejón passed us empty on their way back south. In the distance, two huge cranes on the wharf at Puerto Bolívar came into view. Beyond them, the sunlight was glittering on the Caribbean. We crossed the tracks to drop off the girl and her sister at the workers' compound, then spent another half-hour twisting and turning between the thorn bushes, along a makeshift track that followed the gulleys cut by flash floods.

The few Wayúu in the remote north of La Guajira live in huts of knotted-together sticks of *yotojoro*, the inner core of the local cactus, under roofs that let the rain in, unless they can afford corrugated zinc. They get their power from generators that run from sundown until bedtime and their drinking water from butts set under the eaves of their shacks. They had seen little benefit from the coalmine or the row of towering wind turbines that we came to a little further on.* Twin anomalies from the modern world they, like the *chupacabra*, seemed to have come to La Guajira only to suck the blood of the living before jetting back into the depths of space.

At long last the driver let us off at a tiny settlement of three huts and drove back the way he had come. I waited with what was left of the passenger list, as the rain came down in occasional big drops and the sun gradually lost its power. Then we were in another old Land Cruiser with all the electrics wrenched out and windows that wouldn't wind up, on another winding desert road, paved in three portions of about ten yards each, interspersed with stretches of rock and sand that went on for miles.

Cabo de la Vela turned out to be no more than a handful of huts strung along the beach. I made for the nearest lodgings. Doña Flor's was a *yotojoro* hut with two pokey rooms for guests, which gave onto a small concrete patio, where her husband Jorge strung up a hammock for me to use the next day. The patio led right onto the short beach. Though there was no electric light to see by, the moon illuminated the phosphorescent bodies of millions of underwater animals. It had been a long journey, so I made my excuses and went to bed, though only after Jorge had been around my hut with a pump-action insect fumigation pump.

With the first light of the next day, the women of Cabo de la Vela came out to rake the little patch of sand in front of their

* The wind power of the Guajira region has the potential to generate electricity to meet the demand for power in Colombia twice over.

properties. Between carefully raked stretches there was loads of rubbish that no one felt obliged to pick up, but as the mayor's office seemed to be regarded as no more than a source of booty, there was no collective action to tackle the litter. There were signs telling the tourists not to drop litter, but as there were no tourists, the litter must have been dropped by the locals, the signs a tidy way of ducking the blame for it. The women kept their patch clear; the bits in between that belonged to no one went neglected.

Though there was no music to be heard that morning, a little girl was gyrating with a beachside statue of the Virgin Mary to the *reggaeton* rhythm in her head. I walked along the beach towards the lighthouse, following the curve of the bay along a track that led between enclosed *ranchería* homesteads onto the bare headland. There the sand gave way to rusting red rock, whose outer layer had been cracked into countless tiny pebbles by the sun. The lighthouse stood atop a bluff, on the far side of which I sat for a while, looking down at a solitary canoe. I didn't have a watch, but even after walking for two hours, it couldn't have been long past eight in the morning by the time I got back to Doña Flor's hut.

Around eleven o'clock, the sun came out for an instant, but the sky quickly loomed dark over the milky blue-white sea and it began to rain. The sun didn't re-emerge until sunset, when a crack of golden light stole out from under its cloudy blanket, giving me a tantalizing glimpse of what Cabo de la Vela might look like if only it would stop raining.

The guidebook had said that Cabo de la Vela was like a tropical version of the west coast of Ireland, but I seemed to be the only tourist to have believed them. There was next to nobody there and nothing to do. The following morning, I watched a pelican fly by. In the afternoon, I watched two dogs mating on the beach. At five o'clock, the hem of the curtain of cloud that had cast a thrall over the day lifted an inch, and a stream of tropical light gave me a late glimpse of the electric-blue and white Cabo that I had come here to see. By six, it was dark and by nine, I was asleep.

Back at Doña Flor's, we ate red snapper for lunch and we had it again for dinner. Jorge, a black man from Riohacha, told me that he had come up here to marry Flor, who was Wayúu. But conversation didn't come easily to anyone in Cabo de la Vela, and Jorge preferred to eat in silence at the bench where he repaired his fishing nets. Flor, whose girth was so perfectly round that her behind and her belly were effectively one and the same, ate at a chair by the door. When she wasn't cooking, she spent the day looking out onto the empty sand road that ran past her hut. Her feet didn't touch the ground, so she dangled them in the air, gently kicking in time with some unheard rhythm. Such was Cabo de la Vela, where the land and everything else ran out. After two days, I felt as if I knew the contours of life there in their entirety. The only way now was back.

10.   The Emerald Cowboy

Eishi Hayata is an *esmeraldero*, and was until recently one of the most powerful men in the emerald business. He is also the only foreigner to have made it big in Muzo, the humid village in the mountains of Boyacá, sixty-five miles northwest of Bogotá, from whose seams 80 per cent of the world's emeralds are hewn. When I'd tried to track down Eishi Hayata in 2001, I was told that he was in Hollywood, hawking around a script of his life story. Since then I had seen no trace of him – until the day I happened to be in the office of a professor at the Universidad de los Andes and saw a poster for *Emerald Cowboy* on the wall. The professor told me that he was a good friend of Eishi Hayata – I was in.

In the interim before we were due to meet, I went online to see what I could find out about *Emerald Cowboy*. Apparently, the Japanese emerald don had approached Jason Priestley to play the part of himself, but the *Beverly Hills 90210* actor had turned the script down. Eventually, tiring of looking for backing in Los Angeles, Eishi decided to make the film himself. He named himself executive producer, and even took the lead role, at least in the present-day sequences. I was impressed by his verve, but I hadn't seen the end result. The *New York Times* had – and wasn't. Its reviewer wrote, '*Emerald Cowboy* must surely occupy a unique place in film history as the most solipsistic film ever made . . . The movie is crushingly mundane and is unlikely to attract any audience beyond close relatives.' No matter: I was looking for somebody who could tell me more about Colombia's emerald miners, not a film-maker.

Although by now most *bogotanos* were winding down for the Christmas holidays, the emerald traders along the Avenida Jiménez were still huddled under the awnings of the shops around Plaza del Rosario, carefully unwrapping squares of white paper to inspect the tiny stones inside. They held them to the light with tweezers, searching for imperfections and the highly prized dark-green 'garden' at the heart of every stone.

I threaded my way through the crowd of buyers and sellers thronging the pavement outside the Henry Faux building and took the lift, a scrupulously maintained brass-trimmed relic from the 1950s, to the fifth floor. Eishi Hayata's office was behind a reinforced-steel door at the end of a long, echoing corridor. I knocked as loudly as I could and a small eye-level panel in the door slid back. A large, impassive face appeared close to my own. I told its owner my business; he gestured for me to wait and slid the panel shut. A moment later, the door opened and I was ushered into an adjoining room.

I could hear steam hissing from an urn in the kitchen that filled the air with the sweet aroma of eucalyptus tea. Eishi Hayata was sitting at the dining table, which had been cleared of lunch, looking out of the window at the street below. He was wearing a dark-blue suit that had grown shiny with age and wrap-around Armani shades. When he took them off, his eyes struck me as being at once expressionless and slightly child-like. He ran his fingers through his hair, pushing it back over his head. It was still thick and black and looked unwashed.

He told me that it was the day before his seventieth birthday. 'No be a stupid proud, but I think I can say that I am one of the last adventurers in this world,' he said brightly. 'But not now,' he said with a derisive flick of his fingers. 'Now there is no adventure. Maybe only killing – but that's not adventure.' I recognized the quick, impatient gestures: Eishi had been in Colombia for a long time.

In the 1990s, the Japanese press had dubbed Eishi Hayata 'the king of emeralds'. 'That time, I had fifty million dollar export yearly. Commission eight per cent – imagine, eight per cent of fifty million dollar!' But the recession had hit the jewellery business hard, particularly in Japan, the biggest export market for emeralds. Ever since the collapse of Lehman Brothers, Eishi had heard only bad news. 'Now I don't even have $2 million yearly. In the future, maybe finish.' He winced at the thought and stared out of the window gloomily.

The first outsiders to set foot in the New World had found emeralds all over the northwestern corner of South America. The precious green stones excited their cupidity no less than gold, but it wasn't until 1564 that the conquistadores found the source of the emeralds, when the Spanish captain Juan de Penagos literally stumbled upon the hidden treasure of Muzo, after a strange object hobbled his mount. Lifting the horse's hoof, he found a green rock the size of a child's fist embedded in its frog. Crossing the brow of a hill, de Penagos found what until then only a few chosen members of the Somondoco tribe had been permitted to see. On a mile-long spur of the hill, he watched in fascination as native diviners, inspired by a hallucinogenic brew prepared from the ayahuasca plant, tried to locate the richest veins of emeralds. Once found, they prised the stones loose with long sticks before flushing them down the mountainside through a system of water channels, to be graded and cut.

Having located the source of Colombia's emeralds, the Spanish were keen to take control of it. But good Christians couldn't just help themselves to what wasn't theirs, so their priests set about devising some justification for the plunder that was to come. The Jesuit naturalist José de Acosta ventured that it was part of God's design to hide the world's precious stones in its remotest parts, among its most primitive peoples. 'God placed the greatest abundance of mines (in such remote places) so that this would invite men to seek those lands and hold them, and in this way to communicate their religion of the true God to those who did not know it.'

It was an elegant justification for the pillage of the Americas by Spanish adventurers, and de Acosta also came up with a simple metaphor to illustrate God's intentions: 'A father with an ugly daughter gives her a large dowry to marry her; and this is what God did with that difficult land, giving it much wealth in mines so that by this means he would find someone who wanted it.'*

Unfortunately for God and the Spanish, the ugly daughters of Boyacá didn't see it quite like that. They put up fierce resistance to the invaders, so it was another twenty years before the conquistadores got their hands on what were to become the richest emerald mines in the world. Having secured control of Boyacá, the Spanish expelled the Somondoco's diviners and brought in African slaves to work the mines alongside the local indigenous men. Together, they made a handful of impoverished European noblemen very wealthy.

The history of the mines has been no less bloody since the Spanish were driven out of Colombia. In 1848, Congress decreed that the country's emerald deposits be worked under the direction of the nation. But this noble writ from Bogotá was easily bypassed by the men who ran the department of Boyacá. Government ministers, seeing that they had no way of enforcing the laws they had drafted, happily signed contracts with private parties. Despite a glaring lack of qualified geologists and engineers, and chaotic management, the emerald mines at Muzo have been worked almost continuously ever since. In the 1950s the mines

---

* John Hemming, *The Search for El Dorado* (Michael Joseph, 1978), p. 11.

fell under the control of Efraín González, one of the best-known Conservative bandits of the era of *La Violencia*.

But the man whose name has become practically synonymous with emerald mining in Colombia is Victor Carranza. Born into a poor family in Guateque, a village set amidst the sacred lakes of highland Boyacá, Carranza knew little of his father, who deserted the family when he was still a baby. A few years later, his older brother found a large emerald and went to Bogotá to sell it, promising to return with the proceeds and buy a plot of land for the family – that was the last they ever heard of him. Young Victor vowed that he would find an emerald of even greater value, and set to work as a prospector in the mines. Some say he was only seven at the time; others, that he was already ten. None dispute that he achieved his goal, for Victor Carranza went on to become the biggest emerald don of them all.

Eishi Hayata had other motives for going into the emerald mines. 'When I was young, two movie I like only. *Adventure* – American guy went Guatemala, Nicaragua and Chile. Other one is *Arabe Lawrence*. I loved that type life. I wanted to go somewhere. Maybe Latin America. Somewhere like war.'

Eishi had been born in Tokyo, but his family was evacuated to Kyushu, in the far west of Japan, for the duration of the Second World War. He was four years old when the war ended in 1945. 'That was very rough countryside of conservative age in Japan. Hard place. Hard people. Everything hard. I was good family, not strong like country bear. But Kyushu people like to give a shit to Tokyo people and I had to fight to protect my family.'

At high school, Eishi became the leader of his gang. 'I don't like to be beaten by that shit yakuza. But I never hit anybody – somebody attacked and I react. That's defence. Always shit guys run.' After graduating in 1957, Eishi went to the United States in search of adventure. 'I went Arizona, Nevada, Indian reserve area. Just hitch hiking, living like Indian. About one year and a half, I was looking for adventure. But nineteen century is over. No more gold rush. Old western doesn't exist!'

So Eishi went back to Japan, trained to be an aircraft mechanic, and went to work for Northwest Airlines. 'Mechanic engineer chief O'Higgins telling, "Oh, you go Latin America with smuggler."' Cigarette and alcohol smuggling was rife in the Caribbean in the late 1960s, so Eishi decided to try his luck in Costa Rica, where he soon found work maintaining the smugglers' planes. It was while living in Costa Rica that he first heard about Colombia's emerald mines. They seemed to promise the kind of adventure he had been searching for, so in 1973 he moved his young family to Bogotá and started buying rough stones in the mining villages of Boyacá. From there, he would take them back to the capital, where his team of Japanese gem cutters would prepare them for sale.

'The first couple years get back by bus, because poor *esmeraldero*. Then, 1975, I bought Land Rover – like a cowboy get a horse.' Eishi had come to Colombia at a time of great change in the emerald mining business. Increasingly, miners needed bulldozers and high-pressure water pumps to expose new seams. The mine owners had to borrow money to buy the equipment, but the emerald mining business was fraught with risk and they couldn't guarantee potential backers any return on their investment.

In the early 1980s, the mines of Muzo found themselves in the sights of Pablo Escobar, the head of the Medellín cartel. The newly minted cocaine baron was flush with US dollars and keen to find a reliable way of laundering them. At first it seemed a mutually advantageous partnership, but Escobar wasn't content to play banker to the mine owners, and soon began muscling his way into the emerald business. The local bosses refused to roll over for the upstart from Medellín and before long Muzo found itself on the front line of a bloody turf war. Between 1984 and

1990 rival clans of miners banded together to resist the cocaine cartels, then fractured as they set to fighting amongst themselves over ownership of the mines. Locals called it the Green War.

'Victor Carranza like to take everything,' said Eishi. 'But other emerald mine owner, they can't stand. Of them, chief was Martin Lojas. Not only Carranza and Lojas fighting – everybody want their benefit. Kill, kill, kill!' The words came out of his mouth as if they were punches. By 1989, when Pablo Escobar's cartel was being wracked by spasms of internecine suspicion and retribution, the most dangerous part of Colombia was not Medellín but the mining district of Boyacá. During the six years of the Green War, the number of murders committed in Muzo soared. In 1990, the homicide rate peaked at 439 per 100,000, a staggering figure when you consider that in Honduras, currently the most murderous country in the world, the homicide rate is 82 per 100,000. Up to 5,000 people – a full 6 per cent of the population of Muzo and the surrounding villages – died in the fighting.[*]

The violence soon reached Bogotá, where most of the mine owners had their offices. 'Every day, killing in front of me,' said Eishi. 'Beside me, guy sitting down, we were talking, young guy running and coming to look for his enemy. "Bang, bang, bang!" Only a few minutes ago he was here and now dead!' He laughed and I found myself laughing along with him. When I had first met Eishi, his skinny, stooped figure, surrounded by deferential security guards, had made it easy for me to forget that he was a don, well accustomed to dispensing violence in a controlled and comprehensive way. If at first he hadn't unnerved me, he did now, and my laughter came out hollow.

In 1990 the Bishop of Chiquinquirá brokered a truce between the mine owners and the cartels. Pablo Escobar and his associ-

---

[*] Jacinto Pineda Jiménez, *Veinte años de los acuerdos de paz entre los esmeralderos: Una reflexión desde la paz y el desarrollo* (ESAP Boyacá, 2010).

ates acknowledged that winning control of the gem trade would be impossible. Thereafter, emerald mining became a public–private venture, with much less scope for interference from the cocaine business. The softly spoken Carranza, backed by his own private army, emerged as the undisputed don of the mines.

That same year, Eishi Hayata bought his first mine; the following year, he bought two more; the year after that, he went into partnership with a consortium of mine owners to expand into five more mines. Before long, he had a 5 per cent stake in Cosquez, one of the biggest and most lucrative mines in Boyacá. As his profits increased, he upped his stake and took on more miners. In his biggest mine, he employed 300 men. 'After 1985, I start export. Then become biggest. Victor Carranza number one. I'm number two.'

Emerald miners were expected not just to find emeralds, but also to defend their boss when jealous rivals went on the attack. Every mine owner had a retinue of armed guards, who regularly shifted their grip from pickaxe to pistol. In return for their loyalty, Eishi took care of their families' medical bills and their children's school fees. 'My mine worker, my family. In the end, I am Indian chief tribe. System like that.'

Eishi and his men soon found themselves fighting a war of their own in Cosquez. The neighbouring mine belonged to Martin Lojas, one of the dons who had fought and lost the Green War with Victor Carranza. As the rival *esmeralderos* pushed further underground, disputes broke out over the boundary between their mines. Overground, fighting would flare up over the smallest things and the working day often ended with a shoot-out. 'Countryside mine area, his worker go a bar and then met my worker and *"hijo de puta!"* He kill my worker! At night, put body in jeep and taking to his father's place. "Your son, accident killed." Never say "fighting". Otherwise revenge like that. Revenge!' he said, stabbing the table with a bony finger.

Revenge was a recurring motif in the isolated villages of Boyacá. Without laws respected by both sides, violence could only become cyclical. Eishi often found himself adjudicating in conflicts between families that went back generations, if only because he was the only person who could. There was no police station to take a complaint to. Title deeds meant nothing in Muzo and Cosquez, where lawyers were only hired to cover the tracks of the private armies. And Eishi knew all too well that his rivals would exploit the first sign of vacillation. If he didn't retaliate to attacks, his men would doubt his resolve and might be tempted to supplant him. 'Colombia is revenge country,' said Eishi. 'That's why no need death penalty. Because has a thousand professionals. Easy to get cheap.'

Lawlessness could be terrifying, but it was also a great leveller. The seventeenth-century philosopher Thomas Hobbes wrote that we enjoy a kind of equality when any of us can kill anyone else. Until President Uribe brought down his 'hard hand', violence was a fact of life, not only in the emerald mines but in hundreds of towns and villages across the country. Abiding by the law and deferring to the writ of Bogotá made no sense in the anarchy of Boyacá. In the absence of laws, what a miner needed was a patron and the loyalty of his fellow miners. Unfortunately, that loyalty was always at risk of being undermined by bribes or threats, so the balance of power was never stable. While for the most part the miners thrived on the camaraderie that existed between them, nothing was dependable and there were times when the colder, more calculating characters among them came to the fore.

It was a contradiction well expressed by the *salsero* Alfredo 'Chocolate' Armenteros, when he sang *'Tu no tienes problema conmigo si no te lo buscas* – You'll have no problem with me unless you're looking for one.' It was a line from a salsa song that I often heard in bars and cafés in the countryside. Many of the peasant farmers I met on my travels were great individualists. On meeting, they would offer one another an open hand, but were always ready to turn feisty if need be. *Campesino* culture could be violent, but it was also free, and the earthiness of many of the country people I met on my travels was as appealing as it was unnerving.

Back in London, I had often found people to be indifferent or downright rude, because there is no law against bad manners. But in Colombia's villages, offending somebody without good reason can still get you shot. When there is no police officer to turn to, people become surprisingly well mannered. Like most British people, I am not in the habit of using violence to negotiate my way through the world. When civility breaks down, most Londoners are more likely to sign up for classes in anger management than to wade in with their fists. But wherever the law is less than resolute, assertiveness training won't get you very far. Generations of Colombians who have grown up on the lawless frontiers have learned to fight or risk losing everything. Was it any surprise that, if they made it to university, their children studied 'violentology' and 'conflict resolution'?

Martin Lojas was in no mood to resolve the conflict with Eishi Hayata. He would accept nothing less than total control over the disputed mine. 'Then, he like to kill me,' Eishi said, sounding a little hurt at the idea. 'I don't like to kill him. But I like to give back shit.' Both dons began to invest a rising share of their profits in men and weapons. 'I had hundreds of fighters. I don't say how many killed!' Not for the first time, Eishi made his emerald war sound like just another scrap in the school playground in Kyushu. But then he would remember something closer to home and the smile would fade from his face. 'Lojas send hitman lot time here. But they can't do. Rich man, always half dozen bodyguard in jeep.'

The final denouement wasn't long in coming. Hayata contracted 300 mercenaries to come to Cosquez from Medellín. 'I have paramilitary chief friend. Lots. Medellín paras very strong.' They headed down to the Magdalena and then up into the mountains of Boyacá in a fleet of nine coaches.

'But then call from Victor Carranza.' The other mine owners were worried that the feud between Hayata and Lojas was about to become a second Green War. As the ultimate powerbroker in the region, only Carranza could avert that eventuality. 'Mr Hayata, you can't do that,' Carranza told him. 'If you put your paramilitaries in Cosquez, you'll have to fight all of us.'

Even Eishi's bank manager felt moved to intervene, warning his client that he would have no choice but to cut off his line of credit if he were to provoke another war. So Eishi bowed to Carranza. 'You have to make friends with Martin Lojas,' Carranza told him. 'You have to give him a hug.'

Peace-making didn't come easily to Eishi. 'Brother Carranza,' he begged, 'let me fight. Otherwise, they never respect me. They think I'm fucking weak foreigner. I'm not.' But Victor Carranza persisted, and in 1994 he had the thirty mine owners of Boyacá, including Eishi Hayata, negotiate terms for another peace agreement.*

The onset of peace in the mines raised hopes that Boyacá might flourish on the back of its emerald wealth. But Colombia's economy has always been at the mercy of world markets and the emerald business is no exception. The mine owners' truce coincided with the collapse of Japan's bubble economy. Suddenly, the biggest market for Colombian emeralds dried up. Reserves of emeralds had run low during Eishi's feud with Martin Lojas, but with international prices at rock bottom,

* 'Fighting Colombia's Green War: Treasure of the Emerald Forest', *Independent*, 29 April 2006.

there was no incentive for anyone to replenish their reserves. Colombia's biggest emerald exporter lurched from one crisis to another until eventually he was forced to sell up.

The hundreds of *campesinos* from all over the country who had followed him into the mines, anxious to strike it rich, now found themselves jobless. Few of them had seen any lasting benefit from the emerald business. They had laboured in poverty, beset by the threat of an early death in a region that the government had abandoned to the dons. Many of them left for the cities. Others turned to coca cultivation, for the international market in cocaine has always been an oasis of relative calm in the stormy world of global commodity prices. 'Nowadays, only money laundry people making money,' Eishi told me. 'This country really shit working nicely drug capital. Government completely rotten. Drug people invited me many, many times, but I never accept, because I'm too proud.' Eishi seemed miles away, lost in his scorn.

I knew that he'd been back to Japan a few times, so I asked him what he thought of the country it had become. He sighed. 'When I get there, one day, "Oh, nice modern country. Organized way. Restaurant good. People gentlemen." But second day, bored. Nothing happen.' Modern Japan had been built on peace, democracy and prosperity, and he could find few reminders of the Japan that he had grown up in. His childhood friends seemed glad, but Eishi couldn't help wondering what his home country had lost, as law conquered chaos and the traditions of righteous anger and vengeance faded away. Estranged from what was once familiar, he was always quick to get a flight back to Bogotá.

'Japan collect logic. But Colombia is not logic. Is not collect. Colombia is . . . ' He rooted around for the right expression. 'Ridiculous disorder.' He looked half disgusted, half thrilled by the idea. 'But that's original human nature, I think. When we are born we need food and steal. Colombia looks like modern, but it is not. Too many poor people.'

I also knew that, having grown up with their father in Bogotá, his children now lived in the States. I wondered if he ever considered following them there. He said that he did, though only reluctantly. 'My children say, "Father, we know you're a man likes shit country." Yeah, I like this shit country. Because I'm complete adventurer. Samurai spirit, I have. Maestro look for a place and a time to die.'

Eishi told me that he had always admired Saigo Takamori, the samurai from Kyushu who had led the revolution that brought down Japan's Tokugawa government in 1867. Despite the success of his revolution, Takamori soon grew bored of peace and threw himself into planning an ill-fated invasion of Korea. The new Meiji government was near bankrupt and didn't have the means or the inclination to back Takamori's plans. But his supporters were outraged by the new government's reluctance to support their leader, so 40,000 of them marched on Tokyo from Kyushu, determined to avenge the slight. They were vastly outnumbered by the 300,000 soldiers that the government sent to meet them. Takamori was pushed back towards his hometown of Kagoshima, where he found refuge in a cave on Mount Shiroyama. 'He had everything, but don't care,' Eishi said. 'He want another adventure.' Saigo Takamori gathered a handful of loyal followers and committed *hara-kiri* – ritual suicide. 'He lost, but he won't be sorry."*

I'd spoken to countless Colombians who told me that theirs was a 'normal' country, blighted by the cocaine trade and the pariah status that foreigners afforded it. It was an understandable reaction, though it went hand in hand with a reluctance to

---

* The story of Saigo Takamori's battle with the Meiji government was dramatized in the 2003 film *The Last Samurai*.

admit, much less tackle, the source of the violence that has until recently plagued their country. Eishi Hayata, on the other hand, seemed to revel in the lawlessness that he found in Colombia. Now that it looked to be on the road to 'normality', and Eishi on the road to a comfortable if boring retirement with his kids in Miami, I wondered how he pictured the country's future 'I think Colombia will modernize and then become weak,' he told me. 'Nowadays young generation all looks same. Corner of London, corner of Thailand – everywhere, nice, educated gentleman. No more roughness!'

A few days after meeting Eishi Hayata, I was introduced to one of the 'nice, educated gentlemen' who are gradually taking over from Colombia's emerald cowboys. I was back in the north of Bogotá, where the boutiques and bars of the Zona Rosa were festooning their windows with tinsel and baubles in the run-up to Christmas. I had spent the afternoon with Richard Emblin, a Colombian-Canadian long-term resident of Bogotá and editor of the *City Paper*, the capital's only English language newspaper.

Richard was a familiar dynamo of coffee-fuelled intelligence and rapid-fire diction. He had been regaling me with stories of running the picture desk at *El Tiempo*, a job he held for most of the 1990s, and one that gave him a front row view of the saga that culminated in Colombia practically being labelled a failed state. Now it was getting dark and he had to rush to meet a client who owed him some money for advertising space. So we walked a few blocks to one of the upmarket Juan Valdez coffee shops that had mushroomed across the city with the good times.

There we met Kurt Winner, the American director of an online business-networking organization. Kurt was a new arrival, keen to catch a ride on the rising fortunes of the Colombian economy. In the lapel of his blazer he wore a three-inch-square flat-screen TV that was running an advert for Corona beer in mute. He must have been in his early fifties, and had the look of a one-time college athlete. He sat with his legs wide apart and flashed his smile like a weapon, revealing perfectly shaped, slightly opaque teeth. His very blue, wide-open eyes lent him an appearance of unnerving earnestness. Somebody had polished his brogues to a high shine.

Once he'd given Richard his cheque, Kurt started telling us about the skills he was teaching to Colombia's business executives. 'There are three types of people in the world,' he said, as he drew a square, a circle and a triangle on a paper napkin. He asked us to choose the shape that we most identified with. Richard and I both chose the triangle; Kurt said that he too was a triangle 'That's because we're all kinda spikey'. Squares tended to be intelligent, he said, while circles liked sex and drugs. It sounded as if Kurt didn't like squares or circles.

The smart bars and restaurants in the north of the city were swarming with entrepreneurial Americans like Kurt. Former president Álvaro Uribe's 'democratic security' policies had given foreign companies the confidence to start making long-term investments in Colombia. As the dollar and euro continued to decline in value, the price of gold had hit an all-time high. British companies were investing millions to expand production in the country's gold mines. Australian, Canadian, Brazilian and even Indian mining companies were also combing the Colombian countryside for opportunities. The Chinese were after the country's iron, but also had ambitious plans to build a new city on the Caribbean coast and even a new canal through the swamps of the Darien Gap, which would allow their container ships to bypass Panama.

On paper, Colombia has all the makings of a twenty-first-century success story: in addition to its wealth of minerals, it has a biodiversity rate that is second to none, huge wind and

water resources, and millions of hectares of potentially bountiful farmland. The United Nations has identified seven countries
that, together, have the potential to increase global food production by half in the next fifty years.* Colombia is one of
them; although currently near-roadless, the great eastern plains
may yet become one of the world's biggest suppliers of maize,
rice, soya, sugar cane and all kinds of tropical fruit, not to mention cattle, pigs, rubber and hardwoods.

Such talk makes the coterie of diplomats, academics,
politicians and journalists responsible for Colombia's image
management giddy with excitement. *The Economist* has named
Colombia the 'C' in CIVETS, the select group of emerging
economies poised to boom in the next ten years. There are sticking points, but everyone (or at least everyone in the north of
Bogotá) seems to agree that a turning point has been reached in
the government's battle with the FARC. By a combination of
American arms and multinational capital, Colombia's new
friends in the international community are determined to make
up for the years in which Bogotá, Cali and Medellín were no-go
zones for investors. The Colombian government has sealed the
deal by signing a free-trade agreement with the United States
and would like to do the same with the European Union. As
Eishi Hayata said, this is no longer an adventurers' country.
Thanks in large part to Álvaro Uribe, Colombia is on its way to
becoming a neo-liberal showcase.

But Richard, the honorary Colombian who had braved the
worst of the bad times, wasn't convinced. He referred to the
new arrivals as the country's fair-weather friends, all primed to
jump ship the next time a bomb went off in the capital. I wasn't
convinced either; I wanted to share in the optimism of people
like Kurt, but after several months of travelling Colombia's

* 'El Cerrado Colombiano', *Semana*, 6 November 2010.

highways and byways, I couldn't help but remember the one-way mirror that David Hutchinson had looked through when he was with his FARC captors in the mountains overlooking Bogotá in 2002. The stock market might have been booming, but most Colombians I had met had yet to see any improvement in their living standards, and nothing I had witnessed suggested that would change any time soon.

In most developing countries, the children of the poor have traditionally escaped poverty through the education system. There is a public education system in Colombia, but since few people with any money use it graduates often find that they don't have the right contacts to get the few well-paid jobs to be had in the private sector. The public sector is more accessible, but it is shrinking, and most of the bureaucrats that run the country also hold degrees in business management or international relations from American or European universities.

Shepherded away from their own country, elite Colombians are schooled in the thinking of the transnational business community and graduate as firm believers in the dogma that foreign investment will be Colombia's saviour. But despite the fanfare in *Newsweek* that had sparked my trip, the 'technology transfers' that the poor world expects from the rich have yet to be made. GDP has grown, but mainly because of rising prices for the oil, coal and minerals under Colombia's soils, and a one-off wave of investment that was bound to follow in the wake of the FARC as they fled to the most remote parts of the country. Foreign journalists might be impressed by the giddy excitement of stockbrokers, but the vast majority of Colombians remain spectators.

In unguarded moments of exasperation, the same elite Colombians who have spent the past twenty years blaming their country's poverty on the FARC will lambast imperialist domination of the developing world – rub him hard enough, and even the most dyed-in-the-wool free trader will revert to resentful to isolationism. But in fact, the rich nations' trade with Latin America is currently so small as to be insignificant: only 6 per cent of the United States foreign trade is with Latin America. Far from being bled dry through its 'open veins', countries like Colombia would probably benefit from some mutual blood sucking.*

Another chimerical source of faith is trickle-down economics, which supposes that sooner or later a healthy chunk of the nation's wealth has to pass from its upper to its lower echelons. This might be realistic if Colombian businesses were more ambitious, but generally speaking they're not. Colombia exports fruit, gold and oil, but the best parts of all three sectors is owned by foreigners. The one business still in Colombian hands is coffee – and even that is processed abroad.

Two conglomerates dominate Colombia's economy: the Santo Domingo group and the Ardila Lulle group. The conglomerates make their money from banking, insurance and air transport. They also control most of the Colombian media. What production there is focuses on processing food and drinks for the masses, and luxury goods for the rich. The near-monopolies they enjoy make for huge profits. Until his death in 2011, Julio Santo Domingo was one of the richest men in the world, reputedly worth $6 billion.

When Pablo Escobar first started exporting cocaine to the United States in the early 1980s, Colombia was a country of 28 million people. Today, its population is closer to 45 million. If prospects for education and employment were better, the country would be well placed to take advantage of the huge growth

* J. F. Hornbeck, *US–Latin American Trade: Recent Trends* (CRS Report for Congress, May 2004); *Open Veins of Latin America* is Eduardo Galeano's classic exposé of how the developed world has robbed Latin America of its natural wealth.

in population it has seen in the past thirty years, as other once poverty-stricken countries like Japan and South Korea did in the 1950s. But Colombia has yet to develop the high-value export industries that might offer a way out of poverty and soak up the productive energies of its young workforce. There is little industrial production, and Colombian businesses have yet to export anything with added value, bar cocaine.

Instead, its most powerful sectors have been seduced by the temptations of the captive market. Their insularity is part and parcel of their long-term occupation of the moral high ground, from where they alternate between ignoring, provoking and admonishing the country's large reserve of idle hands. For the only way the poor can survive is by working in the informal economy, by nature unregulated, shadowy and an endless source of anguish for law-and-order enthusiasts.

Officially, joblessness in Bogotá stands at 10 per cent, but even the bureaucrats acknowledge that another 34 per cent of the workforce is 'under-employed'. Those confined to the informal economy soon abandon the rules of the formal market economy, which has in effect abandoned them. Hundreds of thousands of *bogotanos* spend their working day not in offices, factories or shops, but on the street, flogging bootleg CDs and DVDs, knock-off car parts and stolen mobile phones.

Bogotanos depend on the underground economy for all kinds of illegal goods and services. They borrow money from loan sharks, who charge exorbitant and illegal interest rates – eleven *bogotanos* were killed in 2010 because they couldn't pay their creditors. In neighbourhoods like Suba, Kennedy and Barrios Unidos, which no denizen of the north ever ventures into, they buy and sell fake euros, fake drivers' licences, fake passports, and even clean criminal records. They build houses without planning permission and steal power from the nearest overhead cable. They get illegal abortions and buy dodgy knock-offs of prescription drugs, which from time to time put somebody in hospital – if they can afford to go to hospital, that is. They drink copies of brand-name whiskies, chilled with ice from fridges that have been smuggled into the country without paying import taxes, part of a trade in contraband that has long been used by cocaine smugglers to launder the dollars and euros they earn abroad.* Illegality is rampant in Colombia, and has to be, because the legal economy only has room for half the population.

After my meeting with Richard and Kurt, I took a southbound bus back to my flat in La Candelaria. I decided to take a break from my carnivorous diet by making a salad; the very idea of raw, crunchy vegetables seemed almost subversive. I searched the fridge for the ingredients for a dressing, but the cream cheese was off, even though the sell-by date said 13 January – almost a month away. The phoney Cheddar was off too, and the sell-by date on that was 30 January.

But what was I going to do? Sue? Of the 15,000 murders recorded in Bogotá in the past three years, in only a third of cases has a defendant been brought to trial, let alone convicted. When it comes to robbery, hold-ups and burglary, the legal system is even more shambolic. Of 180,000 cases reported to the police since 2007, only 15 per cent have made it to a courtroom.† With such a pitiful clear-up rate, what chance did I stand of convincing the supermarket to reimburse me for mouldy cheese? My salad went un-garnished.

Neither politicians nor journalists seem able to square their love of 'democratic security' with the rampant criminality and impunity that most of Colombia's people have to live with.

---

* 'El top de los actos ilegales que cometen los bogotanos', *El Tiempo*, 28 November 2010.
† 'En Bogotá la justicia cojea . . . y no llega', *El Tiempo*, 29 September 2010.

Looking through the country's one-way mirror from the comfort of a seat in one of the Andean Centre's upscale restaurants, the root causes of its problems seem a world away. The patrons of Bogotá's snazzier restaurants live big city lives, and though overwhelmingly schooled in progressive, liberal ideas, the elite that runs Colombia is at heart indifferent to the rolling crisis the rest of the country lives with.

Despite all the simple-minded talk of Colombia being a democracy under siege from terrorists, my travels had shown me that the FARC is just one of many threats to democracy, and the country is ruled not by the people, but by a clique. Even poor Colombians who voted for Juan Manuel Santos know that he is a member of an oligarchy, and that the meaningful choices are made before, not after, their ballots are cast. The Colombian version of democracy is an incestuous affair, with many spectators and few participants, and every one of them on first-name terms with everyone else.

Corruption and intimidation ensure that most Colombians put little faith in press, courts, Congress, or the other institutions that democracy depends upon. Instead, the pervasive lawlessness creates an incessant demand for law and order, which is how populist authoritarians like Vladimir Putin and Álvaro Uribe come to be elected. I remembered an anecdote Ricardo had told me as we were climbing Moguy, of a TV vox pop of attitudes to then-president Uribe's proposal to put the death penalty on the statute books. Most passers-by were broadly in favour of capital punishment and nodded away to the sound of Uribe dishing out the ultimate punishment. The last of those interviewed was an impoverished old man. When asked what he thought of the death penalty, he thought for a moment. 'Well, it doesn't seem to have worked so far,' he replied. His words came from the other side of the mirror, where vigilantes and *sicarios* take the place of police officers and judges. Those on the receiving end of their rough justice have all of the wisdom but none of the power needed to act upon it.

Ricardo told me another story that day, of the time he spent working as a pollster. The survey was conducted by researchers from a British university, who wanted to find out more about living conditions in the poorest parts of Bogotá. Ricardo's job was to go into people's homes and confirm that indeed, the father had left a while ago, the three children shared a single bed, and the mother cooked on a single hob, using power that she filched from the power lines running overhead.

The part of the survey that dealt with work gave respondents the option of describing themselves as unemployed, but nobody did. Despite mass unemployment, there was no welfare system, at least not for the jobless, so everybody did something, even if it was only touting boiled sweets on buses or packs of felt-tip pens outside Juan Valdez.

According to the survey, all such workers were to be listed as 'independent trades people'. To Ricardo's surprise, far from feeling aggrieved by the phoney poll, the respondents felt pleased to be called 'independent trades people'. They were not 'unemployed', but 'determined lone operators'. The flattering picture that the outside world drew of their poverty was, well, flattering. Ricardo told me that he couldn't handle the duplicity and quit the same day (no wonder he couldn't afford the bus fare).

I have spent time in other countries where the young make up the best part of the population. In the Ghanaian capital of Accra, I watched young women minding their stalls in the marketplaces; their eyes fixed on the mid-distance and seemed to stay there all day. Their passivity was dispiriting, or so I thought until Sunday, when I went to a local church and saw ranks of young women singing their praises to Jesus and crying their eyes out over the unhappiness of their earthly existence.

In Ghana, most young people grow up with little prospect of escaping the poverty they were born into, but still choose to obey the law – or did, until Colombian cocaine traffickers started teaching them how to get ahead. But Colombia isn't a country in which the law is held in high regard. I have met many young Colombians who are well aware that the opportunities that the one in ten takes for granted will never be theirs, not because they lack merit or determination but because they were born on the lower rungs of an oligarchy. They will not take a life of poverty lying down. Five hundred and twelve years after the first European dropped anchor off Cabo de la Vela, Colombia is still part of the New World; it is a project, not an inheritance, and it demands ambition, not stewardship. Like all the countries of the Americas, Colombia was born of hope – first for riches; then order; and lastly for justice. Until those hopes are realized, it will continue to simmer with accumulated frustration and resentment.

11.   Merry Crisis and a Happy New Fear

Over a period of four days in the run-up to Christmas 2010, 200 soldiers from the Colombian Army's elite FUDRA counter-insurgency force secreted themselves into one of the guerrillas' main supply corridors in La Macarena national park. They found a 75-foot-high tree, decorated it with 2,000 Christmas lights, and beat a hasty retreat under the protection of several Black Hawk helicopters. The Ministry of Defence called it 'a Christmas present for the FARC', part of its campaign to encourage guerrillas to hand in their weapons over the holiday season. 'Demobilize this Christmas: anything is possible' ran their slogan.*

Days later, President Juan Manuel Santos delivered a Christmas message to the troops at the Tolemaida military fort. 'This has not been an easy year,' he told them. 'The beast, as President Uribe used to call it, is still alive. We have him cornered and he's weak. But weak, cornered beasts are more dangerous and more cowardly. That's why we have to persevere. We won't let our guard down for a single minute until we have secured complete peace for this country.'†

Resolute, honourable and united, the president's speech seemed the perfect end-of-year message for a country emerging from decades of internecine strife. But the stirring team talk masked a rather messier reality. The Army's success in pushing

---

* 'FF.MM. le regalan a las Farc un árbol de Navidad', El Espectador, 17 December 2010.
† Presidencia de la República de Colombia, press release, 24 December 2010.

the FARC ever further up the slopes of the southern Andes or into the jungles of the *llanos* has been mired in controversy ever since what came to be known as the 'false positives' scandal was brought to light. In the closing months of 2008, nineteen young men disappeared from Soacha, a sprawling suburb of Bogotá. Their bodies turned up the following day in the department of Norte de Santander, where the Army claimed to have killed all nineteen in fire-fights with the guerrillas. When the victims' families went to collect their bodies, they began to ask questions. How could the deceased have been recruited, trained and sent into battle by the guerrillas only twenty-four hours after disappearing from their homes? One of the dead was known to have had mental health problems; another was physically disabled. Was the FARC really so desperate for new recruits that they would send such men into combat with the Army?

Senator Gustavo Petro, a long-standing critic of the government's 'democratic security' policies who was elected mayor of Bogotá in October 2011, believed that the killings were the logical consequence of 'directive 29'. This Army memorandum entitled any soldier who killed a guerrilla or paramilitary fighter in combat to a reward of around £1,000. Directive 29 had led to a series of illegal killings in towns and villages up and down the country. Soldiers hoping for a cash bonus or time off to visit their families would befriend a civilian – usually a young, unemployed man – and entice him back to base with the promise of work. The victim would then be driven into the countryside, where he would be killed, dressed in the uniform of a FARC guerrilla and taken to the Army morgue, to become another number in the Army's body count and further proof of its successful prosecution of the 'war on terror'.

The practice had started with soldiers from the Fourth Brigade in Medellín, before being taken up by other brigades around the country. Wherever the Army was struggling to overrun guerrilla fronts, soldiers were likely to boost their body count by killing unwitting civilians. Although 'directive 29' was dropped when abuses first came to light in May 2006, this 'body count syndrome' remained unaffected. By October 2009, the Attorney General was investigating over 900 cases of alleged 'false positive' killings.

As news of the scandal spread northwards, members of the US Congress began asking why American taxpayers were supporting human rights abusers. Pressure was brought to bear on the Colombians to clean up their act. With so much money riding on Plan Colombia and the United States' support for the Colombian armed forces, then-president Uribe was determined to stop his 'democratic security' policies being dragged into the mire. The Minister of Defence – the future president, Juan Manuel Santos – insisted that he had 'zero tolerance for violations of human rights and corruption'. The head of the Army, Mario Montoya, was forced to resign, as were thirty other senior officers.

Once the peripatetic gaze of the camera had passed, however, the armed forces returned to time-honoured tactics. The generals agreed to prepare an internal report, but kept a public enquiry off the agenda. That done, the high command closed ranks and President Uribe simply refused to discuss the matter any further. Mention of *falsos positivos* was deemed akin to being unpatriotic; those who sided with the victims were part of an international smear campaign orchestrated by foreign NGOs, whose self-righteous talk of peace and justice only provided intellectual cover for terrorists. Juan Manuel Santos warned that he would have no truck with 'false allegations'. The question of who might be issuing such falsehoods and why was left unanswered.

Some took Uribe and Santos' belligerent response to the false positives scandal as licence to issue death threats against the families of the victims. General Carlos Suárez, who was given the job of leading the inquiry into the killings, told US ambassador William Brownfield that Army officers had even threatened his family. While his inquiry had the support of Santos and the head of the Air Force, the new head of the Army, Carlos Ospina, was opposed to it from the outset. By his reckoning, calling the Army to account for anything was an affront, and would only discourage his soldiers from fighting the terrorists.

The false positives scandal shows how desperate the Colombian Army is to give the appearance of winning. The idea that the FARC can be defeated on the ground is crucial to the legitimacy of both the Army and the government. But success is hard to gauge, which is why the body count is so popular with generals, politicians and the press: it is as easy to understand as it is to manipulate. Worse, the scandal shows that in the name of fighting terror, Colombian soldiers are prepared to kill the very people they are supposed to be protecting from terrorism.

Even the official statements of contrition that followed the scandal soon proved to be window-dressing. A UN report published in May 2010 found that more than 98 per cent of the 900 cases of *falsos positivos* had gone unpunished.[*] And in May 2011, a second scandal broke when it was found that 270 soldiers who had been found guilty of torture, disappearances and extrajudicial killings, and imprisoned in the 'reclusion centre' of the fort at Tolemaida, were in fact living in holiday cabins. 'My general often comes round to my place,' said one convicted soldier, who an undercover journalist found relaxing in the sun outside his cabin. 'He's been a big help.'[†] Most convicts still received wages from the Army; some ran the military fort's taxi services; a

[*] 'Colombia Takes Steps on Killings but Security Forces Still Culpable – UN Expert', UN *News Centre*, 27 May 2010.
[†] 'Tolemaida Resort', *Semana*, 2 April 2011.

lucky few had even been given 'leave' to take holidays on the Caribbean island of San Andrés.

Of course, President Santos made no mention of the 'false positives' in the speech that he gave to the troops gathered at the military fort at Tolemaida. He was there to boost, not sap their morale. 'The whole world has said: "Look at Colombia: it's an example of how a democracy that was once cornered can arise once more, with vigour, while guaranteeing the freedoms and rights of its citizens."' In a country as demonized as Colombia, foreign approval is guaranteed to put a spring in a soldier's step. No mention, then, of the fact that, far from guaranteeing its citizens' rights, the Colombian Army has the worst human rights record of any armed force in the western hemisphere.

In 2006 I accompanied a delegation of British MPs and trade union leaders to Colombia. We flew from Bogotá to the town of Saravena, close to the border with Venezuela, where the Army was fighting running battles with FARC and ELN guerrillas. Both groups had come to depend on the money they extorted from foreign oil companies in the region. Caño Limón is Colombia's biggest oil pipeline and the target of endless sabotage. After intense lobbying by their biggest oil companies, the United States had spent $100 million on the creation of a new battalion of the Colombian Army that was dedicated to protecting the pipeline.

From the landing strip, we were taken past rows of armed Sikorsky and Black Hawk helicopters and the tiny Turbo Thrush planes used to fumigate the coca fields. Once inside the heavily barricaded Army base, the British delegates had a chance to put their concerns to the colonel of the battalion. They wanted to know why trade unionists, community leaders and members of the local peasants' association in Saravena were being killed. The families of the victims claimed that the Army was working in concert with local paramilitaries to 'drain the pond' in which the guerrillas swam. It was classic Vietnam-era counter-insurgency theory, as taught at the US Army's School of the Americas and practised by its graduates in Central and South America ever since.

The colonel nodded solemnly. 'Perhaps a song might better express what I'd like to say,' he suggested. A young man with a bandana around his head and a guitar in his hand came into the room, adjusted his mic stand and proceeded to treat us to a ballad, which I translated for the delegates in a respectful whisper. The song lamented the futility of war, the endless suffering of the Colombian people and their enduring dream of peace. 'Peace one day,' he crooned, before making a deep bow and leaving the room. The MPs clapped politely and exchanged worried looks. The gall of the Colombian Ministry of Defence, in donning the garb of peacemaker while engaging in a bloody counter-insurgency campaign against local people, was lost on none of them.

Colombian politicians do a lot of hand-wringing when foreigners start asking difficult questions. Following Álvaro Uribe's election to the Colombian presidency in 2002, trade unionists and elected representatives on both sides of the Atlantic drew attention to the horrendous repression being meted out to Colombian civil society by its Army and paramilitaries. The Colombian government was negotiating free-trade agreements with the United States and the European Union at the time, and was anxious to reassure them that the matter was in hand. Uribe said that 'not one more trade unionist will be killed'; during his eight years in office, 500 trade unionists were murdered.

Equally mindful of placating foreign critics, President Santos has also tried to draw a line under past atrocities, insisting that those responsible will be brought to justice and that trade unionists' lives will be respected and protected. As ever, the rhetoric has been more encouraging than the reality; forty-eight trade unionists were murdered in Colombia in 2010 and it remains the most dangerous country in the world to exercise democratic labour rights.* The paramilitaries aren't alone in tarring all the government's opponents with the same brush: the Army, police and many local politicians instinctively regard unionized teachers, nurses and *campesinos* as *subversivos* too. The FARC's military offensive doesn't help, nor does their strategy of combining '*todas las formas de lucha*', which has only made it easier for the paramilitaries to lump the trade unions in with the FARC.

This blurring of the distinction between military target and unarmed protester has resisted all clarification to this day. Over the past twenty-five years, Colombian civil society has suffered a near-genocidal persecution. Hardest hit have been the trade unions. Nearly 3,000 of them have been 'disappeared' or murdered since 1985, a cull that has prompted little concern from the government, as shown by the fact that in less than one in ten cases has the killer been brought to justice.†

I spent several years monitoring human rights abuses in Colombia for the TUC's Justice for Colombia campaign. When Colombian trade union leaders, journalists and community activists travelled to Blackpool, Bournemouth and Scarborough to address conference delegates, I translated their descriptions of the death threats and bulletproof cars that had become part of their daily lives. I sent letters to British ministers, in which I pointed out that the Colombian government routinely imprisons its opponents on trumped-up charges of 'rebellion'. I collated statistics to show the extent of the Army's collusion with paramilitary units, and compiled graphs that showed that on many counts, human rights abuses in Colombia far exceed those committed in Burma, Iran or Zimbabwe.

* Luís Eduardo Celis, 'Violencia contra el sindicalismo en Colombia: Una larga y triste historia', *Razón Pública*, 31 January 2011.
† Cal Colgan, 'In the Recent Free Trade Deals, What About Colombian Workers?' *The Nation*, 14 October 2011.

The British Ministry of Defence wrote back with assurances. Of course, allegations of human rights abuses by a friendly government were of great concern, which was why the MoD was teaching Colombian soldiers 'the rules of engagement', the first of which was respect for the distinction between armed insurgents and unarmed civilians. There was talk of 'putting pressure' on their Colombian counterparts and the importance of 'positive engagement'. But this was as close as I was allowed to get. Like the Pentagon, the MoD supplies military aid to the Colombian Army, most of which is spent on cloudy 'counter-insurgency training' and 'counter-narcotics training'. Little distinction is made between the two; there is no parliamentary oversight and no accountability.

Reducing British connivance in the Colombian government's dirty war to grubby money would be a crude simplification, but it can be no coincidence that the UK is the second largest foreign investor in Colombia. Its oil companies in particular have made significant investments in the country; were it not for the guerrilla presence in the *llanos*, they'd be making a lot more.

The British government has long regarded Colombia as an ally. In May 2011, Tony Blair flew into Bogotá to receive the Order of Boyacá. President Santos called it 'a sign of our gratitude for all that you have done and continue to do for us'. Blair had strengthened Colombia's foreign policy, Santos said, and was 'a good ambassador for Colombia'. Blair returned the lauding, saying that the Santos government was 'a dependable ally for those who believe in democracy', and 'enjoyed a great reputation abroad'.*

Tony Blair seemed well aware of the Colombian elite's

* See 'Santos condecoró con Orden de Boyacá a Tony Blair', *El Universal*, 27 April 2011; and ' "Colombia está pasando por un buen momento": Tony Blair', *El Tiempo*, 28 April 2011.

boundless appetite for foreign flatterers, which goes hand in hand with a haughty dismissal of foreign critics. According to its own interpretation of the conflict, the Colombian government is struggling to prevent their country becoming a Marxist state. Of course, the concerns of the Dutch and Swedish ambassadors are always listened to and the annual report of the United Nations High Commission for Human Rights makes for predictably uncomfortable reading. But ultimately, talk of human rights abuses is a naïve, and at times disingenuous, distraction. The Colombian government is at war with fundamentalists of its own. It is a war it cannot afford to lose: a 200-year-old tradition of democratic government is at stake.

A leaked report prepared by the DAS (Colombia's internal security service) in 2005 offers a telling insight into the reality of Colombia's 'war on terror'. The report asserted that as well as 'defending democracy and the nation', one of the duties of the security services was to 'create consciousness about the consequences of a communist system'. It went on to list ways of eliminating political opponents, including sabotage, blackmail and terrorism.

The DAS had just about every one of the government's critics in its sights. Operation Amazonas was a planned smear campaign against the Constitutional Court and the leaders of 'political parties opposing the state'. Since the only opposition party worthy of the name in 2005 was the Democratic Pole, they must have been thinking of Carlos Gaviria, a respected former judge, nicknamed Father Christmas for his white beard and fatherly countenance. He was to be dealt with by 'generating ties to the FARC'.

Piedad Córdoba, a Liberal Party senator and long-time thorn in Álvaro Uribe's side, was to be discredited by 'generating ties to the United Self-Defence Forces of Colombia (AUC)'. Someone at the DAS had drawn a question mark next to this proposal, which is no surprise: having been kidnapped by paramilitaries in 1999, Córdoba was hardly likely to be hobnobbing with them. Nonetheless, five years after the report was drafted, the DAS got their woman: Córdoba was barred from office for 'giving advice to the FARC'.

Among the DAS's other targets were 'NGOs in Colombia and around the world'. There was even a plan for 'Operation Foreigners', by which DAS agents were to find ways to smear organizations such as the TUC's Justice for Colombia campaign by 'establishing their links to narco-trafficking organizations and putting them on trial'.* The government's spooks seemed to consider the very idea of a legal opposition an oxymoron.

But their violent intolerance of dissenters isn't confined to Colombia. On the day before Christmas Eve came news that Jorge Videla, the former dictator of Argentina, had been given a life sentence. Videla told the jury that he accepted responsibility for the terror campaigns orchestrated against the left while he was president between 1976 and 1983. His government had 'waged a just war' against terrorism, he said. In his defence he claimed to have acted to prevent a greater tragedy – the transformation of Argentina from a conservative, Christian society to a Marxist state. Luciano Menéndez, another of the many former generals sentenced that day, remarked that if they hadn't waged that war, Argentina would still be wrestling with the problems that Colombia faces today. Before he was led away to the cells, Menéndez had a parting shot for the press pack. 'Democracy gives dignity to the citizenry,' he declared. 'But you need dignified citizens.'†

Wherever I had been in Colombia, the desire to live *con digni-*

---

* I've referred to Operation Amazonas, but some of those named were targeted as part of other DAS operations, such as Operation Risaralda and Operation Arauca.
† 'Argentina's Former Dictator Jorge Videla Given Life Sentence', *Guardian*, 23 December 2010.

dad – with dignity – was a recurrent plea. Perhaps this is nothing new in Latin America, whose people have long been inspired by the highest ideals, yet still live with the humiliation of endemic poverty, corruption and violence. The continent's 'wars on terror' have always been waged against its own people.

But the generals' defence of their 'just war' has implications that resonate far beyond Latin America. If the rejection of terrorism is to be a pillar of global foreign policy post 9/11, politicians should be clear about what the word means. The FARC and the ELN are not the only terrorists in Colombia. The country's army, in cahoots with its paramilitaries, has been terrorizing its people for the past thirty-five years, to a degree that puts the guerrillas in the shade. The Colombian government has never objected to terrorism per se; what they object to are the 'enemies of the state', who sometimes, but far from always, take up arms against it. The distinction between enemy and unarmed opponent has gone unacknowledged for too long. Until that distinction is made and respected, Colombia's trade unionists, journalists and teachers will always be dealt the same hand as its guerrillas, and Colombia, far from being a bastion of good government, will remain 'a genocidal democracy'.*

My friend Deisy had invited me to the Café Pasaje in Plaza del Rosario, where she and her workmates were planning to have a party before going home to their families for Christmas Day. On my way down to the square, I met up with Ricardo, who I hadn't seen since the communion party at his Uncle Alejandro's house. He'd grown a scraggly beard while I'd been out of town and was wearing a tracksuit with stripes in the African colours,

---

* The phrase was coined by Father Javier Giraldo, who founded the NGO Justicia y Paz – Justice and Peace – in 1988. Justicia y Paz maintains a comprehensive database of human rights violations in Colombia. Giraldo is also the author of *Colombia: The Genocidal Democracy* (Common Courage Press, 1996).

which made him look like the lovechild of Che Guevara and Bob Marley. He told me that his mother had finally tired of having a 37-year-old son living at home, so he had moved around the corner to his cousin's house, where he slept on a mattress in the garage.

There was fresh graffiti in the Journalists Park. The words were in English, as if meant for the outside world – 'Merry Crisis and a Happy New Fear' it read. Ricardo and I had come across acres of street art on our walks around Bogotá. Much of it was just tags, left on soot-blackened shop fronts in the city centre, but there were also fantastic murals – of birds with eight eyes, police officers with the teeth of piranhas, and solitary old men with beating red hearts hidden under their raincoats – that stood as testament to the creativity at work in the frustrated city. A tramp with a hessian sack on his back stopped alongside us to read the Christmas message. Some kindly soul had given him a large slice of cake on a paper plate. The pink and blue of the icing practically glowed amidst the browns and greys of his clothes.

In the Plaza Simón Bolívar, the mayor had installed an ice rink for the Christmas holidays. From the square down to the Parque de la Independencia, Avenida Séptima was decked out in lights. Under them wandered *bogotano* families, who tucked into skewers of chargrilled diced beef with roasted and salted new potatoes, blackened corn-on-the-cob, candyfloss, and plastic cups of pineapple, papaya and mango. They gathered to watch a human statue of a golden angel with huge wings, who was standing on a junction box outside the church of San Francisco. Two clowns teetered through the crowds on stilts, and outside the offices of *El Tiempo* a contortionist vied with a belly dancer for the crowd's attention.

Bogotanos in the north of the city might have been stocking up on Wii consoles and iPhones, but for the most part the custom of buying presents for everyone in the family didn't exist. The Davivienda bank had sponsored the illuminations in the Parque El Virrey, probably because their best-heeled customers lived up that way, but that aside, the corporations left Christmas well alone. For most *bogotanos*, Christmas Day meant no more and no less than an evening meal with the family.

As Ricardo and I came into Plaza del Rosario, we passed a young man sitting on the pavement with his head in his hands. It was one of the few times I'd seen signs of grief in all the time I'd been in Colombia. In a country that has lived through so much murder, I'd expected to see more tears. I must have passed hundreds of hit men, paramilitaries, drug traffickers and corrupt officials on the street or sipping coffee with their friends at the local café. I wished I could spot some telltale sign, but their crimes didn't seem to mark their faces.

Instead, just like the Coca-Cola jingle had said, this was a land of smiling faces. Ever since hearing that Colombians are the third happiest people in the world, I had been trying to square the circle. Measuring happiness seems as tricky as putting a pin on smoke, but if the Happy Planet Index is to be believed, Colombians haven't been dented by tragedy.

Deisy's workmates greeted Ricardo and me as if we were old friends. Rum was poured into little plastic cups, our health was toasted, and down the shots went. It was only four in the afternoon, but the dance floor was already packed. If I'd been in a bar in London, people would have been talking, not dancing. No nightclub opened at four in the afternoon – and even if they had, they'd be playing trance or electronica, the soundtrack to a long night drive under the motorway's glowing sulphur lamps. But the DJ in the Café Pasaje was playing a salsa version of 'Let It Be'. By some miracle, the Beatles' melancholy ballad had become an up-tempo celebration of enlightened resignation. It was raucous *puro salsa*, a cacophony of sounds, led by a bold male voice that rang out clear and strong. The Brazilian singer Gilberto Gil once likened samba to the swagger of one who has negotiated a muddy puddle and still kept his white patent-leather shoes spotless. The same might be said of salsa, the soundtrack to a walk through the potholed lanes of the barrio.

When we were ready for a break from dancing, I couldn't help asking Deisy how such a traumatized country could seem so happy. As I thought, she didn't want to talk about it. She admitted that Colombians weren't much inclined to dwell on their problems. Everyone had been touched by the violence, she told me; there were no winners or heroes in the Colombian story, unless you counted the survivors. It was best to have a drink and a dance and get on with it.

Liliana had just come back to Bogotá after a year of travelling around Latin America. Her time abroad had made her more critical of her compatriots. Compassion counts for less in Colombia than it does in other Latin American countries, she told me. 'Look at the way we treat the millions of people who have been displaced by the fighting.' There was a sneer playing around her mouth, but also a sadness born of frustration. 'Colombians have learnt to keep smiling, because no one is going to pay them any attention if they don't.'

Liliana's assessment was a brutal one, but it was borne out by the Happy Planet Index, which shows that some of the world's happiest countries are also amongst its most violent. At the top of the list are Jamaica and El Salvador. Poverty, corruption and general insecurity top the list of popular concerns in both countries, as they do in Colombia. Domestic violence, street violence and political violence are high in all three, and yet people report being happier with their lot than most Europeans do.

I asked Giovanny how he squared violence and happiness. 'I think you have to be a bit stupid to be happy,' he told me. 'By stupid, I mean fatalistic, ignorant of your rights and deferential to the powerful.' His home department of Chocó is the poorest in the country. The way he saw it, the poverty that his family lived in was a cage, yet their lack of freedom only fuelled their happiness. 'Everything conspires to favour those who bend with the wind, like reeds,' he said. Those who deferred to the powerful felt no personal responsibility for the circumstances that bound their lives. They had stifled Giovanny, which is why he lived in Bogotá, but the rest of his family regarded them as a source of security. Within the confines of their neighbourhood, there was a lot of room for movement. 'They might defer to the powerful, but among those as powerless as themselves, they assert themselves to the full.'

After years of widespread insecurity, it should come as no surprise that as well as being among the happiest people on the planet, Colombians are also among the least trusting.* Outside the circles of family and friends, most people are not to be trusted. This makes the family more important than in countries where people feel safe enough to venture into the company of strangers. Spending time with members of your family requires you to show great tolerance for the expectations and demands of others. It also means sacrificing a lot of freedom, in return for which you get great security. 'But feeling secure doesn't take up much of your attention,' Giovanny said, 'so my family spends a lot of time watching the TV together. Living in the countryside, there isn't much else to do.'

Much of the insecurity and general lawlessness that until recently dominated life in Colombia is down to the rise of the *clase emergente* – the cocaine traffickers. Nouvean riche *narcos* might besmirch Colombia's reputation overseas, but they have

* According to a collation of results from the World Values Survey between 1995 and 2008; see Jaime Díez Medrano, 'Interpersonal Trust', JDS Data Bank, 2012.

played an important – and largely overlooked – role in encouraging poor Colombians to become less deferential and more impatient for material betterment. This new-found assertiveness often works in mysterious ways. Although Bogotá's churches are full on Sundays, priests complain that nobody makes confession any more. Ostensibly, their parishioners are great fans of authority, respect and orderliness. As I knew from personal experience, Colombians can sit in meetings for hours, and love to talk in high-flown bureaucratese. But they make better kings than subjects, and the construction of a truly democratic, pluralist society is still a work in progress. Traditionally they respect those who lay down the law, but not the act of obeying laws. It follows that the smartest – and possibly the happiest – were the *abejas*, the bees – the schemers and charmers; great company, but watch your back.

As I prepared to fly back to London, I thought about what I was leaving behind. Certainly, a love of parties: Colombians are supremely sociable people. I had rarely seen them alone: in parks, bars and cafés, they were always in company, whereas I often went to all three just to read a book. But Colombians are not great readers; nor are they great ones for hobbies, most of which are solitary. Thanks to their love of company, hundreds of model airplanes go unassembled, back gardens untended and sweaters un-knitted.

Their distaste for solitude meant that I had met few shy, reserved or awkward Colombians on my travels. They didn't seem to be hampered by lonely ambition, as many Anglo-Saxons tend to be. In fact, they weren't hampered by loneliness of any kind, which is rapidly becoming the biggest cause of physical and social ills in the west. While they prided themselves on their love of hard work, nobody was striving to improve, better or reinvent themselves. They seemed to have little interest in self-expression, self-discovery or self-anything for that matter.

My time in Colombia had been a welcome break from life in London. While sociable, they weren't ones for the gossip and backbiting I overheard on British streets. There was none of the cutting sarcasm or self-deprecation that comes with British company. Despite their country's fearsome reputation, Colombians seemed more hospitable, better mannered, and kinder—both to themselves and others – than a lot of British people.

In 1800 the French doctor Marie-Françoise-Xavier Bichat, the father of descriptive anatomy, defined life as 'the collection of functions that resist death'. Maybe, after living through so much violence and injustice, Colombians have decided to make a project of life, as a conscious act and endless struggle. While the British seem to enjoy indulging their most gloom-laden imaginings, Colombians don't give voice to them. Maybe they have realized that there is no point in taking serious matters too seriously.

Or perhaps, rather than being a resigned response to the conflict, their happiness precedes it. I am sure that Colombians owe much of their vitality to living on a continent so obviously blessed by nature. However wracked by human folly, Colombia's mountains, rivers and jungles are a source of inspiration to anyone who lives among them. Their sheer abundance is an affirmation of life at its most elemental, one that those eking a living in tundra, desert or concrete jungle will never be able to count on.

Perhaps that explains their striking insularity. For despite having received few foreign visitors and practically no immigrants since the nineteenth century, the Colombians I met on my travels seemed surprisingly lacking in curiosity – not just about the outside world, but their own country. Notwithstanding their strident patriotism, few of them had travelled its country roads, and given the chance of a holiday, most chose to head for Miami. Those who couldn't afford the flight would rather go to the Caribbean than the Sierra Nevada or the Amazon. Perhaps their fear of the open road is a habit picked up when the risk of running into a FARC roadblock was ever-present. Those days are gone, yet the country hostels where I stayed were more likely to host foreign backpackers than young Colombians eager to see the most bio-diverse country in the world.

The first time I visited Colombia in 1999, a man stopped me on the street in Cartagena and thanked me for ignoring the nay-sayers. He was glad to see a foreigner look beyond the one-way mirror and pay a visit to a notorious country. Twelve years later, growing numbers of foreigners are discovering the bounty of Colombia. Despite the ragged contours of its national history, it seems destined to emerge from its years of solitude in the years to come. The world is in for a treat when it does.

ALLEN LANE
an imprint of
PENGUIN BOOKS

Recently Published

Richard Barber, *Edward III and the Triumph of England*

Daniel M Davis, *The Compatibility Gene*

John Bradshaw, *Cat Sense: The Feline Enigma Revealed*

Roger Knight, *Britain Against Napoleon: The Organisation of Victory, 1793-1815*

Thurston Clarke, *JFK's Last Hundred Days: An Intimate Portrait of a Great President*

Jean Drèze and Amartya Sen, *An Uncertain Glory: India and its Contradictions*

Rana Mitter, *China's War with Japan, 1937-1945: The Struggle for Survival*

Tom Burns, *Our Necessary Shadow: The Nature and Meaning of Psychiatry*

Sylvain Tesson, *Consolations of the Forest: Alone in a Cabin in the Middle Taiga*

George Monbiot, *Feral: Searching for Enchantment on the Frontiers of Rewilding*

Ken Robinson and Lou Aronica, *Finding Your Element: How to Discover Your Talents and Passions and Transform Your Life*

David Stuckler and Sanjay Basu, *The Body Economic: Why Austerity Kills*

Suzanne Corkin, *Permanent Present Tense: The Man with No Memory, and What He Taught the World*

Daniel C. Dennett, *Intuition Pumps and Other Tools for Thinking*

Adrian Raine, *The Anatomy of Violence: The Biological Roots of Crime*

Eduardo Galeano, *Children of the Days: A Calendar of Human History*

Lee Smolin, *Time Reborn: From the Crisis of Physics to the Future of the Universe*

Michael Pollan, *Cooked: A Natural History of Transformation*

David Graeber, *The Democracy Project: A History, a Crisis, a Movement*

Brendan Simms, *Europe: The Struggle for Supremacy, 1453 to the Present*

Oliver Bullough, *The Last Man in Russia and the Struggle to Save a Dying Nation*

Diarmaid MacCulloch, *Silence: A Christian History*

Evgeny Morozov, *To Save Everything, Click Here: Technology, Solutionism, and the Urge to Fix Problems that Don't Exist*

David Cannadine, *The Undivided Past: History Beyond Our Differences*

Michael Axworthy, *Revolutionary Iran: A History of the Islamic Republic*

Jaron Lanier, *Who Owns the Future?*

John Gray, *The Silence of Animals: On Progress and Other Modern Myths*

Paul Kildea, *Benjamin Britten: A Life in the Twentieth Century*

Jared Diamond, *The World Until Yesterday: What Can We Learn from Traditional Societies?*

Nassim Nicholas Taleb, *Antifragile: How to Live in a World We Don't Understand*

Alan Ryan, *On Politics: A History of Political Thought from Herodotus to the Present*

Roberto Calasso, *La Folie Baudelaire*

Carolyn Abbate and Roger Parker, *A History of Opera: The Last Four Hundred Years*

Yang Jisheng, *Tombstone: The Untold Story of Mao's Great Famine*

Caleb Scharf, *Gravity's Engines: The Other Side of Black Holes*

Jancis Robinson, Julia Harding and José Vouillamoz, *Wine Grapes: A Complete Guide to 1,368 Vine Varieties, including their Origins and Flavours*

David Bownes, Oliver Green and Sam Mullins, *Underground: How the Tube Shaped London*

Niall Ferguson, *The Great Degeneration: How Institutions Decay and Economies Die*

Chrystia Freeland, *Plutocrats: The Rise of the New Global Super-Rich*

David Thomson, *The Big Screen: The Story of the Movies and What They Did to Us*

Halik Kochanski, *The Eagle Unbowed: Poland and the Poles in the Second World War*

Kofi Annan with Nader Mousavizadeh, *Interventions: A Life in War and Peace*

Mark Mazower, *Governing the World: The History of an Idea*

Anne Applebaum, *Iron Curtain: The Crushing of Eastern Europe 1944-56*

Steven Johnson, *Future Perfect: The Case for Progress in a Networked Age*

Christopher Clark, *The Sleepwalkers: How Europe Went to War in 1914*

Neil MacGregor, *Shakespeare's Restless World*

Nate Silver, *The Signal and the Noise: The Art and Science of Prediction*

Chinua Achebe, *There Was a Country: A Personal History of Biafra*

John Darwin, *Unfinished Empire: The Global Expansion of Britain*

Jerry Brotton, *A History of the World in Twelve Maps*

Patrick Hennessey, *KANDAK: Fighting with Afghans*

Katherine Angel, *Unmastered: A Book on Desire, Most Difficult to Tell*

David Priestland, *Merchant, Soldier, Sage: A New History of Power*

Stephen Alford, *The Watchers: A Secret History of the Reign of Elizabeth I*

Tom Feiling, *Short Walks from Bogotá: Journeys in the New Colombia*

Pankaj Mishra, *From the Ruins of Empire: The Revolt Against the West and the Remaking of Asia*

Geza Vermes, *Christian Beginnings: From Nazareth to Nicaea, AD 30-325*

Steve Coll, *Private Empire: ExxonMobil and American Power*

Joseph Stiglitz, *The Price of Inequality*

Dambisa Moyo, *Winner Take All: China's Race for Resources and What it Means for Us*

Robert Skidelsky and Edward Skidelsky, *How Much is Enough? The Love of Money, and the Case for the Good Life*

Frances Ashcroft, *The Spark of Life: Electricity in the Human Body*

Sebastian Seung, *Connectome: How the Brain's Wiring Makes Us Who We Are*

Callum Roberts, *Ocean of Life*

Orlando Figes, *Just Send Me Word: A True Story of Love and Survival in the Gulag*

Leonard Mlodinow, *Subliminal: The Revolution of the New Unconscious and What it Teaches Us about Ourselves*

John Romer, *A History of Ancient Egypt: From the First Farmers to the Great Pyramid*

Ruchir Sharma, *Breakout Nations: In Pursuit of the Next Economic Miracle*

Michael J. Sandel, *What Money Can't Buy: The Moral Limits of Markets*

Dominic Sandbrook, *Seasons in the Sun: The Battle for Britain, 1974-1979*

Tariq Ramadan, *The Arab Awakening: Islam and the New Middle East*

Jonathan Haidt, *The Righteous Mind: Why Good People are Divided by Politics and Religion*

Ahmed Rashid, *Pakistan on the Brink: The Future of Pakistan, Afghanistan and the West*